THE POLITICAL ECONOMY OF SECURITY

Princeton Studies in International History and Politics

TANISHA M. FAZAL, G. JOHN IKENBERRY, WILLIAM C. WOHLFORTH, AND KEREN YARHI-MILO, SERIES EDITORS

For a full list of titles in the series, go to https://press.princeton.edu /series/princeton-studies-in-international-history-and-politics

The Political Economy of Security

Stephen G. Brooks

PRINCETON UNIVERSITY PRESS

PRINCETON & OXFORD

Published by Princeton University Press
41 William Street, Princeton, New Jersey 08540
99 Banbury Road, Oxford OX2 6JX

press.princeton.edu

GPSR Authorized Representative: Easy Access System Europe - Mustamäe tee 50, 10621 Tallinn, Estonia, gpsr.requests@easproject.com

All Rights Reserved

ISBN 978-0-691-17745-8
ISBN (pbk.) 978-0-691-22659-0
ISBN (e-book) 978-0-691-22658-3

Library of Congress Control Number 2025937130

British Library Cataloging-in-Publication Data is available

Editorial: Dave McBride and Alena Chekanov
Production Editorial: Jill Harris
Cover Design: Haley O'Neill
Production: Erin Suydam
Publicity: William Pagdatoon
Copyeditor: Martin Schneider

This book has been composed in Miller

10 9 8 7 6 5 4 3 2 1

This book is dedicated to my father, Thomas Brooks,
who taught me so much about economics and countless other things.

CONTENTS

ILLUSTRATIONS

TABLES

THE TITLE of this book is a variation on the title of Robert Gilpin's 1987 book *The Political Economy of International Relations*. This allusion to Gilpin's book is intentional. Gilpin's book greatly influenced my thinking as an undergraduate and helped inspire my desire to attend graduate school in order to learn more about the workings of the global economy. Although I admired the book and learned greatly from it, I found it disappointing because it had so little to say about how economic factors influenced security affairs. As I headed off to get my PhD at Yale University in 1994, I presumed that one of my professors there would direct me to a different book that would provide an overall understanding of the economics-security interaction.

Soon after starting my PhD studies, I learned that there was, in fact, no book that sought to systematically delineate the theoretical and empirical fundamentals concerning how economic factors influence security affairs. We still lack such a book today. My aim here is to fill this gap.

In graduate school, I learned that many key elements of the economics-security interaction were either not represented or were unsatisfactorily examined in the literature. A key reason why is that the field of international relations (IR) was artificially divided into two subfields: international political economy (IPE) and security studies. I quickly discovered that although numerous important and interesting questions lay at the intersection of these two subfields, almost all scholars specialized exclusively in one or the other.

Indeed, I learned that for many scholars, the "low politics" of economics and the "high politics" of security affairs were seen as essentially operating in different realms. Significantly, even many analysts such as Gilpin who clearly had a deep interest in both security issues and economic factors shared this view. In his 1987 book, Gilpin brusquely swept aside the need to carefully investigate how the global economy shaped security affairs with his blunt assertion that "economic relations are not in themselves critical to the establishment of either cooperative or conflictual international relations. . . . The character of international relations and the question of peace or war are determined primarily by the larger configurations of power and strategic interest among both the great and small powers in the system."

Whether it was ever appropriate to treat economics and security as separate realms is debatable; it is certainly not reasonable to do this today. To understand security affairs in today's world, it is absolutely vital to understand the influence of economic factors. The purpose of this book is to provide a systematic theoretical and economic portrait of how economic factors influence security affairs in today's world.

So far, this preface reads like the introduction to a textbook. Although this book could serve this function in courses, this book is not a textbook. A textbook is for students only: it summarizes and introduces students to existing scholarship in a subject area. From the start, my aim was to write a dual-purpose book—one that students could learn from and that would also be new and enlightening for scholars.

Our current empirical understanding of the economics-security interaction is inadequate. The first part of this book delineates sixteen core pathways by which economic factors can directly influence security affairs and provides an empirical examination of all of them. New empirical work was needed for a number of these pathways, while the existing literature for the others needed to be more carefully synthesized.

The current theoretical literature that bears on the economics-security interaction is also insufficient. As Chapter 1 explains, there is a set of core conceptual questions concerning this relationship for which the current theoretical landscape does not provide a sufficient range of answers. A stronger theoretical foundation is needed for future work that seeks to develop novel understandings of the economics-security interaction; this is the purpose of the second part of this book.

Although the book covers a lot of ground, it is not comprehensive. Notwithstanding that many important elements of the economics-security interaction have been neglected, it is a substantial topic and a very large amount has indeed been written on it. To discuss "everything" of relevance that has ever been written on this topic would require many volumes. Moreover, reviewing existing work would hardly be enough, since so much new theorizing and empirical work is needed. As Chapter 1 delineates, I use Adam Smith—the founder of the field of political economy—as a "guide" to help bound the subject matter of this book into a manageable size.

ACKNOWLEDGMENTS

THIS BOOK has taken a long time to complete—long enough that it is difficult to accurately produce a full inventory of the various people who helped me. At the risk of overlooking some people who deserve thanks, I would like to express my appreciation to the following individuals.

First, I'm grateful to many colleagues at Dartmouth for their valuable comments and assistance: Mike Mastanduno, Ben Valentino, Henry Clark, Russ Muirhead, Daryl Press, Jennifer Lind, Jim Murphy, Ned Lebow, Doug Irwin, and especially Brian Greenhill.

I would also like to thank the scholars based at other universities who provided expert feedback on some or all of the manuscript: Patrick McDonald, Jonathan Kirshner, Andrew Walter, David Baldwin, James Otteson, Andrew Coe, Alex Wendt, Geoffrey Garrett, Jonathan Markowitz, Bruce Russett, Ben Graham, Rosella Cappella Zielinski, and Megan Becker.

I am grateful to the fourteen Dartmouth undergraduates who helped me over the years as research assistants: Pirzada Ahmad, Rohan Chakravarty, Holland Bald, Sonia Qin, Natasha Kapadia, Julianna Docking, Chelsea Lim, Jae Won Hyun, Holly Jeong, Felicia Jia, Ross Brown, Jessica Merry, Carter Anderson, and particularly Tyler Vergho.

I am also indebted to a range of current and former editors at Princeton University Press for their advice, assistance, and patience: Bridget Flannery-McCoy, Chuck Myers, Alena Chekanov, Dave McBride, and especially Eric Crahan.

Finally, a special word of thanks to Bill Wohlforth. He helped me with this book more than anyone else. After the book had been accepted, Bill ended up becoming one of the editors in the "Princeton Studies in International History and Politics" series that it will be published in. Both before and after he became editor of this series, he was always extremely willing to help me. Over the many years I worked on this book, Bill read multiple drafts and discussed it with me in innumerable conversations. His ideas, incisive feedback, and encouragement were immensely helpful. I am very lucky to have had him not just as my longtime coauthor but also as my longtime colleague.

THE POLITICAL ECONOMY OF SECURITY

CHAPTER ONE

Introduction

ECONOMIC FACTORS NOW arguably have a greater potential to influence world politics than ever before. The global economy is qualitatively different than in previous eras, and the costs of remaining isolated from it have greatly increased in recent decades. Moreover, markets continue to become ever more complex, while the significance of economic capacity as a priority for governments and citizens has arguably never been higher. Although it would be a mistake to think that economic factors will ever deterministically influence political affairs, the premium on thinking carefully about how economic factors influence world politics has never been greater.

And yet the words with which Robert Gilpin introduced his influential 1987 text on political economy remain valid today: "Transformations in the real world have made economics and politics more relevant to one another than in the past and have forced the recognition that our theoretical understanding of their interactions has always been inadequate, oversimplified, and arbitrarily limited by disciplinary boundaries."[1] The view that economic shifts can influence the political world has been prominent for centuries, and so one would think that scholars would by now have a well-developed understanding of how economics and politics interact in world politics. But that is not the case.

The stakes are stark: to properly comprehend world politics, we must develop a better overall understanding of economic factors. This is not because economic factors can explain world politics on their own. Nor is it because economic factors will always have a significant role. It is because economic factors have achieved enough salience that for analysts to not carefully investigate them means that they will either miss some of what is going on in world politics or, at a minimum, will not be in a strong position to evaluate whether the alternative propositions they put forward are valid. A simple injunction that emerges from this book is thus that analysts need to always carefully consider the role of economics in world politics.

My aim here is to provide a systematic theoretical and empirical portrait of how economic factors influence a particular domain of world politics: security affairs. Scholars and statesmen have discussed how economic factors influence the prospects for conflict for thousands of years, resulting in a vast outpouring of writings on this topic.[2] While much useful work has been done on the economics-security interaction, many key elements of this topic still are not adequately understood.

This book aims to improve our state of knowledge regarding the economics-security interaction by making six key contributions. First, we currently lack an established understanding of the range of core pathways by which economic factors can potentially have a direct influence on security affairs. Here, I delineate sixteen such pathways in total, which fall across four general categories. While these sixteen pathways do not cover everything of relevance, they are, in my judgment, the most noteworthy pathways and collectively encompass the vast bulk of what we need to know about the economics-security interaction.

A second contribution the book provides is a thorough empirical assessment of all sixteen of these pathways. In many cases, this assessment is accomplished by surveying and synthesizing the findings from the relevant studies that exist in the current literature. But concerning those pathways where there are no existing empirical studies or where they are not set up to adequately address the relevant question at hand, I undertake new empirical evaluations.

Third, I establish that the relationship between economic factors and conflict is complex and multifaceted. Having identified and assessed these sixteen pathways, my overall conclusion is that economic factors are not helpful for advancing peace and stability, nor are they detrimental; they are both. My overall conclusion is thus that there is no simple overall conclusion; economic factors are complicated, and they have complicated effects. There are understandable reasons why so many analysts over the centuries have been motivated to tell a pithy story about how economic factors influence security affairs, but the examination here clearly reveals the inaccuracy of this kind of approach.

This understanding runs contrary to the prominent and long-standing view that economic factors can have a specific kind of general effect on security affairs—a perspective that has been advanced most frequently regarding global commerce. Numerous Enlightenment philosophers such as Immanuel Kant and Montesquieu argued that international commerce made war less likely. "The natural effect of commerce is to lead to peace," Montesquieu wrote in 1748.[3] One hundred years later, John Stuart Mill proclaimed that "it is commerce which is rapidly rendering war obsolete."[4] But other thinkers over the centuries have strenuously disagreed, arguing that the opposite is true: that commerce overall enhances the prospects for conflict. For example, in 1787 Alexander Hamilton rebuked the notion that the "commerce has a tendency to soften the manners of men," concluding instead that "commerce in many instances administered new incentives" for conflict and that numerous cases of wars were "founded upon commercial motives."[5] The Austrian philosopher Friedrich List argued in 1841 that reducing participation in international markets was the surest route to protecting a country's security.[6] And Vladimir Lenin famously argued in 1917 that the quest for foreign markets made war among capitalist states inevitable.[7]

It was only after the Cold War ended that this age-old debate moved beyond largely theoretical arguments and significant empirical research on how commerce influences conflict finally emerged. By far the most prominent perspective emerging from this empirical literature comes from proponents of the "capitalist peace," who conclude that the optimistic view that commerce promotes peace is correct. The lead champion of this perspective, Erik Gartzke, has argued across numerous publications that free markets, free trade, and the free movement of global capital are all beneficial for peace.[8]

Although there have been notable individual studies supporting the optimistic view that global commerce promotes peace, they are just that—individual studies. Having now undertaken a systematic examination of all the relevant pathways and empirical research, I conclude that the notion that more trade and globalization inherently curtail war is mistaken—yet so is the inverse. I conclude that international financial flows—the cross-border purchase of bonds, stocks, currencies, and so on—do not have a clear influence on conflict. Moreover, the types of global economic ties that are significant appear to have both stabilizing and destabilizing effects at the same time. I conclude that trade has a mixed effect, sometimes dampening conflict and sometimes fueling it. In turn, I find the globalization of production—that is, the dispersion of economic activity by global firms across borders—has a stabilizing effect among great powers, but it increases the likelihood of conflict among developing countries.

The first three contributions just described, which are all empirical, emerge from analysis in the first part of the book. The next three contributions, all of which are theoretical, are delineated in the book's second part.

The fourth contribution is the identification of a more complete range of answers to the three key conceptual questions that I believe analysts most need to keep in mind when they seek to develop new theories and explanations of how economic factors influence security affairs: (a) How do economic goals relate to security goals? (b) What kinds of economic factors are important to study when analyzing world politics? and (c) How and how much do economic actors influence policies regarding security affairs?

There is no "set" answer to any of these three conceptual questions that analysts now agree upon, nor should there be. The important thing is to have an appropriate range of ready answers available as guides to inquiry, which I show is not the case at present. Instead, analysts are now being directed away from what, in my opinion, are the most useful understandings of these three conceptual questions, thereby unnecessarily constraining our collective ability to generate useful future analyses of the economics-security interaction.

Fifth, I clarify and recast our understanding of the most prominent political economy frameworks that have long been used to understand the economics-security interaction.[9] Analysts could derive their own individual answers to the three just noted conceptual questions and other relevant ones before examining how economic factors influence security affairs. However, for various reasons they instead typically rely—either explicitly or implicitly—upon existing political economy frameworks to guide their research, and there are two in particular that have long been most prominent in this regard. The first—whose leading protagonists include figures such as Alexander Hamilton, Jean-Baptiste Colbert, and Friedrich List—is alternatively called mercantilism, mercantilist political economy, realist political economy, realism, statism, or economic nationalism. The second—which includes figures such as David Ricardo, Montesquieu, and Richard Cobden—is alternatively called liberalism, liberal political economy, free trade liberalism, economic liberalism, or commercial liberalism.

Over the centuries, a wide range of prominent political scientists, philosophers, economists, and historians—including Jacob Viner, Eli Heckscher, Joseph Schumpeter, Paul Samuelson, Edward Mead Earle, David Baldwin, Robert Gilpin, and Albert Hirschman—have extensively discussed the distinctions between these two political economy frameworks. Nevertheless, our current understanding of how they compare and contrast with each other is inadequate; this has caused these two perspectives to be misunderstood and also has led the field to not recognize that there is a middle-ground theoretical space between them that can and should be delineated.

The sixth and final contribution is that I give Adam Smith his proper due as a theorist of world politics. Smith's insights about world politics in general—and the role of economics in security affairs in particular—have been greatly misinterpreted over the centuries and accordingly have been given short shrift.* Here, the core problem is arguably the frequent effort to jam Smith into the conception of world politics that emerged from the writings of later liberal philosophers such as Kant, Ricardo, and Mill rather than reading Smith on his own terms and being comfortable with the prospect that his views are discordant from these later liberal theorists and should be treated as such.[10] As the analysis here will show, Smith's writings provide the basis for a conception of political economy that stands apart from the understanding that flows from the later liberal theorists who wrote after him and that also remains distinct from mercantilist/realist political economy.

In my assessment, Smith is the most useful thinker concerning the economics-security interaction who has ever lived, and his significant insights on this topic have been neglected over the centuries, to our great

---

*Given the crucial need to read what Smith has to say within the proper context and given that there are so many different editions of his work, I cite his work in such a way that makes it as easy as possible for readers to locate all of the quotations I use and understand for themselves how they appear within his narrative. I therefore follow the standard method regarding citations used in the literature on Smith's work and use the definitive edition of his volumes—*The Glasgow Edition of the Works of and Correspondence of Adam Smith*. The abbreviations used in the footnotes are as follows:

WN: *An Inquiry in the Nature and Causes of the Wealth of Nations*, edited by R. H. Campbell, A. S. Skinner, and W. B. Todd

TMS: *The Theory of Moral Sentiments*, edited by D. D. Raphael and A. L. Macfie

LJ (A): *Lectures on Jurisprudence*, report of 1762–63, edited by R. L. Meek, D. D. Raphael, and P.G. Stein

LJ (B): *Lectures on Jurisprudence*, report dated 1766, edited by R. L. Meek, D. D. Raphael, and P.G. Stein

References to *The Wealth of Nations* and *The Theory of Moral Sentiments* use both the typical citation method in the social sciences (referring to the specific pages of the editions noted above, which are noted at the end of each reference) as well as the particular citation practice used in the Glasgow Edition, which is to cite the relevant section of the book along with the associated paragraph number in that edition. For example, WN,IV.vii.c.80, p. 626 should be read to mean *The Wealth of Nations*, Book 4, Chapter 7, Section C, paragraph 80, page 626.

collective detriment. I will use Smith as kind of a "guide" to this subject; employing his work as a fulcrum of the book provides an ideal platform for the theoretical and empirical work that is necessary. *The Wealth of Nations* points to eight of the sixteen pathways that are examined in the first part of the book. Additionally, the theoretical space occupied by Smith delineated in the second half of the book provides, in my view, the best foundation for future theorizing about the economics-security interaction—a point I will underscore in Chapter 10 by using the end of the Cold War case as an exemplar.

With its aim of systematically evaluating and recasting our understanding of the economics-security interaction, this book has a very wide scope. To allow readers to have a proper understanding of the breadth of the analysis, the remainder of this chapter delineates in more detail the range of empirical and theoretical contributions the book makes.

Because the book covers so much ground, each chapter has been specifically designed so that it can be read "à la carte." In other words, each chapter is effectively freestanding, with a distinct set of conclusions that can be absorbed on their own. As the chapters all make an independent contribution, as is the case with a scholarly article, readers are encouraged to consult the introduction to each chapter in the same manner that they would first read the abstract of an article when deciding how to engage its contents.

Along the same lines, the empirical part (Chapters 2–5) and the theoretical part (Chapters 6–10) of this book can also be read separately from each other. The respective focus of these two parts is distinctly different, and not merely because one is empirical while the other is theoretical. The empirical part is backwards-looking, concentrating on the pathways that now exist concerning the economics-security interaction and how they have operated so far. In contrast, the theoretical part is forward-thinking, analyzing how to think theoretically about the economics-security interaction with an eye toward understanding what analysts should bear in mind when formulating novel understandings of how economic factors influence security affairs, whether new general theories or specific explanations of individual cases.

Overview of Empirical Contributions

To derive a systematic understanding of how economic factors can directly influence security affairs, we would need a list of the key pathways that need to be examined.[11] But there is no existing list of this kind. To help generate such a list, I first carefully consulted the book that founded the field of political economy: Adam Smith's *The Wealth of Nations*. While this is not often recognized, Smith's book contains a remarkably wide-ranging discussion of the economics-security interaction. Notably, Smith's thinking was not circumscribed by the artificial separation of the academic study of economics and politics—a later intellectual development that has done much to constrain our collective thinking about the extent to which economic factors influence security affairs.

All told, Smith points toward eight pathways by which economic factors can directly influence security affairs. When put together, these eight pathways address a large portion of the most significant issues that lie at the intersection of economics and security in world politics. For some of the pathways, the essentials that are needed to frame them as testable theories are spelled out directly by Smith himself. But for the majority of the pathways, I generalize and/or update arguments advanced by Smith. I begin with the relevant insight that he puts forward in *The Wealth of Nations* and then delineate a theory that resonates with the nature of economics in our current era. I then empirically evaluate each of these theories.

The eight pathways Smith points toward do not tell us everything we need to know about the economics-security interaction. In asking what other key pathways by which economic factors can directly influence security also should be considered, I consulted a range of other scholars who, like me, focus much of their research on the economics-security interaction. This led to the identification of the eight additional pathways that are included in this book. Regarding these additional eight pathways, I empirically evaluate the variable(s) in question but do not outline a particular testable theory that pertains to them; in some cases, however, a single clear theory regarding the security effects of that variable has already been specified.

These sixteen pathways can be grouped into four general categories. The first category concerns how the global economy shapes security affairs. There are four pathways within this first category that are analyzed in Chapter 2.

> Pathway 1: how global commerce influences conflict
> Pathway 2: how international finance influences conflict
> Pathway 3: how the global economy influences the ability of powerful states to secure needed resources and supplies via economic means without the need to use or threaten military force

Pathway 4: how the global economy influences the choice between maintaining autonomy in the production of weaponry versus pursuing openness in defense production

The second category concerns the influence of economic actors and other societal interests—how the former can potentially affect security policy and how the attitudes of the latter toward conflict are sometimes influenced by economic changes. There are four pathways within this second category that are delineated and evaluated in Chapter 3. These pathways are:

Pathway 5: how poor economic conditions (such as low growth or high inflation) influence whether leaders use military force to distract the public

Pathway 6: how the public's support for war depends upon whether the war's economic costs are financed via borrowing versus a tax increase

Pathway 7: how public attitudes toward conflict are influenced by the overall fiscal costs of war and the extent of burden sharing (that is, how war costs are distributed across different countries)

Pathway 8: how the global economy influences whether economic actors are likely to lobby for war

The third category of pathways concerns the influence of domestic economic structure, which Smith conceives as being what a society's economy is primarily geared toward producing. There are three pathways within this third category that are analyzed in Chapter 4. These pathways are:

Pathway 9: how economic development influences the gains of conquest

Pathway 10: how economic development alters both the capacity and willingness of potential initiators of conflict

Pathway 11: how a natural resource–based economic structure influences conflict

The fourth and final category of pathways concerns how economic factors influence civil conflict and terrorism (both transnational terrorism and domestic terrorism). There are five pathways in this fourth category that are evaluated in Chapter 5.

Pathway 12: how economic development influences terrorism

Pathway 13: how economic globalization influences transnational terrorism

Pathway 14: how economic growth influences terrorism

Pathway 15: how economic development influences civil conflict

Pathway 16: how economic globalization influences civil conflict

Most of these sixteen pathways have already been extensively examined empirically. However, the accumulation of knowledge from this existing empirical work has been inadequate. For many of these sixteen pathways, the task at hand is thus to undertake the painstaking work to bring together all of the relevant empirical studies under a single roof to get a sense of what their findings collectively show.

Yet for some of these sixteen pathways, we lack a sufficiently strong empirical base of existing studies upon which to draw any conclusions. Sometimes a hypothesis has been evaluated, but it can and should be evaluated in a different manner; if so, I undertake such a revised empirical evaluation. In other cases, there is no existing empirical work; if so, I undertake such analysis.

Overview of Theoretical Contributions

The analysis of the sixteen pathways examined in the first part of the book covers a great deal of ground. But economic factors are powerful and dynamic, and as time progresses we will need to develop novel general theories regarding their influence on security affairs. And regarding the security behavior of particular states, we will also need new explanations regarding the past or current influence of economic factors as well as fresh predictions about the likely future effects of such factors.

This new theorizing will not emerge from nowhere; it will be shaped by our deeper conceptual understanding of the economics-security interaction. To help further our future theorizing, the theoretical portion of this book concentrates on providing a more complete range of answers to arguably the three most significant conceptual questions regarding the economics-security interaction that analysts should consider when formulating new understandings, both general ones and those pertaining to particular cases.

The first conceptual question concerns how economic goals relate to security goals. Clearly, both goals are important for governments. How do governments balance these objectives? Do they favor one goal over the other in a consistent manner and, if so, which goal has priority? Or do they make trade-offs between these two goals and, if so, in what way? The overall relation of economic goals to security goals is a significant but not straightforward matter for analysts to gauge.

A second conceptual question concerns what economic factors to consider when examining world politics. Economic factors are variegated and become ever more so as domestic markets and the global economy increase in complexity. Out of the range of potential economic factors that could influence security affairs, which one(s) should an analyst consider? Answering this question is important but it is also not easy, especially for those analysts of security affairs who do not have much knowledge of economics and/or interest in its intricacies.

The final conceptual question pertains to the role of economic actors in the formation of security policies. To what degree do government leaders form policy distinct from pressures from economic actors and other societal interests? Do leaders make security policy in a "top-down" manner without reference to economic actors and other societal interests? Or is security policy formed in a "bottom-up" manner, in which policy shifts occur in response to what economic actors and other societal interests want? Or does the answer lie in between, in which economic actors and other societal interests are sometimes, but not always, the drivers of policy change? Conceptualizing the role of economic actors in policy formation is, again, a vital matter without an obvious answer.

There is simply no consensus answer to these three conceptual questions. Individual analysts of security affairs could in theory work to answer these questions themselves. Yet for a variety of reasons, it is simultaneously convenient and understandable to rely upon "off-the-shelf" answers to these conceptual questions from existing political economy frameworks that bear on the economics-security interaction.

However, the range of existing answers to these three conceptual questions that are readily available has been too limited in scope. The collective responses to these questions have accordingly been incomplete, with the result that some of the influence of economics on security affairs is prone to be missed or misunderstood.

Regarding the first question, analysts have generally not conceptualized the relationship between economic and security goals as involving a complex, dynamic trade-off. Concerning the second question, the kinds of economic factors that, in my assessment, would now be most profitable to focus on when examining the economics-security interaction have all too frequently been overlooked; specifically, insufficient attention has been paid to the potential influence of economic structure (both domestic economic structure and global economic structure) on security affairs. And regarding the third question, analysts have failed to adequately consider a political role for economic actors that occupies a middle-ground space in between the bottom-up formulation of policy making and the top-down conception.

The core problem is the absence of a theoretical framework that articulates the critical importance of carefully considering the complex, dynamic nature of the trade-off between economic and security goals, that emphasizes the crucial need for scholars to consider the potential influence of economic structure on world politics, and that sees economic actors and other societal interests neither as subservient to the government nor as dominating the formulation of policy. The tragedy is that a theoretical framework with these exact characteristics is available to scholars. It has, in fact, *been* available for a very, very long time—ever since 1776, when Smith published *The Wealth of Nations*.[12]

For many reasons, the existence and significance of this theoretical framework outlined by Smith has been missed. For centuries, Smith's views on world politics have frequently been caricatured: over and over, he has been incorrectly characterized as being just another example in a long line of liberal thinkers rather than as having his own unique conception.

Smith is indeed a canonical theorist of liberalism, which has "constituted the principal current of modern politics in Europe and the West . . . for almost three centuries" and has long occupied a central place within the study of world politics.[13] But exactly because of its prevalence, liberalism has attracted many thinkers over the centuries. Liberal political economy is diverse, but this diversity has not been sufficiently recognized by analysts of world politics; the interpretation of Smith's views is the greatest casualty in this regard. As I will show, Smith provides the foundation for a conception of political economy that competes with, rather than being compatible with, the standard understanding of liberal political economy—what I term "conventional liberal political economy." Smith is ultimately best understood as occupying a theoretical space between mercantilist/realist political economy and conventional liberal political economy.

The organization of the theoretical portion of this book is as follows. In Chapter 6, I show that our current understanding of how liberal and mercantilist/realist liberal political economy compare and contrast with each other is deficient, that the most appropriate means of differentiating these frameworks is to concentrate on their answers to the three conceptual questions noted above. I also delineate that there is more diversity in liberal political economy regarding these questions than has been understood to this point.

Chapters 7 through 9 will then outline the answers to these three conceptual questions that flow from Smith and, in so doing, will show that his understanding forms the basis for a second, alternative conception of liberal political economy. Chapter 7 examines why Smith places great importance in conceptualizing the trade-off between economic goals and security goals as being complex and dynamic. Chapter 8 reveals Smith's argument for the critical need to focus on the role of economic structure when analyzing world politics. And Chapter 9 unpacks Smith's understanding of how economic actors and other societal interests affect security policy, revealing that he articulates a conceptualization that is neither top-down nor bottom-up.

There are many potential terms that could be used to describe the theoretical space that Smith occupies, including "Smithian liberalism," "Smithian political economy," "classical liberal political economy," "Smithian commercial liberalism," and "neo-commercial liberalism"; I am agnostic as to which one, if any, is used. The important thing is for analysts to recognize that Smith provides the basis for a unique, valuable approach for thinking about the role of economics in world politics.

Chapter 10 then looks at the most momentous shift in security affairs since 1945—the end of the Cold War—as a means of showing in practice what a Smithian theoretical understanding of the role of economic factors can do. As I show, Smith's respective answers to these three key conceptual questions point to three different lessons that analysts would be wise to bear in mind when examining the influence of economic factors on world politics. I use the end of the Cold War case to illustrate that the value of paying heed to these three lessons is hardly hypothetical.

In my assessment, if a Smithian theoretical understanding had existed as a prominent guide to thinking regarding the role of economic factors in world politics, then the end of the Cold War would have been far less surprising and may even have been predicted. Scholars missed a number of factors that we now see as critical to the end of the Cold War that our existing theoretical frameworks did not illuminate. Analysts would have been more attuned to these factors if a Smithian theoretical framework had been available as a conceptual guide. The underlying takeaway is that we will be less likely to be caught off guard if we pay heed to the lessons that flow from a Smithian theoretical understanding.

With its aim of unpacking the underlying theoretical and conceptual issues I see as most relevant and important for improving our future understanding of the economics-security interaction, the analysis in the theoretical part of this book is an exercise in what is commonly called "grand theory."[14] This cuts against the grain of recent work examining international relations. Efforts to grapple with general theoretical and conceptual issues, long very prominent, have recently been overwhelmingly replaced by a focus on "middle-range theories" in which an analyst aims to "explore specific problems, to form hypotheses or generalizations explaining limited ranges of phenomena."[15]

Drawing on the arguments of Robert Merton regarding the importance of what he called "general theoretical orientations," I believe grand theory can helpfully perform four key roles[16] that aid in the construction of middle-range theories:

(1) helping us to select certain variables for investigation out of a large number of potential causal factors;
(2) pushing us to make clear our underlying assumptions;
(3) giving us clues as to the type of causal connections to establish and directing us toward certain kinds of phenomena to investigate; and
(4) making it easier to distinguish our hypotheses from competing ones—including competing hypotheses that feature the same independent variable—that are drawn from different underlying assumptions.

Regarding the study of world politics, I maintain that grand theory should not aim to do more than these limited roles. Understood in this way, grand theories should—as Merton aptly puts it—only be used "tentatively," since they provide "only the broadest framework for empirical inquiry. . . . [T]hey constitute only the point of departure for the theorist. . . . and facilitate the progress of arriving at determinate hypotheses."[17] Ultimately, I believe grand theory should be seen as a tool that helps us determine "where to look" when we try to understand the world and to be cognizant and explicit about the choices we make in this regard. Although this is an important role, it is a much more "minimalist" function for grand theorizing than has typically been propounded by its proponents.[18]

PART I

Empirical Examination of the Economics- Security Interaction

CHAPTER TWO

The Global Economy and War

THIS CHAPTER BEGINS the empirical examination of the sixteen pathways by which economic factors can influence security affairs; four of them will be analyzed here. The focus of this chapter is on how the global economy shapes security affairs, with particular emphasis on the influence of changes in global economic structure; the last two pathways, as well as much of the first, specifically concern structural shifts in the global economy.

The first section examines how global commerce influences the likelihood of conflict; I synthesize the findings from the massive literature on trade and conflict and then discuss how the globalization of production influences security affairs. The second section then turns to an analysis of the other main element of economic globalization: international finance.

The third section examines a theory—termed "conquest substitution theory"—concerning how the structure of the global economy influences the ability of powerful states to secure needed resources and supplies via economic means without the use or threat of military force. The final section then analyzes a theory—"the weapons autonomy trade-off theory"—concerning the influence of recent changes in the structure of the global economy on the choice between pursuing openness in defense production versus maintaining autonomy in the manufacturing of weaponry.

Pathway 1: Contingent Commerce Theory

The notion that international commerce can significantly influence the prospects for war and peace between states is one of a very small number of foundational arguments about international relations that has been prominent for hundreds of years. Over the centuries, Kant, Mill, Ricardo,

Montesquieu, Cobden, and numerous other liberal theorists famously argued that increased trade would enhance the prospects for peace by, most notably, making war too economically costly. As Montesquieu puts forward this argument: "The natural effect of commerce is to bring peace. Two nations that negotiate between themselves become reciprocally dependent, if one has an interest in buying and the other in selling. And all unions are based on mutual needs."[1] Commerce was seen as a dynamic force that would have a progressively stronger stabilizing effect over time; in the eyes of Kant, for example, "the spirit of commerce, which is incompatible with war, sooner or later gains the upper hand in every state."[2]

Over the centuries, Adam Smith has been repeatedly mischaracterized as agreeing with this liberal notion that trade promotes peace. Yet if one reads Smith's writings, it is clear that he never expresses an expectation of this kind. A reasonable question to ask is: how has Smith been so misinterpreted as being someone who saw trade as always acting as a force for peace? One reason is that a prominent quote from Smith has often been improperly taken out of context.[3] But likely the key reason is the significance of Richard Cobden's work. As van de Haar notes:

> Cobden was the major populariser of the trade-leads-to-peace thesis in the nineteenth century. . . . Cobden acknowledged Adam Smith as the greatest single influence on his thought. He called for the establishment of Smithian Societies, devoted to the promulgation "of the beneficent truths of the *Wealth of Nations*." Cobden and his colleagues actively used the legacy of Smith to further their own aims and to discredit economic protectionists and other opponents of Corn Law repeal and free trade measures. But Cobden seriously misinterpreted Smith's view on international relations. . . . The Scot did not believe in the relation between trade and peace, or in harmony between states. . . . Cobden's big influence on IR theory, well into the first half of twentieth century, largely explains this continued but erroneous linkage of Smith with the trade-leads-to-peace thesis.[4]

To be clear, although Smith was not of the view that trade would lead to peace and did outline some mechanisms by which it could enhance the prospects for conflict, he also did not expect that trade linkages would consistently undermine the prospects for peace in the manner that realist/mercantilist theorists expect. As Copeland outlines, the essence of the realist perspective is that "[s]tates concerned about security will dislike dependence, since it means that crucial imported goods could be cut off during a crisis. . . . Consequently, states dependent on others for vital goods have an increased incentive to go to war to assure themselves of continued access of supply. . . . A state vulnerable to another's policies because of dependence will tend to use force to overcome that vulnerability."[5]

Smith advances his own distinct understanding that departs from realist and liberal political economy. In Smith's view, trade has the potential to simultaneously have positive influences on security affairs (such as by potentially promoting a bond of union and friendship) as well as negative influences (such as by undermining martial spirit and contributing to dangerous power gaps between nations). Ultimately, what emerges from Smith's analysis is the view that trade is likely to have a mixed effect on conflict—that is, that trade can sometimes promote peace while simultaneously having no stabilizing effect or a harmful influence on security relations in other circumstances.

Smith centered his discussion of how commerce influences conflict around trade. In turn, the overwhelming preponderance of the empirical literature examining the influence of the global economy on security affairs does so as well. Yet we no longer live in a world in which trade is the primary driver of global commerce: nowadays, the geographic dispersion of production by multinational corporations (MNCs)—a development that postdated Smith by centuries—has become the key organizing feature of global commerce (this point will be explored in detail in Chapter 8).

Expanding beyond an exclusive focus on trade, a broader proposition—what I here term "contingent commerce theory"—would posit that *all* of commerce, and not just trade, is likely to have a mixed effect on conflict. Contingent commerce theory stands apart not just from the conventional liberal perspective regarding how the global economy influences security affairs but also from contemporary capitalist peace theory.[6] Notably, key proponents of the capitalist peace theory have caricatured Smith as someone who believes that unleashing market forces will be pacifying and have portrayed their own work as building on his.[7] Yet when reading Smith, what emerges is a clear understanding that capitalism—and the commerce that flows from it—is an incredibly dynamic, complex force that has a wide range of effects. While it is of course possible that all of capitalism's varying effects could somehow add up to a consistently pacifying effect, this seems unlikely; certainly, Smith did not foresee such a positive outcome.

ASSESSING CONTINGENT COMMERCE THEORY

How does the massive empirical literature on trade and conflict bear on contingent commerce theory? An initial wave of statistical studies produced during the 1990s that examined the relationship between trade and conflict literature generally found that trade had a pacifying effect.[8] Many of the studies in this initial literature were inspired by the optimistic liberal understanding that trade had an unconditionally positive influence on the prospects for peace, and they generally found support for this view.[9] However, a series of powerful methodological critiques was leveled at this initial wave of analyses,[10] and a second wave of studies then emerged that sought to reexamine the trade/conflict relationship.

I identified 63 statistical studies published during the 2000–2025 period that directly focus on examining the link between trade and peace; they are shown in Table 2.1. In this systematic review and in all others that I conduct throughout the book, my approach is to weight equally the identified studies within a given literature. Now that I have created these various inventories, future researchers may well want to undertake alternative analyses that weight the studies differently.

As the table shows, nine out of these sixty-three studies find that trade has no influence on the likelihood of conflict (category 1). Notably, there is virtually a complete lack of support for the realist notion that trade makes conflict more likely; just one study reaches this conclusion (category 3). For a very long time, this realist hypothesis seemed worthwhile to consider and discuss as plausible. Having undertaken this systematic review of the empirical literature, it is now reasonable to conclude that this realist hypothesis has been falsified.

Although it is not reasonable to conclude the conventional liberal hypothesis that trade promotes peace is falsified, it arguably is on its last legs. The empirical support for this hypothesis is clearly far weaker than seemed to be the case in the 1990s, with just eighteen out of these sixty-three studies finding that trade reduces the likelihood of conflict (category 2). And notably, as the years continue to pass—and as more studies accumulate—this support only continues to diminish further: of the eighteen studies concluding that trade reduces the likelihood of conflict, just six were published after 2010.

It would seem most reasonable at this juncture to conclude that trade has a mixed effect on conflict; thirty-five out of sixty-three of statistical studies find such a relationship, with twenty-one of these studies having been published after 2010 (category 4). In turn, this assessment matches up with the most detailed qualitative analyses of how trade influences conflict.[11]

These mixed-effect studies do not yield consistent, clear insights; the list of conditions regarding the influence of trade on security affairs that emerges from this scholarship is long, unwieldy, and sometimes contradictory. Ultimately, the relationship between trade and conflict has so many asterisks that it simply cannot be boiled down into anything pithy.

Table 2.1. Trade and Conflict

Author(s)	Publish Date	Independent Variable(s)	Years	Main Finding(s)
Category 1: Trade Does Not Affect Conflict				
Fordham[1]	2008	Exports	1918–2001	Exports do not have a significant direct effect on the probability of US intervention.
Gartzke/Li Boehmer[2]	2001	Trade dependence	1951–1985	In most models, trade dependence does not have a statistically significant influence on conflict.
Goenner[3]	2004	Trade	1950–1992	Trade does not affect conflict.
Keshk et al.[4]	2004	Trade	1870–2000	Trade does not affect conflict.
Keshk et al.[5]	2010	Trade	1950–1992	Trade does not affect conflict.
Kim/Rousseau[6]	2005	Trade	1960–1988	Trade does not affect conflict.
McDonald[7]	2004	Trade and free trade policies	1960–2000	Trade does not affect conflict, but free trade policies do: the likelihood of conflict within a dyad decreases as protectionism decreases, and increases as the level of protection increases.
Ward/Hoff[8]	2007	Trade	1980–2001	No significant relationship between trade and cooperation in international disputes.
Ward/Siverson/ Cao[9]	2007	Trade	1950–2000	High levels of trade do not reduce conflict.
Category 2: Trade Reduces the Likelihood of Conflict				
Boehmer/Sacko[10]	2023	Trade	1870–2010	More trade = less conflict.
Dorussen[11]	2006	Trade	1970–1997	More trade = less conflict.
Dorussen/Ward[12]	2010	Trade networks	1948–2000	Trade networks (in the form of both direct and indirect linkages) reduce interstate conflict.
Gartzke[13]	2007	Trade and others	1950–1992	Globalization (as measured by trade and other indicators) reduces conflict.
Gartzke/Li[14]	2003	Trade and others	1950–1992	Globalization (as measured by trade and other indicators) reduces conflict.
Goenner[15]	2011	Trade	1950–1992	More trade = less conflict.
Hegre[16]	2009	Trade	1885–2001	More trade = less conflict.
Hegre et al.[17]	2010	Trade	1950–2000	More trade = less conflict.
Kim[18]	2023	Trade	1950–1992	More trade = less conflict.
Lee/Pyun[19]	2016	Trade and global trade openness	1950–2000	Increased trade interdependence and global trade openness both significantly increase peace.
Lee/Rider[20]	2016	Trade	1870–2001	Trade reduces conflict directly and indirectly.
Maoz[21]	2006	Trade	1816–2001	More trade polarization/interdependence = less conflict.

Continued on next page

Table 2.1. (*continued*)

Author(s)	Publish Date	Independent Variable(s)	Years	Main Finding(s)
Category 2: Trade Reduces the Likelihood of Conflict (continued)				
Maoz[22]	2009	Trade	1816–2001	More trade = less conflict.
Oneal[23]	2003	Trade	1886–1892	More trade = less conflict.
Oneal/ Russett/ Berbaum[24]	2003	Trade dependence	1885–1992	Economically important trade substantively reduces dyadic militarized disputes.
Seitz/Tarasov/ Zakharenko[25]	2015	Trade	1993–2001	More trade = less conflict.
Xiang et al.[26]	2007	Trade	1870–1992	More trade = less conflict.
Yakovlev/Spleen[27]	2022	Trade	1950–2000	Trade dependence and concentration increases peace.
Category 3: Trade Increases the Likelihood of Conflict				
Barbieri/Peters[28]	2003	Trade	1949–1992	More trade = more conflict.
Category 4: Trade Has a Mixed Effect on Conflict				
Aaronson/ Abouharb/ Wang[29]	2015	GATT/WTO membership	1950–2001	GATT/WTO membership alone does not reduce the likelihood of conflict, but when pairs of states are both GATT/WTO members and benefit from increased trade, they are less likely to engage in conflict with each other.
Akoto[30]	2021	Trade	2000–2016	Inter-industry trade increases the incidence of aggression, but intra-industry trade has the opposite effect.
Bell/Long[31]	2016	Trade	1948–2000	Trade decreases militarized conflicts when the issue under dispute is territorial or military/diplomatic; but trade increases militarized conflicts for other issues (regime, policy, humanitarian, and economic reasons).
Benson[32]	2005	Trade	1948–1992	Trade by itself does not affect conflict, but increased trade between dyads with larger economies can lead to less conflict.
Chang (CC)[33]	2005	Trade	1958–1967	The influence of trade on conflict depends on the relationship between the third party and the dispute participants: conflict will decrease if the target and the third party are friends, and will increase if they are rivals.

Table 2.1. (*continued*)

Author(s)	Publish Date	Independent Variable(s)	Years	Main Finding(s)
		Category 4: Trade Has a Mixed Effect on Conflict (continued)		
Chatagnier/ Kavakli[34]	2017	Similarity of dyad's export portfolios	1962–2000	Bilateral trade may have pacifying effects, but countries that produce and export similar goods are more likely to be in conflict.
Chen[35]	2021	Trade	1951–2010	Trade with a potential target's allies reduces the likelihood of conflict, but trade dependence on the prospective target or on the target's nonaggression-pact partners does not.
Choi[36]	2023	Trade	1900–2001	While trade generally deters conflict, these pacifying effects do not apply to highly nationalist leaders.
Cyrus[37]	2022	Trade	1950–2014	Trade raises the likelihood of conflict for countries that do not belong to the same trade agreement.
Garfinkel/ Syropoulos/ Yotov[38]	2020	Trade	1986–1999	Bilateral symmetric trade decreases military spending and the risk of conflict, but trade with a third party in the same export market increases the risk of conflict.
Gartzke/ Westerwinter[39]	2016	Trade dependence	1948–1978; 1966–1992	Only states that share symmetric economic ties experience fewer militarized conflicts; states that are asymmetrically dependent are more likely to experience militarized conflicts.
Gelpi/Grieco[40]	2008	Trade	1950–1992	Trade is not a constraint on the conflict behavior of autocracies; democratic countries are slightly more averse to initiate conflict with trading partners.
Goenner[41]	2010	Trade	1962–2000	The influence of trade depends on the elasticity of import demand, export supply, and ease of expropriation of strategic commodities. Trade in energy, non-ferrous materials, and electronics increases conflict; trade in chemicals and arms reduces conflict.
Goldsmith[42]	2006	Trade	1921–1992	Effect of trade interdependence is subject to regional variation; trade does not affect conflict in developing world.
Goldsmith[43]	2007	Trade	1950–2000	More trade = less conflict for Asian states.
Goldsmith[44]	2013	Trade (volume and interdependence)	1992–2001	Trade volume increases conflict onset, but decreases conflict escalation; trade interdependence slightly decreases conflict onset, but is insignificant for escalation.

Continued on next page

Table 2.1. (*continued*)

Author(s)	Publish Date	Independent Variable(s)	Years	Main Finding(s)
Category 4: Trade Has a Mixed Effect on Conflict (continued)				
Hegre[45]	2000	Trade	1950–1992	More trade = less conflict, but only for dyads with relatively developed countries; for less developed dyads, trade may increase the likelihood of conflict.
Hegre[46]	2004	Trade	1951–1992	Trade reduces the incentives for conflict, but this effect is most clearly seen in relatively symmetric dyads.
Jackson/ Nei[47]	2015	Trade	1823–2003	Countries with high levels of trade with their allies are less likely to be involved in wars with any other countries.
Jungblut/Stoll[48]	2002	Trade	1950–1978	Lower trade dependence = less conflict; higher trade dependence = more conflict.
Li/Reuveny[49]	2011	Trade	1970–1997	If a country expects conflict to lower (raise) the price of its import, it has an incentive to raise (reduce) conflict toward the country when its import rises. The reverse occurs for exports.
Lu/Thies[50]	2010	Trade	1885–2000	High interdependence levels strongly reduce conflict, but moderate/middle levels do not.
Lupu/Traag[51]	2013	Membership in trading community	1816–1976	States within the same trading community are less likely to experience conflict with each other.
Martin et al.[52]	2008	Trade	1950–2000	Effect of trade on war depends on geography and type of trade: bilateral trade reduces conflict; multilateral trade increases conflict.
McDonald[53]	2009	Trade and free trade policies	1970–2001	The links between aggregate trade flows and conflict depends on the level of protection: only at lower levels of protection do increased trade flows between two states reduce conflict.
Nieman[54]	2015	Trade	1870–2001	Trade initially has no impact on conflict (1870–1938), but later exerts a pacifying effect (1938–2001).
Peterson[55]	2014	Exit costs of cutting trade	1984–2000	Unilaterally high exit costs of cutting trade increase conflict, while jointly high exit costs decrease conflict.
Peterson/ Thies[56]	2012	Trade	1963–2001	Development and intra-industry trade are both needed to decrease conflict.

Table 2.1. (*continued*)

Author(s)	Publish Date	Independent Variable(s)	Years	Main Finding(s)
Category 4: Trade Has a Mixed Effect on Conflict (continued)				
Peterson/Wen[57]	2021	Trade	1994–2012	Pacifying effect of trade is high for countries with strong democratic institutions.
Peterson/Zeng[58]	2021	Trade	1995–2012	States will initiate cooperation and conflict with trading partners; higher global economic exposure for the initiator is associated with a preference for cooperation over conflict.
Pevehouse[59]	2004	Trade	1951–1958	Trade can simultaneously increase the probability of a conflict while decreasing the frequency of that conflict.
Reuveny[60]	2001	Trade	1963–1992	Conflict level may rise or fall with trade and the relationship generally varies across goods.
Sadeh/ Feldman[61]	2020	Trade	1970–2009	High levels of trade decrease the opportunity costs of conflict via the ability to substitute trade partners.
Xiang[62]	2010	Trade	1870–1992	The predicted probability of conflict is nonmonotonic, increasing at low levels of trade and decreasing at high levels.
Zeng[63]	2024	Trade	1962–2009	In bilateral trade relationships, more trade increases the risk of conflict when the weaker state can convert trade gains into military capability.

[1] Benjamin Fordham, "Power or Plenty? Economic Interests, Security Concerns, and American Intervention," *International Studies Quarterly*, Vol. 52, No. 4 (2008), pp. 737–758.

[2] Erik Gartzke, Quan Li and Charles Boehmer, "Investing in the Peace: Economic Interdependence and International Conflict," *International Organization*, Vol. 55, No. 2 (2001), pp. 391–438.

[3] Cullen Goenner, "Uncertainty of the Liberal Peace," *Journal of Peace Research*, Vol. 41, No. 5 (2004), pp. 589–605.

[4] Omar Keshk, Brian Pollins, and Rafael Reuveny, "Trade Still Follows the Flag: The Primacy of Politics in a Simultaneous Model of Interdependence and Armed Conflict," *Journal of Politics*, Vol. 66, No. 4 (2004), pp. 1155–1179.

[5] Omar Keshk, Rafael Reuveny, and Brian Pollins, "Trade and Conflict: Proximity, Country Size, and Measures," *Conflict Management and Peace Science*, Vol. 27, No. 1 (2010), pp. 3–27.

[6] Hyung Min Kim, and David L. Rousseau, "The Classic Liberals Were Half Right (or Half Wrong): New Tests of the 'Liberal Peace', 1960–88," *Journal of Peace Research*, Vol. 42, No. 5 (2005), pp. 523–543.

[7] Patrick McDonald, "Peace through Trade or Free Trade?" *Journal of Conflict Resolution*, Vol. 48, No. 4 (2004), pp. 547–572.

[8] Michael Ward and Peter Hoff, "Persistent Patterns of International Commerce," *Journal of Peace Research*, Vol. 44, No. 2 (2007), pp. 157–175.

[9] Michael Ward, Randolph Siverson, and Xun Cao, "Disputes, Democracies, and Dependencies: A Reexamination of the Kanatian Peace," *American Journal of Political Science*, Vol. 51, No. 3 (2007), pp. 583–601.

Continued on next page

Table 2.1. (*continued*)

[10] Charles Boehmer and David Sacko, "Economic Growth's Catalyzing Effect on War," *Defence and Peace Economics*, Vol. 34, No. 7 (2023), pp. 931–962.

[11] Han Dorussen, "Heterogeneous Trade Interests and Conflict: What You Trade Matters," *Journal of Conflict Resolution*, Vol. 50, No. 1 (2006), pp. 87–107.

[12] Han Dorussen and Hugh Ward, "Trade Networks and the Kantian Peace," *Journal of Peace Research*, Vol. 47, No. 1 (2010), pp. 29–42.

[13] Gartzke, "The Capitalist Peace."

[14] Gartzke and Li, "War, Peace, and the Invisible Hand," pp. 561–586.

[15] Cullen F. Goenner, "Simultaneity between trade and conflict: Endogenous instruments of mass destruction," *Conflict Management and Peace Science*, Vol. 28, No. 5 (2011), pp. 1–20.

[16] Håvard Hegre, "Trade Dependence or Size Dependence?: The Gravity Model of Trade and the Liberal Peace," *Conflict Management and Peace Science*, Vol. 26, No. 1 (2009), pp. 26–45.

[17] Håvard Hegre, John Oneal and Bruce Russett, "Trade Does Promote Peace: New Simultaneous Estimates of the Reciprocal Effects of Trade and Conflict," *Journal of Peace Research*, Vol. 47, No. 6 (2010), pp. 763–774.

[18] Kyeongbae Kim, "Trade and Peace Revisited," *Journal of Economic Integration*, Vol. 38, No. 4 (December 2023), pp. 529–544.

[19] Jong-Wha Lee and Ju Hyun Pyun, "Does Trade Integration Contribute to Peace?" *Review of Development Economics*, Vol. 20, No. 1 (2016), pp. 327–344.

[20] Hoon Lee and Toby Rider, "Evaluating the Effects of Trade on Militarized Behavior in the Context of Territorial Threat," *Foreign Policy Analysis*, Vol. 14, Issue 1 (January 2018), pp. 44–63.

[21] Zeev Maoz, "Network Polarization, Network Interdependence, and International Conflict, 1816–2002," *Journal of Peace Research*, Vol. 43, No. 4 (2006), pp. 391–411.

[22] Zeev Maoz, "The Effects of Strategic and Economic Interdependence on International Conflict Across Levels of Analysis," *American Journal of Political Science*, Vol. 53, No. 1 (2009), pp. 223–240.

[23] John Oneal, "Measuring Interdependence and Its Pacific Benefits: A Reply to Gartzke & Li," *Journal of Peace Research*, Vol. 40, No. 6 (2003), pp. 721–725.

[24] John Oneal, Bruce Russett, and Michael Berbaum, "Causes of Peace: Democracy, Interdependence, and International Organizations, 1885–1992," *International Studies Quarterly*, Vol. 47, No. 3 (2003), pp. 371–393.

[25] Michael Seitz, Alexander Tarasov and Roman Zakharenko, "Trade Costs, Conflicts, and Defense Spending," *Journal of International Economics*, Vol. 95, No. 2 (2015), pp. 305–318.

[26] Jun Xiang, Xiaohong Xu, and George Keteku, "Power: The Missing Link in the Trade Conflict Relationship," *Journal of Conflict Resolution*, Vol. 51, No. 4 (2007), pp. 646–663.

[27] Pavel Yakovlev and Brandon Spleen, "Make Concentrated Trade Not War?" *Review of Development Economics*, Vol. 26, Issue 2 (May 2022), pp. 661–686.

[28] Katherine Barbieri and Richard Alan Peters II, "Measure for Mis-Measure: A Response to Gartzke & Li," *Journal of Peace Research*, Vol. 40, No. 6 (2003), pp. 713–719.

[29] Susan Ariel Aaronson, M. Rodwan Abouharb and K. Daniel Wang, "The Liberal Illusion Is Not a Complete Delusion: The WTO Helps Member States Keep the Peace Only When It Increases Trade," *Global Economy Journal*, Vol. 15, No. 4 (2015), pp. 455–484.

[30] William Akoto, "International Trade and Cyber Conflict: Decomposing the Effect of Trade on State-sponsored Cyber Attacks," *Journal of Peace Research*, Vol. 58, Issue 5 (2021), pp. 1083–1097.

[31] Sam Bell and Andrew Long, "Trade Interdependence and the Use of Force: Do Issues Matter?" *International Interactions*, Vol. 42, Issue 5 (2016), pp. 1–24.

[32] Michelle Benson, "The Relevance of Politically Relevant Dyads in the Study of Interdependence and Dyadic Disputes," *Conflict Management and Peace Science*, Vol. 22, No. 2 (2005), pp. 113–133.

Table 2.1. (*continued*)

[33] Yuan-Ching Chang, "Economic Interdependence and International Interactions: Impact of Third-Party Trade on Political Cooperation and Conflict," *Cooperation and Conflict*, Vol. 40, No. 2 (2005), pp. 207–232.

[34] J. Tyson Chatagnier and Kerim Can Kavakli, "From Economic Competition to Military Combat: Export Similarity and International Conflict," *Journal of Conflict Resolution*, Vol. 61, No. 7 (2017), pp. 1510–1536.

[35] Frederick Chen, "Extended Dependence: Trade, Alliances, and Peace," *The Journal of Politics*, Vol. 83, No. 1 (January 2021), pp. 246–259.

[36] Seung-Whan Choi, "When Does Liberal Peace Fail? Trade and Nationalism," *Review of International Political Economy*, Vol. 30, No. 5 (2023), pp. 1907–1932.

[37] Teresa Cyrus, "Conflict or Cooperation: A Survival Analysis of the Relationship between Regional Trade Agreements and Military Conflict," *Peace Economics, Peace Science and Public Policy*, Vol. 28, Issue 3 (September 2022).

[38] Michelle Garfinkel, Constantinos Syropoulos, and Yoto Yotov, "Arming in the Global Economy: The Importance of Trade with Enemies and Friends," *Journal of International Economics*, Vol. 123 (March 2020).

[39] Erik Gartzke and Oliver Westerwinter, "The Complex Structure of Commercial Peace Contrasting Trade Interdependence, Asymmetry, and Multipolarity," *Journal of Peace Research*, Vol. 53, No. 3 (2016), pp. 325–343.

[40] Christopher Gelpi and Joseph Grieco, "Democracy, Interdependence, and the Sources of the Liberal Peace," *Journal of Peace Research*, Vol. 45, No. 1 (2008), pp. 17–36.

[41] Cullen Goenner, "From Toys to Warships: Interdependence and the Effects of Disaggregated Trade on Militarized Disputes," *Journal of Peace Research*, Vol. 47, No. 5 (2010), pp. 547–559.

[42] Goldsmith, "A Universal Proposition?"

[43] Benjamin E. Goldsmith, "A Liberal Peace in Asia?" *Journal of Peace Research*, Vol. 44, No. 1 (2007), pp. 5–27.

[44] Benjamin Goldsmith, "International Trade and The Onset and Escalation of Interstate Conflict: More to Fight About, or More Reasons Not to Fight?" *Defence and Peace Economics*, Vol. 24, No. 6 (2013), pp. 555–578.

[45] Hegre, "Development and the Liberal Peace."

[46] Håvard Hegre, "Size Asymmetry, Trade, and Militarized Conflict," *Journal of Conflict Resolution*, Vol. 48, No. 3 (2004), pp. 403–429.

[47] Matthew O. Jackson and Stephen Nei, "Networks of military alliances, wars and international trade," *Proceedings of the National Academy of Sciences of the United States of America*, Vol. 112, No. 50 (2015), pp. 15277–15284.

[48] Jungblut and Stoll, "The Liberal Peace and Conflictive Interactions."

[49] Quan Li and Rafael Reuveny, "Does Trade Prevent or Promote Interstate Conflict Initiation?" *Journal of Peace Research*, Vol. 48, No. 4 (2011), pp. 437–453.

[50] Lingyu Lu and Cameron Thies, "Trade Interdependence and the Issues at Stake in the Onset of Militarized Conflict: Exploring a Boundary Condition of Pacific Interstate Relations," *Conflict Management and Peace Science*, Vol. 27, No. 4 (2010), pp. 347–368.

[51] Yonatan Lupu and Vincent Traag, "Trading Communities, the Networked Structure of International Relations, and the Kantian Peace," *Journal of Conflict Resolution*, Vol. 57, No. 6 (2013), pp. 1011–1042.

[52] Philippe Martin, Thierry Mayer and Mathias Thoenig, "Make Trade Not War?" *Review of Economic Studies*, Vol. 75, No. 3 (2008), pp. 865–900.

[53] McDonald, *The Invisible Hand of Peace*.

[54] Mark David Nieman, "Moments in time: Temporal patterns in the effect of democracy and trade on conflict," *Conflict Management and Peace Science*, Vol. 33, No. 3 (2015), pp. 273–293.

[55] Timothy Peterson, "Dyadic Trade, Exit Costs, and Conflict," *Journal of Conflict Resolution*, Vol. 58, No. 4 (June 2014), pp. 564–591.

Continued on next page

Table 2.1. (*continued*)

[56] Timothy Peterson and Cameron Thies, "Beyond Ricardo: The Link between Intra-Industry Trade and Peace," *British Journal of Political Science*, Vol. 42, No. 4 (2012), pp. 747–767.

[57] Timothy Peterson, Shaoshuang Wen, "International Trade, Cooperation, and Conflict: The Role of Institutions and Capabilities," *Foreign Policy Analysis*, Vol. 17, Issue 4 (October 2021).

[58] Timothy Peterson and Yuleng Zeng, "Conflict and Cooperation With Trade Partners," *International Interactions*, Vol. 47, No. 2 (2021), pp. 266–290.

[59] Jon Pevehouse, "Interdependence Theory and the Measurement of Conflict," *Journal of Politics*, Vol. 66, No. 1 (2004), pp. 247–266.

[60] Rafael Reuveny, "Disaggregated Bilateral Trade and Conflict: Exploring Propositions in a Simultaneous Framework," *International Politics*, Vol. 38, No. 3 (2001), pp. 401–428.

[61] Tal Sadeh and Nizan Feldman, "Globalization and Wartime Trade," *Cooperation and Conflict*, Vol. 55, No. 2 (2020), pp. 235–260.

[62] Jun Xiang, "Relevance as a Latent Variable in Dyadic Analysis of Conflict," *The Journal of Politics*, Vol. 72, No. 2 (2010), pp. 484–498.

[63] Yuleng Zeng, "Microchips and Sneakers: Bilateral Trade, Shifting Power, and Interstate Conflict," *Journal of Peace Research*, Vol. 61, Issue 4 (July 2024), pp. 659–672.

FACTORING IN THE GLOBALIZATION OF PRODUCTION

What about the second, now central, driver of global commerce: the globalization of production? Does it also have a mixed effect on security affairs?

The few statistical studies that have sought to examine the influence of dyadic foreign direct investment (FDI) linkages have generally found that they reduce the likelihood of conflict. However, the FDI data these studies have used is plagued with various limitations (the quality and scope of FDI data is very poor relative to trade data).[12] Moreover, FDI data only partially reflects the intra-firm dispersion of production across borders and also does not capture other core components of the globalization of production that involve third parties (most notably, the significance of international subcontracting and inter-firm alliances).

In my 2005 book, *Producing Security*, I sought to systematically examine the security repercussions of all of the various components of the globalization of production through an analysis of the full range of pathways—eight in total—by which it can potentially influence security affairs.[13] Looking across these eight pathways, I concluded that the globalization of production has a mixed effect on security affairs: "The unfortunate conclusion of this book is that while the geographic dispersion of MNC production is stabilizing among the great powers, it will not promote peace elsewhere in the world. Indeed, the analysis . . . shows that this global production shift is likely to have a net negative influence on security relations among developing countries."[14]

Regarding developing countries,[15] the analysis in *Producing Security* reveals that the globalization of production is likely to be harmful for security relations principally because it exacerbates the problem of weapons proliferation.[16] A developing country that pursues globalization in defense-related production can gain access to certain weapons systems they would not otherwise have had. This can make it possible for some developing countries to quickly gain a relative advantage over regional rivals and/or to project military power over longer distances, thereby increasing the number of potential flashpoints.

Regarding the great powers, two findings from *Producing Security* concerning the globalization of production have especially great significance. The first is that the geographic dispersion of production has greatly reduced the economic benefits of military conquest among the most advanced countries (the underlying reasons why this is the case are outlined in Chapter 4). The second is that no state can now consistently remain on the cutting edge of military technology if it does not pursue significant internationalization in weapons production (this finding will be discussed further later in this chapter).

Both of the changes caused by the globalization of production are stabilizing for security relations among the great powers. In short, when the economic benefits of conquest are low and great powers cannot effectively go it alone in defense production, it will be structurally harder for a great power to "run the tables"—that is, to use one instance of conquest as a springboard for the next, and so on, and overturn the fundamental nature of the system through force.[17] Had the globalization of production existed at the time of World War II, Nazi Germany would have been much less successful: it would not have been able to effectively seize resources from the advanced societies it conquered, nor would it have been able to remain generally competitive in military technology while under an extensive economic cutoff. And today, China does not have anything like the same capacity for undertaking successful territorial revisionism that past rising powers have had in part because of these changes flowing from the globalization of production. Unlike previous rising powers, Beijing is simply not in a position to dramatically augment its power via conquest and, moreover, it also faces a historically unique, punishing trade-off between economic efficiency and strategic vulnerability in the development of defense-related technologies.[18]

OVERALL CONCLUSION

In the end, it appears that trade has a mixed influence on security relations and that the same is true regarding the globalization of production. This corresponds with the contingent theoretical understanding that Smith puts forward and runs contrary to the optimistic viewpoint that has long been championed by conventional liberalism and has recently been prominently articulated by capitalist peace theory.

What is surprising is not that global commerce has a mixed effect on security affairs—but that many will find this surprising. It would have been incredible if something as dynamic, complex, and crosscutting as global commerce had a uniform effect on war and peace. The problem here is that the arguments made by so many prominent analysts—for century after century—in favor of such an overarching effect have been too influential. There were some, most notably Smith, who advanced a more nuanced understanding, but the influence of their voices unfortunately was largely drowned out.

Pathway 2: How Does International Finance Influence Conflict?

International capital flows are now an essential element of the modern global economy: the incredible speed and volume of financial transactions across borders during recent decades is historically unprecedented. It is evident that financial flows can have dramatic effects on the economies of countries. It is therefore reasonable to think that these dramatic financial flows could have a significant influence on the likelihood of conflict.

There are some theoretical reasons to think that international capital flows may reduce the likelihood of conflict, as proponents of the capitalist peace theory would expect. Gartzke and other scholars argue that financial flows can potentially play an informational role by acting as a mechanism for states to credibly communicate resolve to each other, thereby making it easier to avoid wars due to uncertainty about how other states will act.[19] The most prominent argument for why financial flows can promote peace, however, concerns costs: in this view, financial investors will "punish" states for going to war. In his bestselling book *The Lexus and the Olive Tree*, Thomas Friedman famously outlined such a hypothesis regarding investor reactions to the onset of conflict:

International investors write investment checks to make profits. . . . Not only will international investors not fund a country's regional war . . . they will actually punish a country for fighting a war with its neighbors by withdrawing the only significance source of growth capital in the world today. As such, countries have no choice but to behave in a way that is attractive to international investors or . . . pay the price of living without them.[20]

On the other hand, there is an equal if not stronger set of theoretical reasons to think that international capital flows will not promote peace—that they will have little or no effect on the likelihood of conflict or could even potentially increase it. Regarding the potential informational role of financial flows, even some of those scholars who advance this theoretical line of argument concede that "the impact of information effects . . . may be marginal, as the reduction in uncertainty will at most be partial."[21] Concerning the argument that financial investors will punish states that engage in war, a significant number of states historically have had very little access to international capital, either by choice (such as North Korea) or by virtue of the fact that they have never had much to offer foreign investors (such as Syria); states that lack capital to begin with of course cannot suffer from capital flight in response to a conflict. In turn, for those states that do have significant access to foreign capital, conflict is just one of many factors influencing investment decisions and may not on its own be significant enough to cause financial investors to consistently flee, especially over the medium or long term.[22] Moreover, even if global capital does depart in response to conflict for an extended time, it may have already provided a state with much more access to financial resources beforehand than it would otherwise have had, thereby increasing its overall capacity to engage in aggression.[23]

Empirically, there are two related questions concerning the link between conflict and financial flows that need to be scrutinized; a range of existing analyses has looked at each. One set of studies examines whether international finance has an influence on the likelihood of conflict. And a second set of studies investigates how war influences financial markets and thus speaks to the question of whether financial investors punish states for going to war. No one has yet sought to systematically review and pull together the findings of these two literatures. This is the task I undertake below.

INTERNATIONAL FINANCE AND
THE LIKELIHOOD OF CONFLICT

Eight studies have empirically examined the relationship between some variable associated with international finance and the likelihood of conflict. The essential details regarding these analyses and their findings are shown in Table 2.2. The analyses are grouped together on the basis of the kind of independent variable they focus on: (1) global financial flows to and/or from a state, (2) the attractiveness of a state in the eyes of global financial investors, or (3) policies that governments enact to try and increase their access to global capital markets.[24]

Overall, these studies do not produce a clear result regarding how international finance affects conflict. Regarding the question at hand—do capital flows have an influence on interstate security relations?—the first group of four studies is the most relevant since they directly examine an element of financial globalization. The second group—which contains just two studies—is also very pertinent since it examines a state's creditworthiness in the eyes of financial actors, which will have a direct influence on its ability to engage in foreign borrowing. As the table shows, none of the studies in these first two groups finds that financial flows facilitate peace, as capitalist peace theory would expect: two conclude there is no effect, while three find that a greater capacity to engage in foreign borrowing increases the likelihood of conflict to some degree.

In contrast, all of the studies in the third group produce optimistic findings. Yet the variable that is used by all four of these studies—government restrictions on foreign exchange and capital account transactions—is by far the most removed from the question at hand. Specifically, these studies employ a measure of government preferences regarding foreign capital rather than actual exposure to it; this is useful for testing the influence of free-market policies regarding global capital, not financial flows.

DOES INTERNATIONAL CONFLICT
AFFECT FINANCIAL MARKETS?

How do financial investors respond to war? I identified eleven empirical analyses that directly address how wars influence financial markets in the post–World War II era. Three of these studies examine how wars influence bond yields, while eight analyze the influence of international conflict on stock prices.

Table 2.2. International Finance and Conflict

Author(s)	Publish Date	Independent Variable	Years	Main Finding(s)
Independent Variable Type 1: Financial Flows to and/or from a State				
Gartzke/Li[1]	2003	Exposure to portfolio flows	1950–1992	Exposure to portfolio flows is not statistically significant.
Helfstein[2]	2012	Foreign borrowing	1970–2001	Foreign ownership of government debt increases the likelihood of conflict.
Shea[3]	2016	Bond yields	1946–2008	Military regimes with decreasing bond yields are more likely to be the target of militarized disputes.
Rosecrance/ Thompson[4]	2003	Portfolio investments	1890–2002	International portfolio investments have no effect on the likelihood of conflict.
Independent Variable Type 2: Assessment of State by Global Financial Investors				
DiGiuseppe[5]	2015	State creditworthiness	1981–2001	Creditworthy states are more likely to initiate conflict.
Shea[6]	2020	Lending behavior	1815–1914	States that receive loans are less likely to be involved in conflict.
Independent Variable Type 3: State Policies concerning Openness to Global Capital Markets				
Boehmer/ Gartzke/Li[7]	2001	Governmental openness to capital	1951–1985	Governmental openness to capital decreases the likelihood of conflict.
Gartzke[8]	2007	Governmental openness to capital	1950–1992	Governmental openness to capital decreases the likelihood of conflict.
Gartzke/Li[9]	2003	Governmental openness to capital	1950–1992	Governmental openness to capital decreases the likelihood of conflict.
Kim[10]	2013	Governmental openness to capital	1950–2001	Governmental openness to capital decreases the likelihood of conflict.

Continued on next page

Table 2.2. (*continued*)

[1] Gartzke and Li, "War, Peace, and the Invisible Hand."

[2] Helfstein, "Liabilities of Globalization."

[3] Patrick Shea, "Borrowing Trouble: Sovereign Credit, Military Regimes, and Conflict, International Interactions," *International Interactions,* Vol. 42, Issue 3 (2016), pp. 401–428.

[4] Rosecrance and Thompson. "Trade, Foreign Investment, and Security," pp. 377–398.

[5] DiGiuseppe, "The Fiscal Autonomy of Deciders."

[6] Patrick Shea, "Money Talks: Finance, War, and Great Power Politics in the Nineteenth Century," *Social Science History,* Vol. 44, No. 2 (Summer 2020), pp. 223–249.

[7] Gartzke, Li, and Boehmer, "Investing in the Peace."

[8] Gartzke, "The Capitalist Peace."

[9] Gartzke and Li, "War, Peace, and the Invisible Hand."

[10] Nam Kyu Kim, "Testing Two Explanations of the Liberal Peace: The Opportunity Cost and Signaling Arguments," *Journal of Conflict Resolution,* Vol. 58, No. 5 (2013), pp. 894–919.

Regarding bond yields, no clear answer emerges; if anything, the few existing studies so far seem to suggest a contingent effect on conflict. Thomas Chadefaux's study, which primarily focuses on the effects of wars on government bond yields prior to the modern era of financial globalization (he examines bond yields across the entire 1816–2007 period), concludes that "on average, wars lead to a jump in bond yields. Yet many do not."[25] A second analysis that looks at the effects of recent nuclear threats by North Korea finds that government bond yields in South Korea were significantly lowered in response to North Korea's first nuclear test in 2006, but that subsequent periods with an increased nuclear threat did not produce such an effect on bond yields.[26] Finally, an examination of the Israel's military offensive in the Gaza Strip in 2008/09 shows that the onset of the offensive initially reduced Israeli government bond yields, but that this effect reversed as the conflict continued.[27]

Concerning how stock returns are influenced by conflict, Table 2.3 shows the key details of the eight relevant studies and their findings.[28] Six of these eight analyses show a mixed effect, while two of them find that stock returns decline in response to conflict. Notably, the two studies showing declines both stand apart from the others in important respects. The Hoffman and Neuenkirch study examines stock returns in Russia and Ukraine, two stock markets that differ in many ways from the more established markets examined by the other studies. Meanwhile, the Wisniewski article uses a different dependent variable than the other studies (how stock prices correspond to their expected value based on earnings).

Table 2.3. Conflict and Financial Markets

Author(s)	Publish Date	Independent Variable	Dependent Variable	Main Finding(s)
Brune et al.[1]	2015	Major U.S. wars from WWII onward (WWII, Korean War, Vietnam War, First Gulf War, Afghanistan War, Iraq War)	U.S. stock market	For wars with a "lengthy prologue," the onset of war significantly increases stock prices. In contrast, wars that occur "out of the blue" tend to decrease stock prices.
Gerlach/Yook[2]	2016	13 North Korean military attacks against South Korea from 1999–2010	South Korean stock market	After an attack, foreign investors increase holdings of South Korean stocks, while domestic investors reduce their stock holdings.
Guidolin/La Ferrara[3]	2010	Intra- and inter-state conflict onsets from 1971–2004	Stock market indices for U.S., UK, France, Japan, & world	US stock markets mostly react positively to conflicts, while the reactions of other stock markets are typically mixed.
Hoffmann/Neuenkirch[4]	2017	Russia/Ukraine conflict from 2013–2014	Stock markets in Russia and Ukraine	Conflict escalations lead to decreased returns in Russian and Ukrainian stock markets.
Huh/Pyun[5]	2018	North Korea nuclear threats from 2004–2015	South Korean stock market	Enhanced nuclear threats from North Korea sometimes reduce stock prices in South Korea, but other times have no effect.
Kollias et al.[6]	2010	Israeli military offensive in Gaza Strip from 2008–2009	Stock index for Israeli Exchange	The onset of the conflict saw negative stock market returns; as the conflict continued, this outcome reversed and the market rebounded.

Continued on next page

Table 2.3. (*continued*)

Author(s)	Publish Date	Independent Variable	Dependent Variable	Main Finding(s)
Schneider/ Troeger[7]	2006	First Gulf War, the Israel-Palestine conflict, Wars in Ex-Yugoslavia	Stock market indices for France, UK, and U.S.	Stock market reactions to international crises were most often negative, but "war rallies" occasionally occur.
Wisniewski[8]	2009	WWII, Korean War, 1958 Lebanon crisis, Vietnam War, Lebanon 1982/3 engagement, Panama invasions, Persian Gulf War, Afghanistan War, Iraq War.	U.S. stock market	During first year of conflict, the market value of stocks relative to their estimated fundamental values is lower than usual.

[1] Brune et al., "The War Puzzle."

[2] Gerlach and Yook, "Political Conflict and Foreign Portfolio Investment," pp. 178–196.

[3] Massimo Guidolin and Eliana La Ferrara, "The Economic Effects of Violent Conflict: Evidence From Asset Market Reactions," *Journal of Peace Research*, Vol. 47, Issue 6 (2010), pp. 671–684.

[4] Manuel Hoffmann and Matthias Neuenkirch, "The Pro-Russian Conflict and Its Impact on Stock Returns In Russia and the Ukraine," *International Economics and Economic Policy*, Vol. 14 (2017), pp. 61–73.

[5] Huh and Pyun, "Does Nuclear Uncertainty Threaten Financial Markets?"

[6] Kollias et al., "Armed Conflict and Capital Markets."

[7] Gerald Schneider and Vera Troeger, "War and the World Economy: Stock Market Reactions to International Conflicts," *Journal of Conflict Resolution*, Vol. 50, No. 5 (October 2006), pp. 623–645.

[8] T.P. Wisniewski, "Can Political Factors Explain the Behaviour of Stock Prices beyond the Standard Present Value Models?" *Applied Financial Economics*, Vol. 19, No. 23 (2009), pp. 1873–1884.

Three other significant points are worth noting regarding this literature. First, almost all of these studies focus just on short-term effects. Yet the Kollias et al. study reveals that although the Israeli stock market initially declined when conflict was initiated in 2008, this outcome reversed as the conflict proceeded, with the stock market rebounding in 2009. More attention should be paid to this timing issue in future work, since what matters most is how foreign capital reacts to conflict over the long term, not the short term.

Second, the research to date indicates that not all stock markets respond to conflict in the same way. In particular, there are indications the U.S. stock market is more prone to change significantly in response to conflict and also more likely to generate "war rallies" than other exchanges.[29] That being said, even the U.S. stock market does not come anywhere close to reacting to conflicts in a uniform, consistent manner: Guidolin and La Ferrara report that in response to international conflict, U.S. stock returns were positive in 13.8 percent of cases and negative in 6.9 percent of cases.[30]

Third, the Gerlach and Yook analysis deserves special attention since it is the only study that directly contrasts the actions taken by foreign investors versus domestic investors. As Gerlach and Yook underscore, it is important to "distinguish the roles played by foreign and domestic investors," since "a host country's political risk may have different implications for foreign investors than for domestic investors, leading them to respond differently."[31] They find that although domestic investors withdrew from the South Korean stock market after North Korean attacks, foreign investors actually increased their holdings of South Korean stocks—a result they argue is consistent "the well-documented benefits of international diversification" that these investors are well positioned to reap.[32]

CONCLUSION

In the end, the literature does not provide clarity regarding the nature of the relationship between international finance and conflict. A wide range of results emerge from the studies that analyze international finance as an independent variable that may influence the likelihood conflict. And the lack of clarity emerging from these studies is hardly surprising given the results from the literature on how conflict influences financial flows: bond prices and stock market returns both seem to respond in a very contingent manner to the onset of war.

At this point, we have no basis for concluding that financial flows have a clear influence on the likelihood of conflict. This conclusion will no doubt be a disappointing one for capitalist peace proponents in academia and those in the public sphere, such as Thomas Friedman, who expect global finance to promote peace. But the international financial system is clearly unstable, with two global financial crises having occurred in just the past few decades (the 1997 Asian financial crisis and the 2007–08 global financial crisis). Given this instability, it is perhaps more reasonable to lower our expectations about the potential role of international finance on conflict: so long as it does not have a significant *destabilizing* effect on security affairs, we should probably be grateful.

Pathway 3: Conquest Substitution Theory

Smith is well known for his arguments concerning the cost/benefit ratio for colonialism. He was a scathing critic of colonialism, arguing forcefully that it overall does not "pay" and that establishing "normal" trading relations with these territories would be a more preferable and profitable policy.

On the cost side, Smith underscored that colonies are costly to run. Of note, he presciently emphasized that it would likely become progressively more difficult for colonial powers to rule over their subjects because the latter would become more able to resist the former over time. Specifically, with respect to the discovery of America and the East Indies, he notes:

> At the particular time when these discoveries were made, the superiority of force happened to be so great on the side of the Europeans, that they were enabled to commit with impunity every sort of injustice in those remote countries. Hereafter, perhaps, the natives of those countries may grow stronger, or those of Europe may grow weaker, and the inhabitants of all the different quarters of the world may arrive at that equality of courage and force which, by inspiring mutual fear, can alone overawe the injustice of independent nations into some sort of respect for the rights of one another.[33]

Smith also emphasized that colonialism was costly because it stirred up conflict with other powerful countries and distorted economic activity.

On the benefits side, Smith argued—as will be stressed in Chapter 9—that reliance on colonial markets was a sign of commercial economic weakness, not strength. In his view, only uncompetitive firms would have incentives to lobby for the creation and maintenance of colonial territories they would have preferential access to.

Smith's overall conclusion regarding colonialism is nicely summarized by Earle, who notes that Smith

> clearly believed that a colonial policy did not "pay." ... The values of colonies in an imperial system should be measured, in his judgment, by the military forces they provided for imperial defense and by the revenue that they furnished for the general support of the empire. Judged by these criteria, the American colonies were a liability, not an asset, to Great Britain; they not only contributed nothing to imperial defense,

but they required British forces to be dispatched to America and they had involved the homeland only recently in a costly war with France. Stated in terms of a financial and commercial balance sheet, England would be better off without the colonies.[34]

Smith's general argument that England's interests would be best served by moving away from colonialism and aggressively pursuing free trade was an early manifestation of a notion that eventually became very prominent: that trade can serve as a substitute for conquest. According to this line of argument, it is more cost-effective for states to buy needed products and supplies in the global marketplace than to directly seize them via extraction from conquered territory.[35]

This notion, that trade can potentially serve as an effective substitute for conquest, still has force today, but it has become less relevant in recent decades; this is because—as will be emphasized in detail in Chapter 8—we no longer live in a world in which trade is the most important integrating force in global commerce. Instead, commerce today is primarily shaped by the geographic dispersion of production by MNCs. Smith and other early liberal writers who argued that trade could serve as a substitute for conquest understandably did not foresee a world in which FDI by MNCs would have the kind of prominence it has today for serving foreign markets and accessing foreign inputs and supplies.

Theoretical updating is needed given the onset of the globalization of production and its great relative significance as a driver of global commerce as compared to trade. Delineated below is theory along these lines, which I term the "conquest substitution theory." The essence of the theory is captured by Figure 2.1, which I will now explain in more detail.[36]

On the far left-hand side of Figure 2.1, the increased opportunity cost of closure to FDI is a well-established fact. To put it simply, states that close themselves off to MNCs will have greater difficulty gaining access to technologies, knowledge, and capital, thus harming their overall competitiveness in global markets.[37]

The increased ease and greatly lowered cost of both transportation and communications are also well-established facts. Dramatic advances in communications technology have made it far easier for managers to coordinate far-flung business holdings than in earlier eras. At the same time, marked recent improvements in transportation (due to factors like the advent of shipping containers on cargo ships) have made it far more economical to transport inputs and goods across vast distances than was the case in previous eras.

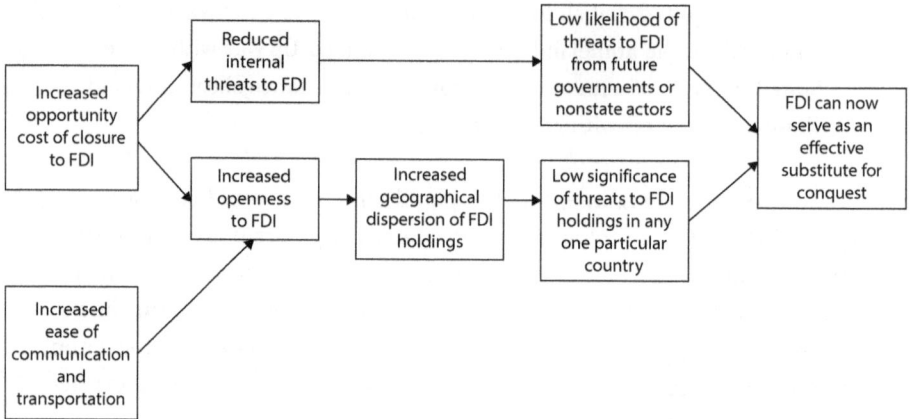

FIGURE 2.1. Conquest Substitution Theory

Moving rightward to the next column in the chart, the general response of states to these powerful new incentives is also well established. First, states in recent decades have generally rushed to change their policies to make themselves more attractive investment sites for MNCs. As a result, the overall level of openness to FDI throughout the system has greatly increased.[38]

Second, governments have generally sought to ensure that no internal threats will emerge that might threaten the interests of MNCs. Two points are of critical importance here. The first is that countries have generally sought to put in place a positive legal and institutional environment for MNCs that would be difficult for future governments to overturn.[39] In turn, governments who are hosts to FDI have overall shown a great willingness to act against threats to MNC assets that emerge from non-state actors within their territory. This dynamic is very different from previous eras, when powerful states where MNCs were based often had to intervene in order to protect MNC assets from non-state actors due to inaction by host countries.[40]

Moving rightward on the chart again, MNCs have responded to this new investment climate in a very clear manner: they have greatly increased the geographic dispersion of their FDI holdings as compared to previous eras. MNCs have always faced strong incentives to geographically diversify their FDI in order to reduce risk and to reap various locational efficiencies. However, pursuing extensive geographic dispersion in previous eras was structurally difficult for various reasons, including the difficulty of monitoring and coordinating far-flung assets. As a result, in previous eras MNCs tended to concentrate their FDI holdings in a relatively limited number of countries. Recent advances in communications and transportation have made it far easier to geographically disperse FDI holdings than in previous eras.

Moving rightward yet again to the next columns in the chart, two underlying points emerge. First, in today's world, the likelihood that governments or non-state actors will significantly threaten FDI holdings is much lower than in previous eras. Beyond the points stressed above regarding why this is the case, an additional consideration is that the purpose of most FDI has greatly changed from previous eras. In the nineteenth century and the first part of the twentieth century, the vast majority of FDI was based around the exploitation of natural resources. By the end of the twentieth century, in contrast, only around 10 percent of FDI was devoted to natural resource extraction.[41] This shift is very significant, since natural resource investments are much more tempting to seize than are service-based FDI and manufacturing-based FDI.[42] This is in large part because raw materials FDI by definition has site-specific rents. As Jeffrey Frieden notes in this regard:

> For example, the income stream created by a copper mine is specific to the place where it is located. The mine, and the resource rents associated with it, can be seized by a host country with relative ease. On the other hand, the income stream accruing to a branch plant of a manufacturing multinational corporation typically is specific to its participation in a global enterprise—it relies on managerial, marketing or technological inputs available only within the firm. While the host government can seize the factory, it cannot appropriate the rents.... Host governments have little incentive to take assets whose value disappears with the takeover.[43]

Second, the significance of threats to FDI in any one particular country is also greatly reduced as compared to previous eras. When FDI is geographically concentrated in just a few countries, threats to MNC assets in any one individual country are very concerning. But when FDI is more geographically dispersed, threats to MNC holdings in an individual country are much less threatening because other countries where the MNC has assets can likely make up the difference.

We can grasp the significance of this point is by looking at the example of Japan. In the 1930s, 82 percent of Japan's FDI was based in just one country—China—with nearly two thirds of this total based specifically in the region of Manchuria. As a result, the rise of internal unrest in

Manchuria from the mid-1920s onwards was very threatening to a number of Japanese firms with investments there and also to the Japanese government.[44] The growing threat to Japanese FDI holdings in Manchuria led to demands by many Japanese firms for protection and contributed to the onset of the Japanese military intervention in China in 1931. By the end of the twentieth century, in contrast, Japan's FDI holdings were very widely dispersed throughout the world. With this high degree of geographic dispersion, a challenge to Japanese FDI holdings in any one country would be much less threatening and hence would be much less likely to either lead to lobbying for intervention or to a government response.

The bottom line is that it has now become structurally easier for MNCs and their associated host governments to gain access to needed inputs and supplies via FDI than in previous eras. This is very significant given the significance of FDI as a driver of commerce and also because FDI is a comparatively more secure means of securing resources and supplies as compared to purchasing them in international markets; in times of scarcity, the owners of resources and supplies will have first priority in their allocation. Overall, therefore, it has now become much easier for powerful states to secure resources and supplies via non-military means.

ASSESSING CONQUEST SUBSTITUTION THEORY

How can we evaluate conquest substitution theory? One observable implication of the theory is that we should not expect to find many recent examples of states intervening militarily to protect MNCs whose assets are threatened. In fact, I am not aware of a single case of military intervention since at least 1970 in which threats to FDI holdings were the trigger for the use of military force. This dovetails with the comprehensive analysis of international crises undertaken by Michael Brecher and Jonathan Wilkenfeld.[45] They examine 412 crises across the twentieth century and code for numerous triggers, including the presence of an "economic threat." After 1965, they identify no cases in which threats to FDI holdings triggered the use of military force.

A 2012 article by Hoon Lee and Sara Mitchell empirically evaluates the underlying proposition of conquest substitution theory in another way. For similar reasons as the theoretical analysis above, Lee and Mitchell emphasize that FDI has the potential to act as "a mechanism for states to peacefully extract wealth from other countries, as opposed to extraction of resources through military conquest."[46] They then posit that "increases in global FDI flows reduce the chances for new border disputes because states can gain more from a peaceful, economic exchange of goods and services" and more specifically hypothesize that higher levels of "foreign direct investment reduce the likelihood that a pair of states becomes involved in a geopolitical issue claim."[47] Their statistical analysis strongly supports the underlying hypothesis. As Lee and Mitchell note, "Our empirical analyses provide strong support for the idea that there are declining benefits of territorial conquest in an economically globalized world. As world FDI levels have increased, states have become significantly less likely to make new diplomatic claims to other states' land or water territories. This reflects the sheer size of FDI globally today, which was not felt in earlier time periods."[48]

It is important to recognize that not all states can rely on MNCs to effectively secure external resources and supplies: states that lack significant MNCs are not in this position. Yet it is notable that the three countries that were long the largest three sources of FDI in the world (the United States, the United Kingdom, and France) all have also long been at the leading edge in terms of their material potential to project military force across large distances (by virtue of the size, nature, and especially the mobility of their military forces). Moreover, it is significant that FDI from China has been so high in recent years and that the country now has the second largest outward FDI stock (after the United States).

Pathway 4: Weapons Autonomy Trade-Off Theory

On the question of what balance a state should strike concerning the trade-off between pursuing autonomy in defense-related production versus promoting economic efficiency, Smith arguably considered this question in greater depth than any other theorist prior to the twentieth century. Mercantilist/realist political economists such as List certainly discussed the question of how a state can best provide for its defense to a significant degree, yet they never spent much time considering the autonomy-efficiency trade-off: for them, the obvious answer was that autonomy in defense-related production should be prioritized over economic efficiency when such a trade-off existed. Smith, in contrast, was far more sensitive to the need to carefully consider this trade-off and had a very conditional view as to when autonomy should be prioritized in defense-related production.

Smith's conditional assessment was rooted in his overall understanding of the trade-off between military security and economic capacity: as will be delineated in Chapter 7, he saw military security as the highest priority, but he did not see governments as privileging it over economic capacity in the short or medium term to the same degree as mercantilist/ realist political economists. Smith is clear in noting that he favored promoting autonomy only under certain specific circumstances and that he did not generally see it as "advantageous to lay some burden on foreign, for the encouragement of domestick industry."[49] This position resonates with Smith's broader argument that pursuing protectionism was very costly and instead that the best route for maximizing productivity, and thus long-term power, was to pursue free trade.

A limitation with Smith's analysis is that he only focuses on the security rationale for why pursuing autonomy in defense-related production is sometimes the best course. In explaining why he strongly supported the Navigation Acts prohibiting the use of foreign ships, he notes, "The defence of Great Britain . . . depends very much upon the number of its sailors and shipping. The act of navigation, therefore, very properly endeavors to give the sailors and shipping of Great Britain the monopoly of the trade of their own country."[50] But Smith does not specify how economically costly it was for Britain to pursue the Navigation Acts, and yet this also clearly influenced the viability of pursuing autonomy. One can only speculate as to whether his support for the Navigation Acts was partly based on an underlying, though not stated, assessment that it would not have a very high long-term economic cost for Britain.

THE PRESSURE TO GLOBALIZE DEFENSE PRODUCTION IN TODAY'S ERA

In the present era, carefully scrutinizing the economic cost of pursuing autonomy in defense-related production is of paramount importance due to the onset of the globalization of production. An essential argument that permeates *The Wealth of Nations*—that pursuing protectionism is to be avoided because it is harmful to the productivity of a state and thus to its long-term military security—now appears to apply with incredible force: these pressures now seem to be the decisive influence regarding how states approach the trade-off between pursuing autonomy in defense-related production versus promoting economic efficiency.

Specifically, the opportunity cost of closure now appears so high that even if states are willing to pay a substantial premium for the pursuit of autonomy in defense-related production, they will nevertheless still be unable to consistently remain on the cutting edge in military weaponry.

This is the underlying theory I analyzed in a portion of my book *Producing Security* (the part that examines the influence of the globalization of production on military weaponry competitiveness).[51] The hypothesis of this theory—which can be termed the "weapons autonomy trade-off theory"—is that if a state today does not pursue significant internationalization in defense-related production, it will be unable to consistently remain on the cutting edge in military technology.[52]

We can understand the essential reason why the pressure to pursue globalization in defense-related production is now so extraordinarily strong if we recognize the connection between two relevant facts. The first is that advanced weapons systems generally have incredibly long, complex production chains that are now significantly comprised of dual-use technologies (that is, technologies can be used for both civilian and military applications).[53] The second relevant fact is that the pressure to globalize production has been most intense in the very dual-use sectors that comprise the backbone of modern weaponry: when one examines the sectors that became the most globalized in recent decades, it indeed reads like a "who's who" of modern defense-related technologies. Specifically, the sectors that have had the highest degree of intra-firm trade are the following: computers, machinery, electronic components, chemicals, electrical equipment, transportation equipment, and electronic products. In turn, the sectors that have had the highest levels of international inter-firm alliances are new materials technology, microelectronics, telecommunications, chemicals, computer technology, computer software, industrial automation, and aviation.[54]

GLOBALIZATION IN DEFENSE-RELATED PRODUCTION IN TODAY'S ERA

The bottom line is that as the significance of dual-use technologies grew in defense production and, in turn, as the productivity of firms in these sectors increasingly became tied to the extent to which they globalized production, this created immense pressure to move away from autarkic defense production strategies. As the summary of the empirical analysis of weapons production in my book *Producing Security* notes, "[A]utarkic defense production has been fundamentally undermined. This is true not just for some states, but for all of them. It was already true in the 1980s, and has only solidified as the geographic dispersion of production in areas related to weaponry increases."[55] The book also states, "[E]ven those states with the largest and most advanced economies in the system—the great powers—now must strongly pursue globalization of defense-related production if they wish to remain on the leading edge in military technology."[56]

In particular, I highlighted the experience of the United States, which had "long been the country in the best position to pursue an autarkic defense production strategy due to its economic size and domestic technological capacity." In the final phase of the Cold War, the United States decided to move "away from its long-standing approach of minimizing its reliance on international sources for key aspects of defense production" and "strongly pursued globalization in defense-related production during the 1970s and 1980s."[57] This American production shift "was undertaken because defense policymakers and defense firms recognized the significant gains to be accrued by internationalizing production"; in turn, "U.S. military technological competitiveness was, in fact, enhanced by a strategy of openness during the final phase of the Cold War; isolation from the globalization of production had an independent, negative effect of Soviet ability to remain competitive with the United States in key dual-use industries and defense-related production during the 1980s."[58]

Subsequent empirical research examining other, more contemporary cases has confirmed the great underlying pressure to pursue globalization in weapons production today. Most notably, Mark Devore's detailed 2013 examination of weapons production by Israel, Sweden, and South Africa concludes that "defense-industrial self-sufficiency is no longer a feasible option for states desiring armaments that are militarily and economically competitive. . . . The case studies . . . provide additional evidence of the globalization pressures that Stephen Brooks identifies." Devore goes on to emphasize:

> Even in states strong with traditions of defense-industrial autarky, such as those examined here, defense industries are subject to a new form of globalization wherein flows of foreign direct investment and the trade in intermediate goods are becoming increasingly important. Foreign direct investment was indeed an integral component for two-thirds of the examined states' adaptive strategies, and all three engaged in the intermediate goods trade. Thus, South Africa's defense industries today largely survive as producers of components for European weaponry, and the Swedish and Israeli defense-industrial bases depend on a wide range of foreign subsystems in each of the weapons systems they produce.[59]

CONCLUSION

Smith was prescient in emphasizing the trade-off between pursuing autonomy in defense-related production versus the promotion of economic efficiency; in recent decades, this nature of this trade-off has shifted decisively. The pressure for states to move away from autonomous defense production has augmented dramatically due to the enhanced significance of dual-use technologies in weaponry and the importance of pursuing globalization in these sectors for firms seeking to maintain competitiveness. Put simply, states can no longer be self-reliant and consistently be on the cutting edge in developing military technology at the same time; they must choose.

This change in the parameters of weapons development has particularly strong significance for China. Past rising powers could consistently produce cutting-edge weaponry using just domestic producers, but this will not be a viable course for China. And because so many of the key dual-use technologies employed in modern weaponry are dominated by firms from the United States and its allies, relying on significant inputs from abroad in its defense production would be strategically risky for China.

CHAPTER THREE

Societal Actors, Economics, and War

THIS CHAPTER EXAMINES four additional pathways by which economic factors can influence security affairs. The specific focus of this chapter is the role of economic actors and other societal interests—how the former can potentially affect security policy and how the attitudes of the latter toward conflict are sometimes influenced by economic changes.

The chapter begins by examining whether poor economic conditions make leaders prone to use military force as a means of distracting the public. The second section analyzes a theory—termed the "taxes and peace theory"—which concerns how the public's support for war depends upon whether its economic costs are financed via borrowing versus a tax increase. The third section then examines how public attitudes toward conflict are influenced by the overall fiscal costs of war and by how war costs are distributed between different countries (that is, the extent of burden sharing). The final section then analyzes a theory—"the structural theory of security lobbying"—concerning the influence of the global economy on whether domestic economic actors are likely to lobby for war.

Pathway 5: How Do Poor Economic Conditions Influence Conflict?

A large literature exists concerning the "diversionary theory of war."[1] The central hypothesis in this literature is that when a leader is suffering politically, they will be more likely to use military force to distract the public. This literature largely developed in response to the "rally 'round the flag" finding that emerged in the early 1970s, which showed that presidential approval ratings increase after the use of force.[2] Yet the theory is seen as being pertinent for all states, not just democracies, whose leaders have reason to care about public approval: authoritarian leaders also face incentives to distract the public when their political fortunes are poor.

Notably, the diversionary theory of war has wide currency beyond the academy. Oneal and Tir helpfully review a series of recent instances in which U.S. politicians were seen by other politicians or journalists as acting as the theory would predict:

> In September 2002, the *New York Times* claimed in a lead editorial that "many Democrats in Congress" agree with former Vice President Gore, "who accused the White House of botching the campaign against terrorism and mobilizing the United States for war with Iraq to avoid having to talk about its economic failures." President Bush's father, George H. W. Bush, had to defend himself against similar charges in 1990 and 1992. The veteran journalist R. W. Apple Jr. argued that a president is apt to gain politically when he acts forcefully overseas, which 'has led America into a number of adventures over the last 45 years.' In 1994, the French defense minister criticized a deployment of U.S. marines to Kuwait, suggesting that the buildup was "not unconnected with domestic politics"; and in 1996, Ross Perot accused President Clinton of using military force to increase his electoral prospects.[3]

There are many poor domestic circumstances that might create incentives for a leader to use force to divert the public. However, scholars have paid particular attention to the influence of a faltering economy, which is most commonly measured by an economy's growth rate, followed by the inflation rate. Beyond these two economic variables, scholars have also examined the unemployment rate, stock market performance, recessions, and the misery index (a combination of the inflation rate and the unemployment rate).

Do poor economic conditions lead to conflict, as the diversionary theory of war predicts? Table 3.1 shows the range of findings from the 25 published studies since 2000 that examine this relationship.

Just six of the twenty-five studies find that economic weakness increases the likelihood of conflict, as the diversionary theory of war predicts. In turn, four of the twenty-five find that economic weakness lowers the likelihood of conflict—that is, the opposite of what the diversionary theory of war would expect—while five find that economic distress has no effect on the use of force. The remaining ten studies conclude that

Table 3.1. Poor Economic Conditions and Conflict

Author(s)	Publish Date	Independent Variable(s)	Years	Main Finding(s)
Category 1: Poor Economic Conditions Do Not Affect Use of Force				
Bloomberg/ Hess[1]	2002	Recessions	1950–1992	Recessions do not affect conflict.
Enterline/ Gleditsch[2]	2000	Economic growth and inflation	1948–1982	Weak economic growth does not affect conflict.
Kisangani/ Pickering[3]	2007	Economic growth and inflation	1950–1996	Growth and inflation have no impact on use of force.
Meernik[4]	2001	Unemployment and inflation	1948–1990	Unemployment and inflation do not impact Presidential use of force.
Oneal/Tir[5]	2006	Economic growth	1921–2001	Overall, no clear effect.
Category 2: Poor Economic Conditions Decrease Likelihood of Force				
Boehmer[6]	2007	Economic growth	1920–1992	Decreased growth leads leaders to avoid conflict.
Boehmer[7]	2010	Economic growth	1875–1990	Force is more likely when economic growth is high, not low.
Pickering/ Kisangani[8]	2005	Economic growth	1950–1996	Force is more likely when economic growth is high, not low.
Sirin[9]	2011	Economic downturn	1918–2005	Economic downturn = less force.
Category 3: Poor Economic Conditions Increase Likelihood of Force				
Brule et al.[10]	2010	Economic growth	1945–2001	Lower growth leads to increased dispute initiation.
Brule/ Williams[11]	2009	GDP growth per capita	1950–1997	Declining growth rate = more force.
DeRouen[12]	2000	Unemployment rate	1949–1994	Rising unemployment = more force.
Foster[13]	2006	Inflation rate	1960–1999	Higher inflation = more force.
Mitchell/ Tyhne[14]	2010	Inflation	1960–2001	High inflation = more force.
Prins[15]	2001	Economic growth	1870–1992	Decline in growth rate = more force.
Category 4: Poor Economic Conditions Have Mixed Effect on Use of Force				
Brule/ Hwang[16]	2010	Unemployment and inflation	1949–1995	When unemployment is high and Congress controlled by Democrats, Republican Presidents more likely to use force.
				When inflation is high and Congress is controlled by Republicans, Democratic Presidents more likely to use force.

Table 3.1. (*continued*)

Author(s)	Publish Date	Independent Variable(s)	Years	Main Finding(s)
Category 4: Poor Economic Conditions Have Mixed Effect on Use of Force (continued)				
Foster/ Keller[17]	2014	Economic misery	1953–2000	Economic misery increases the use of force for U.S. Presidents with a distrustful psychological profile, especially if they are low in cognitive complexity.
Foster/ Keller[18]	2020	Economic misery	1945–2007	Economic misery increases the initiation of military disputes by UK Prime Ministers with a distrustful psychological profile.
Fordham[19]	2002	Economic growth and inflation and unemployment	1870–1995	Low or negative economic growth = more force. Increased unemployment = more force. Increased inflation = less force.
Foster/ Keller[20]	2010	Misery index (inflation + unemployment)	1953–2000	Higher misery index = more force (depending on psychological proclivity of President).
Goldsmith[21]	2006	Unemployment	1990–2000	For democracies: higher unemployment = less force. Generally: higher unemployment = more force. Generally: higher unemployment does not lead to more fatal conflicts.
Johnson et al.[22]	2011	Economic growth	1950–1998	For economically closed countries, low growth = more force.
Kisangani/ Pickering[23]	2009	Economic growth and inflation	1950–1996	Increased inflation = less force. Increased economic growth = more force (for mature democracies).
Mitchell et al.[24]	2004	Inflation	1960–2001	Increased inflation = more force for enduring rivals. Increased inflation = less force for nonrivals. Increased inflation = no effect on force for democracies. Increased inflation = more force for non-democracies against enduring rivals.

Continued on next page

Table 3.1. (*continued*)

Author(s)	Publish Date	Independent Variable(s)	Years	Main Finding(s)
Category 4: Poor Economic Conditions Have Mixed Effect on Use of Force (continued)				
Pickering/ Kisangani[25]	2010	Economic growth and inflation	1950–2005	Economic growth has no effect on use of force by autocracies.
				Higher inflation = less force in autocracies.
Tir[26]	2010	Economic growth	1945–1973	Low growth rate = more conflicts, but only for fatal disputes over territory.
				For economically open countries, low growth = less force.

[1] Brock Blomberg and Gregory Hess, "The Temporal Links between Conflict and Economic Activity," *Journal of Conflict Resolution*, Vol. 46, No. 1 (2002), pp. 74–90.

[2] Andrew Enterline and Kristian Skrede Gleditsch, "Threats, Opportunities, and Force: Leaders Externalization of Domestic Pressure," *International Interactions*, Vol. 26, No. 1 (2000), pp. 21–53.

[3] Emizet Kisangani and Jeffrey Pickering, "Diverting with Benevolent Military Force: Reducing Risks and Rising above Strategic Behavior," *International Studies Quarterly*, Vol. 51, No. 2 (2007), pp. 277–299.

[4] James Meernik, "Domestic Politics and the Political Use of Military Force by the United States," *Political Research Quarterly*, Vol. 54, No. 4 (2001), pp. 889–904.

[5] John O'Neal and Jaroslav Tir, "Does the Diversionary Use of Force Threaten the Democratic Peace?: Assessing the Effect of Economic Growth on Interstate Conflict," *International Studies Quarterly*, Vol. 50, No. 4 (2006), pp. 755–779.

[6] Charles Boehmer, "The Effects of Economic Crisis, Domestic Discord, and State Efficacy on the Decision to Initiate Interstate Conflict," *Politics and Policy*, Vol. 35, No. 4 (2007), pp. 774–809.

[7] Charles Boehmer, "Economic Growth and Violent International Conflict: 1875–1999," *Defence and Peace Economics*, Vol. 21, No. 3 (2010), pp. 249–268.

[8] Jeffrey Pickering and Emizet Kisangani, "Democracy and Diversionary Military Intervention: Reassessing Regime Type and the Diversionary Hypothesis," *International Studies Quarterly*, Vol. 49, No. 1 (2005), pp. 23–43.

[9] Cigdem Sirin, "Is it Cohesion or Diversion? Domestic Instability and the Use of Force in International Crises," *International Political Science Review*, Vol. 32, No. 3 (2011), pp. 303–321.

[10] David Brule, Bryan Marshall, and Brandon Prins, "Opportunities and Presidential Uses of Force: A Selection Model of Crisis Decision-Making," *Conflict Management and Peace Science*, Vol. 27, No. 5 (2010), pp. 486–510.

[11] David Brule and Laron Williams, "Democracy and Diversion: Government Arrangements, the Economy, and Dispute Initiation," *Journal of Peace Research*, Vol. 46, No. 6 (2009), pp. 777–798.

[12] Karl DeRouen Jr, "Presidents and the Diversionary Use of Force: A Research Note," *International Studies Quarterly*, Vol. 44, No. 2 (2000), pp. 317–328.

[13] Dennis Foster, "State Power, Linkage Mechanisms, and Diversion against Nonrivals," *Conflict Management and Peace Science*, Vol. 23, No. 1 (2006), pp. 1–21.

[14] Sara Mitchell and Clayton Thyne, "Contentious Issues as Opportunities for Diversionary Behavior," *Conflict Management and Peace Science*, Vol. 27, No. 5 (2010), pp. 461–485.

[15] Brandon Prins, "Domestic Politics and Interstate Disputes: Examining US MID Involvement and Reciprocation, 1870–1992," *International Interactions*, Vol. 26, No. 4 (2001), pp. 411–438.

Table 3.1. (*continued*)

[16] David Brule and Wonjae Hwang, "Diverting the Legislature: Executive-Legislative Relations, the Economy, and US uses of force," *International Studies Quarterly*, Vol. 54, No. 2 (2010), pp. 361–379.

[17] Dennis Foster and Jonathan Keller, "Leaders' Cognitive Complexity, Distrust, and the Diversionary Use of Force," *Foreign Policy Analysis*, Vol. 10, No. 3 (2014), pp. 205–223.

[18] Dennis Foster and Jonathan Keller, "Single-Party Government, Prime Minister Psychology, and the Diversionary Use of Force: Theory and Evidence from the British Case," *International Interactions*, Vol. 46, No. 2 (2020), pp. 227–250.

[19] Benjamin Fordham, "Another Look at 'Parties, Voters, and the Use of Force Abroad,'" *Journal of Conflict Resolution*, Vol. 46, No. 4 (2002), pp. 572–596.

[20] Dennis Foster and Jonathan Keller, "Rallies and the 'First Image,'" *Conflict Management and Peace Scieince*, Vol. 27, No. 5 (2010), pp. 417–441.

[21] Benjamin Goldsmith, "Unemployment and 'Diversionary' Foreign Policy Around the World," in Graham Wrightson, ed., *The Constraints to Full Employment: Fiscal and Monetary Policy, Work Choices, and Job Insecurity* (Callaghan: Centre of Full Employment and Equity, 2006).

[22] Jesse Johnson and Tiffany Barnes, "Responsibility and the Diversionary Use of Force," *Conflict Management and Peace Science*, Vol. 28, No. 5 (2011), pp. 478–496.

[23] Emizet Kisangani and Jeffrey Pickering, "The Dividends of Diversion: Mature Democracies' Proclivity to Use Diversionary Force and the Rewards they Reap From It," *British Journal of Political Science*, Vol. 39, No. 3 (2009), pp. 483–515.

[24] Sara Mitchell and Brandon Prins, "Rivalry and Diversionary Uses of Force," *Journal of Conflict Resolution*, Vol. 48, No. 6 (2004), pp. 937–961.

[25] Jeffrey Pickering and Emizet Kisangani, "Diversionary Despots? Comparing Autocracies' Propensities to use and to Benefit from Military Force," *American Journal of Political Science*, Vol. 54, No. 2 (2010), pp. 477–493.

[26] Jaroslav Tir, "Territorial Diversion: Diversionary Theory of War and Territorial Conflict," *Journal of Politics*, Vol. 72, No. 2 (2010), pp. 413–425.

economic distress has a mixed effect on the likelihood of conflict. Most produce conditional findings showing that poor economic conditions have an influence on the use of force only for certain kinds of political systems, leaders, parties, disputes, and so on. No clear pattern emerges across these conditional studies.

What about the effects of the two most significant economic variables: the growth rate and the inflation rate? Out of the seven studies that examine the influence of inflation, just one finds that high inflation increases the use of force as the diversionary theory of war would expect. Out of the remaining six studies, three find no effect and three find that increased inflation reduces the likelihood of conflict.

In turn, out of the eleven studies that examine the direct influence of low economic growth, only four find that it increases the use of force as the diversionary theory of war would expect. Out of the remaining studies, three conclude that low growth decreases the likelihood of conflict and four find no effect.

The overall pattern of results from these studies is arguably most consistent with the theoretical argument of Ostrom and Job; they maintain that poor economic conditions do not produce clear incentives for political leaders concerning the use of force but instead create contradictory incentives that pull them in multiple directions.[4] On the one hand, they concur that a bad economy does create some incentives for leaders to divert the public's attention by using force, as the diversionary theory of war posits. But on the other hand, Ostrom and Job stress that a bad economy simultaneously creates incentives for leaders to focus on redressing the economic problems at hand and to focus their overall attention on domestic, not foreign, affairs.

Pathway 6: Taxes and Peace Theory

Smith puts forward a clearly specified theory in *The Wealth of Nations* as to why the public's support for war will vary depending upon how the war is financed. Specifically, he avers that wars financed through taxes will receive lower public support than wars financed through borrowing. He notes:

> Were the expence of war to be defrayed always by a revenue raised within a year, the taxes from which that extraordinary revenue was drawn would last no longer than the war. The ability of private people to accumulate, though less during the war, would have been greater during the peace than under the system of funding. War would not necessarily have occasioned the destruction of any old capitals, and peace would have occasioned the accumulation of many more new. Wars would in general be more speedily concluded, and less wantonly undertaken. The people feeling, during the continuance of the war, the complete burden of it, would soon grow weary of it, and government, in order to humour them, would not be under the necessity of carrying it on longer than it was necessary to do so. The foresight of the heavy and unavoidable burdens of war would hinder the people from wantonly calling for it when there was no real or solid interest to fight for. . . . The facility of borrowing delivers [leaders] from the embarrassment which this fear and inability would otherwise occasion.[5]

Until a few years ago, this intriguing theory of Smith's had not been empirically evaluated. In a 2017 article, Gustavo Flores-Macias and Sarah

Kreps outline a theoretical logic along the same lines as Smith, whom they cite and quote.[6] They stress that "taxation has a direct impact on individuals' purchasing power and draws an explicit connection between the individual and the war, whereas the costs of borrowing are deferred. This important difference makes the prospect of a war financed through extraction less palatable than through borrowing, which in turn translates into greater support for war in the absence of taxation."[7]

Using a series of original survey experiments conducted on adults in the United States and the United Kingdom, Flores-Macias and Kreps ultimately find that "individuals are more sensitive to the costs of war when they come into contact with those burdens through taxes rather than debt, a relationship that holds across democracies, types of conflicts, and party identification."[8] In short, their empirical analysis is directly in line with Smith's prediction.

A second article, by Douglas Kriner, Breanna Lechase, and Rosella Cappella Zielinski, examines this same underlying issue, also using survey experiments—which, as they correctly stress, is the most appropriate method for doing so.[9] They helpfully develop and test a more fine-grained hypothesis that considers the kind of taxation instrument that is used: broad-based regressive taxes versus progressive taxes.

In their survey experiments on the U.S. public, Kriner, Lechase, and Cappella Zielinski find that "all war taxes do not automatically decrease public support for war; rather, the influence of a tax on war support is a function of its design. Broad-based taxes that affect all Americans significantly erode public support for war. Narrowly targeted taxes that affect only the wealthy do not."[10] As they explain, "a broad-based regressive war tax, such as a national sales tax, would directly affect every American," while, in contrast, "a war tax that was narrowly targeted to affect only the very wealthy . . . would not directly increase the tax bill of the vast majority of Americans."[11]

The Kriner, Lechase, and Cappella Zielinski study is an interesting and helpful advance on Smith's underlying theoretical argument. Smith only considered the effects of a war tax that is widely felt by the public; he expected that such a tax would decrease public support for war, which is what they find. However, Kriner, Lechase, and Cappella Zielinski are correct that war taxes could be designed such that they would not be widely felt; if so, then the mechanism Smith highlights would not be operative.

Of course, that wars financed through taxes will receive lower public support compared to wars financed through borrowing doesn't necessarily mean that this dynamic will have an influence on the likelihood or severity of conflict. Smith's argument that "wars would in general be more speedily concluded, and less wantonly undertaken" if they had to be financed by taxation presumes that public opinion has an influence on security policy, at least in democracies.

But does public opinion, in fact, influence foreign policy decisions? As Benjamin Page notes, this is not easy to determine since "when opinion and policy correspond, it is extremely difficult to sort out whether public opinion has influenced policy, or policy has influenced opinion, or there has been some mixture of reciprocal processes; or, indeed, whether an outside factor, by affecting both, has produced a spurious relationship."[12] A pathbreaking recent article by Tomz, Weeks, and Yarhi-Milo brought clarity to this important question. Using an experiment in which policymakers in the United States and Israel were exposed to randomized information about public opinion, they find that incumbent political leaders actually do respond to public attitudes toward security policy "out of concern that rebuffing the public could be politically costly. . . . [A]ll else equal, policy makers were more likely to support the use of military force when the public was in favor."[13]

Pathway 7: How Do the Fiscal Costs of War and Burden Sharing Affect Public Attitudes?

It is not an accident that it took almost 250 years before there was an empirical evaluation of Smith's just discussed theory that public support for war is likely to vary depending upon how it is financed. The neglect of this theory is part of a larger pattern: the economic costs of war are rarely examined within the literature on public support for war.[14] The significance of this oversight is especially high for the United States given that its recent wars have been so incredibly costly: a recent estimate found that the combined direct expenditures of the U.S. wars in Afghanistan and Iraq totaled more than US$6 trillion.[15]

The neglect of the economic burden of war by scholars of public opinion is surprising not only because these costs are now so substantively large, but also because economic factors figure so prominently in studies of public attitudes regarding elections and other political issues. Discussed below are the two key economic factors of potential relevance regarding public attitudes toward conflict that require examination: the overall fiscal costs of war and burden sharing—that is, how war costs are distributed between different countries.

FISCAL COSTS AND PUBLIC SUPPORT

Beyond the issue discussed above regarding how a war is financed, the overall magnitude of government spending on a conflict may also be a source of concern for the public. Although borrowing may be seen as relatively less objectionable than paying for a war via taxation, taking on additional debt is likely to create significant unease with some parts of the public, especially economic conservatives.

Of course, one might wonder if the public actually has any awareness of the level of economic expenditures on a war. The evidence indicates that they do:

> Media sources spend considerable effort on portraying and discussing the financial costs of warfare. They thereby provide not only absolute numbers, but often also a contextual interpretation of these data. More-over, survey evidence suggests that at least some of this information is absorbed by the public. Indeed, the share of Americans believing that U.S. spending on defense and the military is "too high" generally strongly increases when the costs of military conflicts mount.[16]

In a 2010 article, Benny Geys undertook the first detailed examination of how the fiscal costs of war influence public attitudes. His analysis of U.S. public opinion during the 1948–2006 period produces only very slight empirical support for the proposition that high fiscal costs of war decrease public support. Geys finds that "the financial cost of the Korean War had a significant negative impact on presidential popularity. . . . Yet, such effect is much weaker in Afghanistan/Iraq and absent in Vietnam."[17] In turn, he finds that "high unemployment strongly mitigates the negative effect of war-induced spending on incumbent popularity. . . . In the absence of unemployment, war-induced spending depresses incumbent popularity in both the Korean and Afghanistan/Iraq conflicts, while increasing levels of unemployment significantly weaken this effect."[18]

Overall, the evidence so far suggests that the fiscal costs of war have only a weak conditional effect on public attitudes. More research on this question would clearly be valuable.

BURDEN SHARING AND PUBLIC SUPPORT

Beyond the fiscal costs of war, the presidency of Donald Trump highlights a second economic consideration that should be carefully investigated: burden sharing, that is, how the costs of wars are relatively distributed between different countries. Anger about "unfair" burden sharing is arguably the strongest and most consistent foreign policy preference of Trump: as a candidate and as president—and indeed for decades prior to the start of his political career—Trump has strongly and consistently repeated his view that it is unjust that the United States spends proportionally more than its allies on wars and on defense.[19] To be clear, Trump's concern is not with U.S. military expenditures in absolute terms; what bothers him is the level of American expenditures relative to its allies.

Reflecting the overall lack of attention to economic costs in the literature on the public support for war noted above, there are no published studies I am aware of that examine whether burden sharing actually affects public attitudes toward a conflict.[20] A key deficiency of the existing literature is that the provision of troops and money by other governments is not distinguished from mere endorsements by other states within international institutions; instead of isolating the influence of burden sharing and institutional endorsements, analysts instead invariably conflate them under the broader conception of "multilateral support."[21]

Yet having "multilateral support" for a military action could mean one of three different things for the United States. First, that the United States receives an institutional endorsement *and* other states contribute substantially in material terms to the operation (as in the 1991 Gulf War and the 2011 military operation in Libya). Second, that the United States receives an institutional endorsement but the military action was dominated by the United States, with virtually no material contributions by other states (as during the 1994 Haiti intervention and the initial phase of the Afghanistan war that began in 2001). Or it could mean that the United States does not receive an institutional endorsement but that other states do contribute substantially in terms of material support (as with the Multinational Force in Lebanon in 1982–1983 and many of the antiterrorism efforts that the U.S. military has conducted with the assistance of local military and law enforcement forces). The effects of these three types of scenarios on public attitudes need to be carefully separated from each other, but no published analysis I am aware of has yet done so.[22]

Because of Trump's extensive focus on burden sharing and because partisan "elite cues" have been shown to have a powerful effect on public attitudes,[23] it is problematic to use any post-2016 polls to determine how the U.S. public thinks about burden sharing (since elite cue effects would be expected to activate especially strong concerns about burden sharing among Republican respondents after Trump's initial election). Moreover, for various reasons polls are simply not well equipped to determine public attitudes toward something like burden sharing.[24]

The best way to study the influence of burden sharing is with a survey-based experiment where some respondents are exposed to a hypothetical military action in which other countries contribute a large amount of money and troops while other respondents are exposed to a scenario that is identical to the first except that the United States is fighting by itself. In such an experiment, respondents would need to react only to the scenario presented to them rather than engaging in the unrealistic exercise of explicitly weighing the causes of their support for a military action.

To study the effect of burden sharing on public attitudes, we would thus ideally use a survey-based experiment that (a) was administered prior to Trump's emergence on the political scene; and (b) carefully differentiates the two kinds of support America can receive from other countries: institutional endorsements and material burden sharing. A coauthor and I conducted such a survey experiment from July 24–31, 2010, using an internet survey delivered to a national sample of 3,000 Americans age 18 years or older by Polimetrix.[25]

In our experiment, subjects were randomly assigned to different conditions and were presented with different versions of similar news stories about a hypothetical conflict. The exact same information about the war and its stakes was reported for all of the conditions. Regarding burden sharing, subjects either read that (1) the United States would be fighting by itself, with no other countries contributing troops and money for the operation, or (2) that the United States would be fighting alongside other states, with other countries providing a substantial amount of troops and money to fight the war. And concerning institutional endorsements, subjects read one of the following: (a) the UN had unanimously endorsed a U.S.-led military intervention; (b) NATO had unanimously endorsed a U.S.-led military intervention; (c) Great Britain, Germany, and Australia had endorsed the intervention; or (d) the United States was acting on its own, with no mention of support from any other countries or institutions.

In combination, these two treatments produce an experiment with the following seven[26] conditions:

(a) the action receives the UN's endorsement, but the United States fights by itself;

(b) the action receives NATO's endorsement, but the United States fights by itself;

(c) key allies (Great Britain, Germany and Australia) endorse the action, but the United States fights by itself;

(d) the action receives the UN's endorsement, and other countries contribute substantial troops and money alongside the United States;

(e) the action receives NATO's endorsement, and NATO countries contribute substantial troops and money alongside the United States;

(f) key allies (Great Britain, Germany, and Australia) endorse the action, and these three countries also contribute substantial amounts of troops and money alongside the United States; or

(g) the United States fights by itself, and the action is not endorsed by any countries or institution.

Respondents then answered a question about their support for using force in that situation on a scale of 1 to 6, with 6 expressing the highest level of approval. The results shown in Table 3.2 indicate that burden sharing increases public support for military force by a notable amount— about half of a point on a 6-point scale. In other words, people are more likely to approve of military action when other countries are also providing troops and money for the operation.

It is also notable that the interaction between burden sharing and institutional endorsement is not significant. In other words, the increased public support for war engendered by burden sharing is not conditional on whether the UN, NATO, or just "key allies" support the action: burden sharing helps to improve support to a reasonably similar degree across all of these conditions. Ultimately, when we simultaneously vary both institutional backing for a war and burden sharing by other states, the data show that it is the latter the American people value and not the former. Interestingly, a UN endorsement actually *reduces* support for military involvement by the United States by a modest margin (.3 between UN approval vs. key allies approval) while a NATO endorsement does not appear to influence public support.

CONCLUSION

Although Smith recognized the vital importance of considering how the economic costs of wars influence public attitudes, contemporary scholarship on foreign policy opinion has neglected this issue. This oversight needs to be corrected in future research. While the initial research suggests

Table 3.2. Burden Sharing and Institutional Endorsements

	D.V. = Approve of Using Military Force	
ANOVA	F-Test	*p*-value
Burden sharing	61.94 ***	0.00
Institutional endorsement	7.85 ***	0.00
Institutional endorsement * burden sharing	0.28	0.76

		MEAN
	NO burden sharing	2.8
	WITH burden sharing	3.3
	UN approval	2.9
	NATO approval	3.1
	KEY ALLIES approve	3.2
A	UN approves with NO burden sharing	2.7
B	NATO approves with NO burden sharing	2.8
C	KEY ALLIES approve with NO burden sharing	2.9
D	UN approves WITH burden sharing	3.1
E	NATO approves WITH burden sharing	3.3
F	KEY ALLIES approve WITH burden sharing	3.4

	MEAN DIFFERENCES	Mean Diff	
A-D	UN NO burden sharing - UN WITH burden sharing	−0.4 ***	0.00
B-E	NATO NO burden sharing - NATO WITH burden sharing	−0.5 ***	0.00
C-F	KEY ALLIES NO burden sharing - KEY ALLIES burden sharing	−0.5 ***	0.00
A-B	UN NO burden sharing - NATO NO burden sharing	−0.2	0.32
A-C	UN NO burden sharing - KEY ALLIES NO burden sharing	−0.2 *	0.07
B-C	NATO NO burden sharing - KEY ALLIES NO burden sharing	−0.1	0.49
D-E	UN WITH burden sharing - NATO WITH burden sharing	−0.2	0.15
D-F	UN WITH burden sharing - KEY ALLIES WITH burden sharing	−0.3 ***	0.00
E-F	NATO WITH burden sharing - KEY ALLIES WITH burden sharing	−0.1	0.18

*** $p \leq .01$, ** $p \leq .05$, * $p \leq .10$

that the fiscal costs of war have very little influence on public attitudes, more research on this topic is clearly needed—both regarding the United States and other countries.

In contrast, the experimental research described above shows that burden sharing by other countries does, in fact, have a significant influence on U.S. public attitudes toward the use of force. Separating out the effects of endorsements by institutions or other countries, the analysis indicates that burden sharing independently increases public support for military force by a notable amount. Additional research on burden sharing should now be undertaken regarding both the United States and other countries.

Pathway 8: Structural Theory of Security Lobbying

As will be emphasized in Chapter 9, Smith saw economic actors as often lobbying the government to adopt specific policies regarding the conduct of foreign policy. Colonialism is a particularly prominent example he highlights. Smith argued contemptuously that it was weak, uncompetitive firms that lobbied for the creation and maintenance of colonies, not strong ones. As he notes: "The sneaking arts of underling tradesmen are thus erected into political maxims for the conduct of a great empire: for it is the most underling tradesmen only who make it a rule to employ chiefly their own customers. A great trader purchases his goods always where they are cheapest and best, without regard to any little interest of this kind."[27]

Although Smith observed that the ability of economic actors to influence policy was frequently very significant, he hardly thought it was absolute: as he maintains, "merchants and manufacturers . . . neither are, nor ought to be the rulers of mankind."[28] Indeed, *The Wealth of Nations* is arguably premised on the notion that economic actors would someday have a lower degree of influence over policy than they did in Smith's time. As Chapter 9 will make clear, there would have been little reason for Smith to write much of what he expressed in this book if he thought that the political significance of merchants and manufacturers would *always* be predominant. Put another way, Smith's analysis appears based on an underlying prediction, that the political role of economic actors could and would eventually be reduced.

This raises a general question: as the global economy shifts over time, will the influence of economic actors on security policy also change over time, either for all states or for some of them? Here, I will examine how recent global economic shifts have altered the significance of lobbying by economic actors regarding security policy.[29] The theory I put forward here—termed the "structural theory of security lobbying"—posits that among the economically advanced states, there is now a lack of economic actors who will be favorable toward war and will lobby the government with this preference.

Before proceeding, let me clearly specify my conceptualization of lobbying by economic actors. Following Smith, my focus is on the political behavior of firms, owners of firms, financiers, banks, industry groups, and other private financial institutions that undertake economic activities; this excludes labor unions as well as the military-industrial complex and elements of the government that deal with economic issues. And by lobbying, I mean the situation in which economic actors have preferences that they seek to actively make known to policymakers to influence their decisions. If economic actors have preferences regarding war and peace (or anything else) but don't make them directly known to policymakers in some fashion, then no lobbying has occurred.

EVALUATING THE PREDICTION

What are the reasons why some economic actors may sometimes lobby for war? This question was long understudied, but it recently was carefully examined in two weighty books by Kevin Narizny and Patrick McDonald.[30] Narizny and McDonald collectively identify a total of five potential mechanisms that can lead a subset of economic actors to have an incentive to push for military force under certain circumstances:

(1) Uncompetitive industries will favor using military force in some circumstances to annex territory to create "colonial monopolies."[31]
(2) Internationally competitive industries will favor using military force in some circumstances to prevent other countries from setting up exclusive economic zones in foreign markets that are potential export markets for these firms.[32]
(3) Raw materials industries will sometimes favor military force to allow them to secure supplies of minerals and raw materials.[33]
(4) Industries with FDI overseas will sometimes favor military force to protect their business interests from instability (coups, civil wars, and unrest) that threatens to disrupt their commercial activity.[34]
(5) Uncompetitive industries will sometimes support military conflict to slow imports.[35]

Many of these mechanisms can be traced to analyses from the pre–World War II period by scholars such as Eugene Staley and John

Hobson.[36] The key question is: are these mechanisms still relevant today, or have there been economic changes since then that reduce or eliminate their relevance? Narizny and McDonald do not address this question.

Notably, Narizny and McDonald do not consider the significance of colonialism's end in their analyses. In my assessment, mechanisms 1, 2, and 3 noted above are likely to have applicability only during the period in which formal colonial control was prevalent throughout much of the developing world (i.e., the period prior to the mid-1960s). While we once lived in a world where powerful states used the military to carve up much of the developing world into exclusive economic zones, this is no longer the case. By all indications, the option of creating colonial monopolies (mechanism 1) seems very unlikely to be operative. In today's world, it would also seem that economic actors and states have little reason to fear that their competitors will gain from the widespread establishment of exclusive economic zones in foreign markets (mechanism 2). At the same time, both states and economic actors do not have much reason to be concerned that a geographic region that is rich in raw materials will fall under the exclusive political control of a single state (mechanism 3).

As for mechanism 4, the analysis from the previous chapter regarding "conquest substitution theory" reveals why this mechanism is unlikely to have any relevance today due to the changed structure of the global economy. As was emphasized, it has now become structurally easier for advanced states with MNCs to gain access to needed inputs and supplies via FDI than in previous eras; moreover, the likelihood that a significant threat will emerge to FDI holdings from governments or non-state actors is now much lower than it was previously.

Finally, mechanism 5 does not seem plausible under any circumstances, especially today. The underlying reasons why are: (a) war may not slow imports, especially for large states and/or states that fight limited wars and (b) there are many other mechanisms for limiting imports which are less costly, more likely to be effective, and face fewer political barriers to enact.

Beyond the seeming lack of current relevance of any of the identified theoretical reasons for why some economic actors will sometimes lobby for war, the absence of recent empirical evidence regarding this dynamic is also telling. Narizny presents no recent examples of this kind. Notably, even during the pre–World War II period that Narizny focuses on, he provides very little direct evidence that economic actors ever lobbied for war (or for peace, for that matter).

As for McDonald's analysis, there are two reasons why the evidence he presents leads us to question whether any economic actors in advanced states are likely to lobby for war in the present day. First, in the pre–World War II cases he identifies in which some economic actors called for war, the examples he points to are not generalizable and/or concern dynamics that have no relevance for the present day.[37] Second, in the only post–World War II case he examines, which concerns the relationship between China and Taiwan, it appears that the variation that exists is not between those groups who favor war versus those who favor peace; rather, it would appear that some groups favor peace while others are essentially neutral—in other words, they are best seen as "not pushing for peace."[38] In turn, for these neutral groups, it seems they have this preference for non-economic reasons.[39]

In sum, all of the identified theoretical mechanisms for why some economic actors in advanced states will lobby for war no longer seem relevant in today's world. In turn, neither Narizny nor McDonald—nor any other scholar I am aware of—presents direct evidence that any such lobbying has ever occurred anytime recently.[40] My overall assessment is that although the lobbying activities of economic actors may once have had a direct influence on the likelihood of war, this is no longer the case among economically advanced states.[41]

CHAPTER FOUR

Domestic Economic Structure and War

THIS CHAPTER EXAMINES three additional pathways by which economic factors can influence interstate security relations. It focuses on the role of domestic economic structure, which is conceived by Smith as being what a society's economy is primarily geared toward producing.

The first two sections of this chapter delineate and evaluate two theories regarding how structural economic shifts can influence conflict. The first theory—"structural theory of conquest gains"—analyzes how recent structural changes in the most economically advanced states influence the potential gains of conquest. The second theory—"wealth and war initiators theory"—analyzes how structural changes associated with economic development alter both the capacity and the willingness of potential initiators of conflict.

Although these two theories together encompass a great deal of what we need to know about how domestic economic structure influences security affairs, an additional important dynamic also requires examination: how is conflict influenced by natural resource–based economic structures? The third section of this chapter examines this issue.

Pathway 9: Structural Theory of Conquest Gains

Smith developed a prominent theoretical argument regarding how changes in economic structure influence the gains of conquest. This theoretical argument was based around the four economic production stages Smith identified that societies progressively pass through as they become more advanced: hunting-gathering, shepherding, agriculture, and commerce (Chapter 8 will discuss these stages in more detail). Smith's understanding of how shifts in economic structure influence the gains of conquest incorporates (a) the opportunity cost of using military force by the conqueror and (b) how much economic benefit the conqueror could extract from the vanquished territory.

OPPORTUNITY COST

Regarding the cost portion of the conquest gains ledger, Smith emphasized that the shift to societies based around commerce increased the opportunity cost of using military force. As Winch summarizes, Smith's view was that "it was easier for agricultural societies to leave their work and yet continue to be supported while under arms. This was not the case where 'a great part of the inhabitants are artificers and manufacturers'; their work stops entirely, and they have to be maintained at public expense. The sheer expense of modern war means that the opportunity cost to society of withdrawing men from productive activities grows."[1]

The specific emphasis in Smith's discussion of opportunity cost is less relevant regarding the volunteer forces prevalent today in economically advanced societies. That being said, there are two reasons why the overall thrust of his argument concerning opportunity cost has especially strong applicability today for today's most economically advanced states. The first reason is that today's most advanced states are extremely productive. This is important because, as Coe and Markowitz emphasize,

> for every asset that is diverted from the civilian economy (or retained in the military) and employed in conquest, the conqueror will lose the value that asset would have produced had it remained in (or been returned to) the economy. This is the opportunity cost of employing the asset in conquest. By definition, the more productive each asset would have been in the economy, the higher this opportunity cost will be. Potential conquerors with higher economic productivity will therefore incur a higher opportunity cost for each productive asset they employ in conquest.[2]

The second reason concerns the shift of the most advanced states toward knowledge-based economies. In this regard, Francis emphasizes:

> Education, training, and other human capital investments provide individuals with skills that are valued in the labor market. Hence,

the opportunity cost associated with military service and, consequently, the amount that the state will have to explicitly or implicitly compensate those who choose to work in the military sector both rise with human capital. This effect holds true whether or not there is a chance of injury or death in military service. As long as the value of time rises, the cost of military personnel increases. Furthermore, the economic value of life increases in human capital. This significantly amplifies the cost of injury and loss of life in combat.[3]

THE BENEFITS OF CONQUEST AND ECONOMIC STRUCTURE

The benefits portion of the balance sheet for conquest concerns how many economic resources a conqueror can extract from a vanquished country; on this issue, Smith maintained that it was crucial to look at the economic structure of the occupied society. Smith argued that the economic benefits of occupation would be lowest during the age of hunters; in this stage of development, Smith argued that there were no real benefits of conquest because in such societies "there is almost no property amongst them" to be seized, since people do not own wild game. In contrast, Smith stressed that the age of commerce was characterized by the highest potential benefits of conquest; such societies were the most productive and thus had the most wealth for a conqueror to potentially seize.[4] And in the middle were the ages of shepherds and of agriculture, which were relatively less prosperous than commercial societies; however, the source of wealth—animals and land, respectively—could potentially be seized and exploited.[5]

Smith was far ahead of his time in making a distinction between the amount of wealth a country possessed versus the amount of wealth that a conqueror could potentially seize and, in turn, in regarding the amount of seizable wealth as a byproduct of the society's economic structure. Understanding the significance of these points has become more crucial in the current era than was the case previously. This is because the leading economies of today are qualitatively very different from the most economically advanced states of Smith's time. Regarding the benefits of occupation, we specifically need to factor in the significance of two key structural economic shifts in the most advanced states: (1) the rise of knowledge-based economies and (2) the geographic dispersion of production.[6] The fundamentals of these two structural economic shifts are delineated in the initial sections of Chapter 8.

KNOWLEDGE-BASED ECONOMIES
AND THE BENEFITS OF CONQUEST

Concerning the first key structural economic shift—the shift to production based around knowledge in the most developed states—Richard Rosecrance and Stephen Van Evera outline some arguments regarding why this recent production change has reduced the benefits of conquest. Rosecrance stresses that land is fixed and can be captured, whereas people, and the information they possess, are mobile and can potentially flee; for this reason, he argues, much of the economic surplus in knowledge-based economic economies is not available to be seized by a conqueror.[7] In his theoretical analysis, Van Evera maintains: "Today's high technology post-industrial economies depend increasingly on free access to technical and social information. . . . But the police measures needed to subdue society require that these technologies and practices be forbidden, because they also carry subversive ideas." He goes on to argue that "critical elements of the economic fabric now must be ripped out to maintain control over conquered polities."[8]

I previously outlined an additional argument for why conquerors will be unable to effectively extract benefits from knowledge-based economies. I stressed the mechanisms of economic control that are likely to be employed by a conqueror will greatly undermine innovation in knowledge-based economies, where it has a far greater salience than in agricultural-based or industrial-based economies.[9] Furthermore, we should expect there to be less available capital within the vanquished territory to bring innovative ideas to the marketplace.[10] Reduced innovation within the conquered country is likely to have strong cumulative effects, which will especially restrict the economic benefits of conquest of knowledge-based economies over the long term.

GLOBALIZATION OF PRODUCTION
AND THE BENEFITS OF CONQUEST

Regarding the second key structural economic shift—the geographic dispersion of production—its onset has meant that conquering an economically advanced country will likely only result in possession of a portion of the value-added chain, perhaps a very small portion. Until recently, if a conqueror invaded an advanced country with, say, an automotive sector, then the conqueror would be able to take possession and resume production of virtually the entire range of inputs necessary to produce the car. In today's world of advanced states having geographically dispersed production, in contrast, the car's engine might be produced in one country, the body panels in a second country, the suspension in a third, the transmission in a fourth, the brakes in a fifth, and so on. Although taking possession of a portion of the value-added chain is still valuable, it is proportionately far less valuable than it would be in a world where a conqueror could take over the complete value-added chain.[11]

Another important consideration is that states with geographically dispersed production have a strong need to ensure that they can maintain continued access to foreign firms. Recognizing this point has significant repercussions for the benefits of conquest. There are strong reasons to expect the inward flow of FDI to decline markedly if an advanced country is conquered.[12] Moreover, we should also expect that it will become much more difficult for firms in the conquered territory to establish and sustain other kinds of production links with foreign firms. Overall, we should expect the economic benefits of occupying territory to decline as the opportunity cost of isolation from foreign firms increases, as has clearly been the case in recent decades. Benefits are likely to be especially constrained over the long term, as reduced access to foreign firms in the conquered country are likely to have strong cumulative effects.

A NONLINEAR HYPOTHESIS CONCERNING THE ECONOMIC BENEFITS OF CONQUEST

In sum, a strong theoretical argument exists for why the rise of knowledge-based, geographically dispersed production in the most advanced states will prevent a potential conqueror from being able to effectively extract economic gains from conquest. Neither Rosecrance nor Van Evera nor my own previous work formulates a direct hypothesis regarding the influence of recent structural economic transformations on the likelihood of being targeted for conquest (all of these analyses focus on developing theoretical arguments about a different dependent variable—the economic benefits of conquest—and none undertakes a statistical analysis). Yet the thrust of these theoretical arguments all clearly point to a nonlinear hypothesis in this regard: at low and medium levels of economic development, increases in economic capacity will augment the probability that a state will become the target of an international conflict since it has a greater pool of wealth for conquerors to seize; in contrast, at high levels of development, the probability of being targeted will be low, given that a country's wealth will be constituted in a knowledge-based, geographically dispersed manner that prevents a conqueror from being able to effectively seize it.

To this point, such a nonlinear hypothesis has not been evaluated empirically. A 2005 article by Charles Boehmer and David Sobek is the only published study of which I am aware that examines the relationship between wealth and conflict using a nonlinear approach, but it does not analyze how economic development influences the likelihood of state being targeted in a conflict (they look only the states that initiate conflict, not the states that are attacked).[13] Moreover, Boehmer and Sobek analyze the link between development and conflict using energy consumption per capita as their measure of economic development and not GDP per capita—which is the preferable, standard measure.[14]

Figure 4.1 shows the results from a nonlinear analysis of the development/conflict link undertaken by Brian Greenhill and me that moves beyond the two limitations of the Boehmer and Sobek analysis: (1) the probability that a state becomes the target of an international conflict is used as the dependent variable; and (2) economic development is measured using GDP per capita.[15] The dependent variable is derived from the Dyadic Militarized Interstate Disputes Dataset; as is commonplace in the study of interstate conflicts, the analysis is restricted to militarized disputes that involve the actual use of force rather than merely the threat or display of force. The statistical model includes the standard control variables from the conflict literature for capturing the effects of important influences on the probability of conflict initiation within a dyad.[16]

The easiest way to interpret the results of the logistic regression is to use a visual presentation of the overall effect of development on conflict that is similar in form to "spaghetti plots."[17] Plotting the results in this way allows us to obtain a more continuous measure of the uncertainty around the estimate simply by judging the extent to which the lines overlap: points in the graph where the lines are clustered more closely together indicate higher levels of confidence in the relationship between GDP per capita and conflict, whereas those that are further apart indicate greater uncertainty.[18] To more clearly view the average effect, an additional line is included (shown in white) that shows the mean of the predicted probabilities at each level of GDP per capita.

Figure 4.1 indicates that an inverse, U-shaped relationship exists between development and the probability that a state becomes the target of an international conflict. The curve rises steadily between GDP per capita values of between around $1,000 to $10,000 dollars before beginning to level off.[19] The probability of conflict reaches a peak at a level of GDP per capita around $14,000. Once the GDP per capita begins to exceed $20,000, the probability of being targeted in a conflict sharply declines.

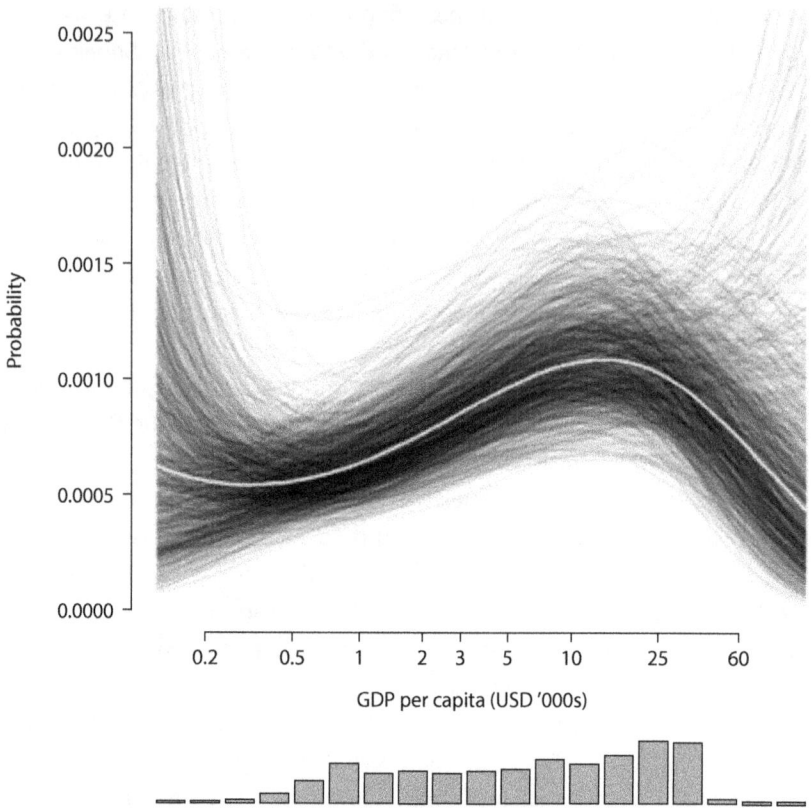

FIGURE 4.1. Wealth and Target

Significantly, the level of development at which we start to see the begin-nings of a significant downturn in the probability of being the target of a conflict—at a value of approximately $20,000 per capita—corresponds with the point at which the most developed states underwent a transition to having more knowledge-based, geographically dispersed economies.[20]

These results are consistent with the nonlinear hypothesis specified above: rising economic development initially makes a state a more tempt-ing as a target of conquest, but at higher levels of development, the rela-tionship reverses. In turn, these results are in line with Smith's two core insights on the topic, first, that it is important to distinguish between a country's wealth and the amount of wealth that a conqueror could poten-tially seize and, second, that changes in economic structure influence the amount of a country's seizable wealth.

Of course, we can only truly have confidence in a finding after a poten-tial relationship has been examined by many analysts in a variety of different ways. And so, additional nonlinear analyses of how economic development influences the likelihood of a state being targeted would now be useful.

FACTORING IN ECONOMIC COSTS AND MEASURING THE OVERALL GAINS OF CONQUEST

The nonlinear hypothesis discussed and evaluated in the previous section concerns the economic benefits of conquest. This takes us part of the way toward understanding how economic structure influences the overall gains from conquest, but we need to go further. As noted above, Smith also emphasizes that we need to factor in the economic costs of conquest—specifically, the opportunity cost of diverting capital and labor to engage in conquest. In turn, we would also ideally derive a specific estimate of the overall cost/benefit ratio for conquest for advanced states today.

The literature had long paid relatively little attention to the economic costs of conquest and had also failed to produce a specific estimate of the overall cost/benefit ratio for conquest by advanced countries. The explanation for this oversight was simple: the dearth of recent cases of extractive conquest by advanced economies to evaluate. Fortunately, this gap in the literature has now been filled by a pathbreaking recent analysis by Andrew Coe and Jonathan Markowitz.

Coe and Markowitz's theoretical argument concerns how increased economic productivity in the most advanced countries during the post–World War II period has greatly increased the opportunity cost of conquest for these countries. They also develop an innovative empirical approach for estimating the economic costs and benefits of conquest by constructing a counterfactual case that relies on data drawn from relevant actual cases. The counterfactual case of conquest that Coe and Markowitz examine is "the oil and gas reserves of Bahrain, Kuwait, Qatar, Saudi Arabia, and the United Arab Emirates."[21] They focus on this target in part since it should be the "most tempting" since its wealth is constituted in such a way that it can be seized by a potential conqueror: "the oil and gas in this territory are by far the most valuable concentration of natural resources anywhere in the world" and "the ratio of the benefits to the costs of conquest offered" is incredibly high.[22] As for their counterfactual conquerors of this target, they examine both the United States and Iraq, since each of them engaged in a similar recent instance of conquest (Iraq's invasion of Kuwait in 1990 and the U.S. invasion of Iraq in 2003) that can be used to generate estimates of the cost of conquest in their counterfactual.

Based on this analysis, Coe and Markowitz conclude that conquering the oil and gas reserves of Bahrain, Kuwait, Qatar, Saudi Arabia, and the United Arab Emirates would be unprofitable for the United States, with the costs of conquest exceeding the benefits by more than two to one. In contrast, they maintain that the benefits for Iraq of conquering these oil-producing countries would exceed the costs by at least a third. They stress that it is varying productivity that plays the "critical role in the difference in profitability between the US and Iraq. The US would employ at least one-fifth of the assets Iraq would use, but the US opportunity cost per asset would be at least seven times that of Iraq. . . . [T]he high productivity of the US economy is enough to drive the profits of conquering the most tempting target in the world well below zero."[23] They conclude that if even the United States—which has a far more advanced military than any other economically advanced state—cannot profit from conquering this especially tempting target, then this means there is no conceivable situation in which an economically advanced state could now profitably engage in conquest.

CONCLUSION

Extractive conquest had been a prominent feature of human history until very recently. The most prolific conquerors have also often been the countries that were among the most economically advanced at the time.[24] But since World War II, extractive conquest has plummeted. Why? One potential reason concerns the influence of changing economic structure on the gains from conquest. It would appear the rise of knowledge-based, geographically dispersed production in the world's most advanced countries means that their wealth can no longer be effectively seized. In turn, the high level of productivity in the most advanced economies—which are the countries with many of the world's most advanced militaries—means that the opportunity cost of conquest for these states has become extremely high; as a result, it appears that it would not be profitable for these states to engage in conquest even in those regions that contain countries with high levels of the kinds of resource-based wealth that can still be seized.

Pathway 10: Wealth and War Initiators Theory

Smith offered a careful, multifaceted understanding of how structural economic changes can alter both the capacity and the willingness of potential initiators of conflict. Regarding initiators, Smith identifies how increasing economic development in commercial societies produces three different dynamics that must be considered: (1) an increase in the opportunity cost of war; (2) a decline in "martial spirit"; and (3) an enhanced capacity to create and pay for advanced weaponry. As we shall see, these three dynamics do not all point in the same direction.

AN INCREASE IN THE OPPORTUNITY COST OF WAR

The first dynamic—that the opportunity cost of conflict increases as states develop more advanced economies—was already delineated in the previous section. It is important to recognize that Smith saw this dynamic as applying generally to all uses of military force, not just to wars of conquest. The key point is that as societies become more economically developed, there is an ever higher opportunity cost in terms of what products and services are otherwise not generated in the civilian economy because labor and capital is instead used by the military.[25] Soldiers must be recruited and deployed who could have worked in the civilian economy. On top of that, some of these soldiers will be injured or killed, which then leads to further opportunity costs in terms of the loss of future output. And fighting of course also requires allocating capital to create and use weapons and other supplies; these resources cannot be used for other purposes in the civilian economy.

A DECLINE IN "MARTIAL SPIRIT"

The second dynamic Smith highlighted was the decline in martial spirit within economically advanced societies. As Winch notes, Smith felt that as societies increasingly focus on commerce, "the populace of civilized nations lose their capacity to undertake war-like ventures."[26] For Smith, "[T]he security of every society must always depend, more or less, upon the martial spirit of the great body of the people."[27] Smith emphasizes that one "bad effect of commerce is that it sinks the courage of mankind, and tends to extinguish martial spirit. In all commercial countries . . . among the bulk of the people military courage diminishes."[28]

Smith's discussion of martial spirit thus centers on how the shift to economies centered around commerce reduces the ability and inclination of citizens to actually engage in combat. This dynamic is obviously less relevant to the most economically advanced countries of today given that they almost all rely on volunteers in their military forces.

A broader version of this argument would be that commerce lowers the overall willingness of the public in economically advanced countries

to undertake conflict. This would correspond strongly with John Mueller's argument concerning how economic development influences the
attitudes of the public toward war and the military. Specifically, Mueller
argues that war is increasingly coming to be seen as barbaric or uncivi-
lized by the citizens of developed states.[29] In his view, just as practices
like dueling came to be seen as inappropriate means of settling disputes
within domestic society, war itself may come to be viewed as "backward"
and rejected by the most advanced states. Mueller posits that it was only
after World War II that this ideational shift began to gain force among
the most advanced states.

In turn, Ronald Inglehart prominently argues that as countries
become highly developed, their citizens and/or leaders will be prone to
deemphasize "traditional" issues such as physical/military security. In
particular, Inglehart maintains that economic development has led to an
ever-increasing shift in the citizens of these countries toward focusing
on "postmaterialistic" values such as the quality of life and the health of
the environment.[30] He underscores that this value shift toward postma-
terialism and away from an emphasis on economic scarcity and physical
security has only occurred in the past few decades (since the 1970s, to be
specific) and is concentrated in the most economically developed countries where survival is no longer regarded as being especially precarious.

In sum, there is reason to expect that a loss of martial spirit will be
a significant societal force that generally pushes economically advanced
states away from the initiation of conflict.

AN ENHANCED CAPACITY TO USE AND
PAY FOR ADVANCED WEAPONRY

The third dynamic Smith highlighted was that economic development
increases the capacity to produce and pay for modern weaponry. As Smith
notes:

> The great change introduced into the art of war by the invention of fire-
> arms, has enhanced still further both the expence of exercising and dis-
> ciplining any particular number of soldiers in time of peace, and that of
> employing them in time of war. Both their arms and their ammunition
> are becoming more expensive. . . . In modern war the great expence
> of fire-arms gives an evident advantage to the nation which can best
> afford that expence; and consequently, to an opulent and civilized, over
> a poor and barbarous nation. In antient times the opulent and civilized

found it difficult to defend themselves against the poor and barbarous nations. In modern times the poor and barbarous find it difficult to defend themselves against the opulent and civilized.[31]

This dynamic Smith discusses with respect to firearms is obviously one that can be generalized: as weaponry becomes more expensive to obtain, this trend will relatively benefit advanced societies, which can better afford to bear the costs of fielding them and can thereby increase their overall capacity for initiating conflict. Moreover, as Erik Gartzke emphasizes, development "greatly enhances the technological ability of states to project power. Nations with ships and aircraft can engage in distant disputes inconceivable for poor countries."[32]

DIVERGING DYNAMICS

It is a tribute to the richness of Smith's theorizing on the relationship between wealth and conflict that the dynamics he established point in different directions, a point that the contemporary empirical literature on the link between economic development and conflict has generally neglected.[33] The first two dynamics Smith identifies (the martial spirit dynamic and the opportunity cost dynamic) point toward the expectation that states will be less likely to initiate conflict as they become more economically advanced. In contrast, the third dynamic (the military technology dynamic) points in the opposite direction. To put it another way, Smith sees development as having an inhibitory effect on conflict in some ways and as having a facilitating effect in another way.

Smith does not lay out how these diverging dynamics he points to interact; as a result, his analysis does not produce a single clear hypothesis concerning how economic development influences the likelihood of initiating conflict. If the military technology dynamic is less significant than the combined influence of the martial spirit dynamic and the opportunity cost dynamic, then we would expect to find that economic development reduces the likelihood of initiating conflict. On the other hand, if the military technology dynamic is of relatively greater significance, then we would expect to find that economic development increases the likelihood of initiating conflict. And if the military technology dynamic is of roughly equal magnitude to the combined influence of the martial spirit dynamic and the opportunity cost dynamic, this would lead to a combined effect of zero, and we would thus expect to see no overall relationship between economic development and conflict initiation.

It is also important to consider that either the inhibitory effect or the facilitating effect of development on conflict could be nonlinear.[34] This could arise if, for example, the facilitating effect begins to taper off beyond a certain level of development, and/or if the inhibitory effect only comes into operation or becomes more pronounced beyond a certain threshold.[35] It seems reasonable to posit that the military technology dynamic will operate in a linear fashion across all levels of development; as states gain resources, they will continuously increase their capacity for using force against other states. Regarding the opportunity cost dynamic, the extraordinarily rapid post–World War II rise in the economic productivity of the most advanced states has caused the opportunity cost of employing productive assets in military operations to increase in a nonlinear fashion. In turn, the arguments reviewed above concerning ideational changes in the views of the public regarding the use of force only become operative at very high levels of development.

A NONLINEAR HYPOTHESIS CONCERNING
WEALTH AND THE INITIATION OF CONFLICT

If (a) the capacity to project power continuously gains force as states advance economically but (b) the opportunity cost of using force increases especially rapidly as states become highly developed and/or states undergo ideational changes that inhibit conflict only at relatively high levels of development, then (c) we would expect to find a nonlinear relationship between economic development and the probability of conflict initiation. At first, the likelihood of conflict will increase as states become more developed because they will gain more capacity to produce weaponry.[36] But eventually, states will reach a point of development where the opportunity cost and ideational change dynamics either negate or overwhelm this facilitating effect.

The analysis below employs the same nonlinear model that was described in the previous section but with a different dependent variable: the probability that a state initiates conflict.[37] Substantively, Figure 4.2 reveals a negative relationship between economic development and the probability of conflict initiation, all else being equal. The figure suggests that a steady downward relationship initially exists between development and conflict initiation, and that the probability of initiating a conflict then declines more sharply once GDP per capita begins to exceed around $25,000. However, the higher levels of uncertainty due to the paucity of observations at the ends of the development scale make the precise nature

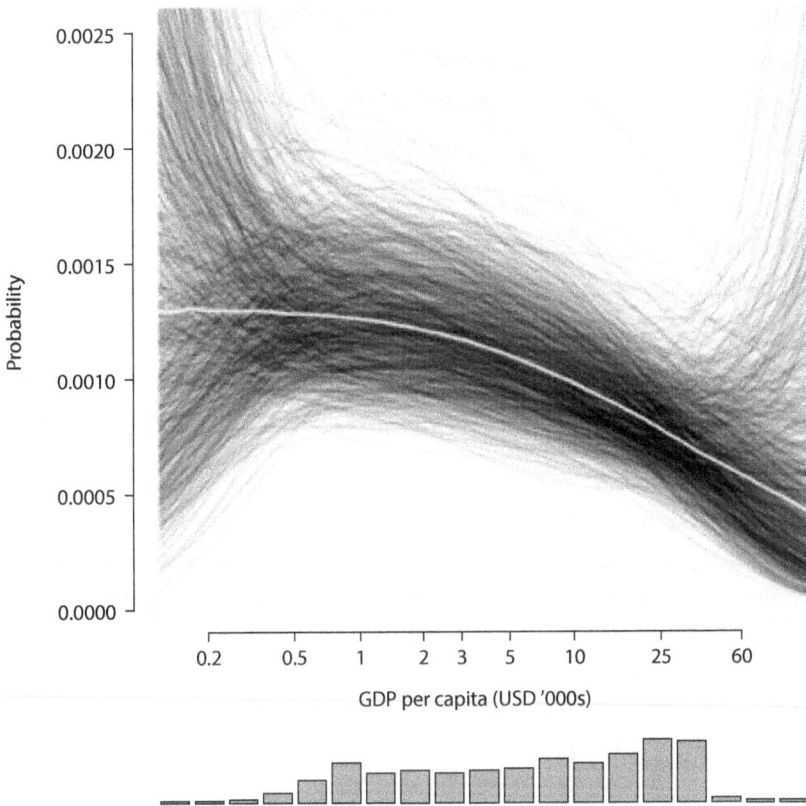

FIGURE 4.2. Wealth and Initiator

of the relationship between GDP per capita and conflict initiation difficult to discern; these results could be consistent with either an inverse, U-shaped relationship or simply a steady downward relationship between development and conflict initiation.

Boehmer and Sobek's 2005 article is the only other analysis I am aware of that examines whether a nonlinear relationship exists between wealth and the initiation of conflict.[38] Their findings point to the existence of an inverse U-shaped relationship, whereby development initially leads to an increased probability of conflict initiation at lower levels of development, reaches an inflection point at medium levels, and is thereafter is followed by a decreased probability of conflict at higher levels of development. As they note, their analysis indicates that states have a period of "violent adolescence" in the middle of their development trajectory: "states at an intermediate level of development have both the opportunity and willingness to pursue territorial claims, which makes them most prone to militarized interstate conflicts. . . . [T]hese states are akin to teens that have matured physically to some degree but require further development and socialization. No state is immune from interstate conflict, though these intermediate-level states are apparently most at risk."[39]

CONCLUSION

Smith identifies a complex relationship between economic development and the initiation of conflict. On the one hand, he maintains there are two reasons why development can have an inhibitory effect on conflict: by increasing the opportunity cost of war and producing a decline in martial spirit. On the other hand, he argues that development can also have a facilitating effect on conflict by enhancing the capacity to produce and pay for advanced weaponry.

At this point, the evidence suggests that the inhibitory effects of development on conflict are generally stronger than the facilitating effect. What is less clear is whether there is a steady downward relationship between development and conflict initiation or whether a nonlinear relationship exists in which the probability of initiating a conflict declines especially sharply after states exceed a high level of economic development. More research on this question would be valuable.

Pathway 11: How Do Natural Resources Influence Conflict?

The prospect of gaining access to natural resources has frequently been a motive for war throughout human history. In the sixteenth century, the Spanish conquered the New World in large part to seize vast quantities of gold and silver. In the nineteenth century, widespread colonialism by European powers in Africa and Asia was fueled to a significant degree by the quest for natural resources such as copper, iron, and diamonds. During World War II, aggression by Japan and Nazi Germany was driven partly by a quest to secure raw materials, especially petroleum. And in the post–World War II era, it was Kuwait's oil supplies that spurred its invasion by Iraq in 1990.

Yet the 1990 invasion of Kuwait was unusual, since wars motivated by a desire to seize natural resources, known as "resource wars," have been much less prominent in the post–World War II period than in previous eras. A key question is what the future holds. Looking forward, many analysts find reasons for pessimism.[40] A particularly prominent concern is that resource scarcity will become a stronger driver of conflict in future years due to the continuing rise in the world's population.

DO OIL SUPPLIES SPUR RESOURCE WARS?

Out of all natural resources that might fuel resource wars, oil is the one that has drawn the greatest attention and for which there is the highest concern. As Coe and Markowitz stress, this is because oil is "the most valuable and concentrated of all natural resources."[41] It is costly for states to use military force to conquer territory in order to seize resources. Conquering vast amounts of territory to seize resources of little value will most certainly not pay, but conquering a small amount of territory to capture resources of high value just might. In the assessment by Coe and Markowitz, seizing geographically concentrated oil fields may well be the only form of conquest that could still be profitable today (although, as was reviewed earlier in this chapter, they find that conquest of oil-rich territory only offers economic gains for poorer conquerors for whom the use of force has a low opportunity cost).

Some recent empirical work finds that the desire to control oil-rich territory does, in fact, still act as a driver of conflict in the current era. Most notably, a 2015 analysis by Caselli, Morelli, and Rohner concludes that conflict is more likely when one country has oil reserves close to a border with a neighboring country that has none.[42]

However, this conclusion of Caselli et al., that gaining access to oil supplies acts as a spur for conflict, has been subjected to two compelling empirical critiques. First, scholars have shown that in those conflicts in which the targeted country has oil, gaining access to oil is generally not the motivating force for aggression. Most notably, in an analysis examining a series of twentieth-century conflicts that are commonly regarded as resource wars, Emily Meierding finds that "the desire to control additional oil resources was not the fundamental cause of aggression in any of these conflicts."[43]

The second critique is advanced by Kenneth Schultz. In a careful reevaluation of the empirical findings from the Caselli, Morelli, and Rohner study, Schultz uses digital mapping data to carve the territory of the targeted state into 50-kilometer grid cells and codes for whether these cells contained oil reserves or not. After doing so, he finds that the likelihood of territorial disputes is actually lower when oil is present: "grid cells that provide access to oil are about 25 percent less likely to be the subject of a claim than those that do not."[44]

OIL AND WAR INITIATORS

Research thus casts doubt on the notion that a desire to seize oil acts as a significant driver of territorial conflict, at least in the current era. But even if oil reserves are not a *target* of conflict, oil can still potentially influence the likelihood of conflict via its influence on the *initiators* of conflict.

In this regard, some scholars have recently concluded that states with economies that are largely based around the extraction of oil, often called "petrostates," are more likely to initiate conflict than other states. Struver and Wegengast find that states with large oil reserves and high oil exports are more likely to initiate militarized disputes.[45] In turn, Hendrix finds that petrostates are more likely to initiate conflict when oil prices are high.[46] And Colgan concludes that "revolutionary petrostates"—states with high oil income and revolutionary leaders—are especially likely to initiate conflict.[47]

A MORE GENERALIZABLE CATEGORY: "LAND-ORIENTED STATES"

Findings regarding how oil-dependent states are more prone to initiate conflict are useful, but there is a more generalizable dynamic at play. As Markowitz has persuasively argued in his solo and coauthored works, oil-dependent states are a subset of a larger category of economies—"land-oriented states"—which have an economic structure that is dependent on either agriculture or natural resources.[48]

Markowitz's theoretical argument about the security behavior of land-oriented states turns the standard dynamic by which resources are seen as contributing to conflict on its head: he stresses that "variation in states' willingness to project military force is not driven by resource *scarcity*, but by *abundance*." More specifically, he argues, "it is states with abundant resources, which become economically *dependent* on the rents these resources generate, that have the strongest preference for controlling additional resources."[49] His core theoretical claim is that "land-oriented states that extract their income from the control of territory and resources have a stronger preference to secure control over territory. . . . [The] more resource-dependent a state is, the stronger its preference for projecting power to seek control over resource rents."[50]

Markowitz empirically evaluates whether land-oriented states are more likely to be assertive in the security sphere by examining a variety of foreign policy behaviors. In his book, he shows that out of the five states that border the Arctic Ocean (the United States, Canada, Denmark, Russia, and Norway), it was only the land-oriented ones—Russia and Norway—that (a) have upgraded their bases and force structure to augment their capacity to project power in the region; and (b) have been willing to deploy military force to bargain over Arctic oil and gas.

In his coauthored work, Markowitz's focus is much broader: he and his coauthors examine whether land-oriented states have a higher preference for territory and will invest more in military competition over territory. In their analysis, they find the "probability of a natural resource dependent state participating in a [militarized interstate dispute (MID)] is approximately 1.4 times higher than a state that is not dependent on natural resources" and that "the probability of a natural resource dependent state initiating a [resource-based territorial] claim is approximately 3.2 times higher than a state that is not dependent on natural resources."[51]

CONCLUSION

Many analysts have predicted of late that the world will be increasingly prone to resource wars. But even regarding oil—the natural resource over which resource wars are most likely—there is a lack of empirical evidence indicating that resource scarcity acts as a significant driver of conflict in the current era. At least so far, pessimistic concerns about the prevalence of resource wars have been overblown.

Although resource wars remain scarce, natural resources are nevertheless still a source of concern in the security realm today; however, the mechanism appears to be different from the standard scarcity dynamic that has so far predominated in the literature. The research by Markowitz indicates that the key problem today is not one of resource scarcity but resource abundance: states with a large supply of natural resources that have largely structured their economies around its extraction appear more likely to engage in conflictual security policies. Additional empirical work by other scholars regarding this line of argument is now warranted.

CHAPTER FIVE

How Do Economic Factors Influence Terrorism and Civil Conflict?

THIS CHAPTER ANALYZES the fourth and final category of pathways by which economic factors influence security affairs. Whereas the previous three chapters focused on interstate security relations, this chapter focuses on terrorism and civil conflict.

The first three sections evaluate a series of pathways regarding the link between economic factors and terrorism. The first pathway concerns how a country's level of economic development influences both forms of terrorism, domestic and transnational.[1] The chapter then examines how economic globalization affects the likelihood of transnational terrorism. The third section analyzes how economic growth influences both domestic and transnational terrorism.

The final two sections then examine how economic factors influence civil conflict. The fourth section evaluates a theory termed "wealth and civil peace theory," which concerns how a country's level of economic development influences the likelihood of civil conflict. The final section then analyzes how four different elements of the global economy influence the prospects for civil conflict.

Pathway 12: How Does Economic Development Influence Terrorism?

After the terrorist attacks on the United States on September 11, 2001, there arose immense interest in the question of whether poverty was a contributor to terrorism. In the immediate aftermath of these attacks, numerous policymakers and academics asserted that such a relationship did exist. Most prominently, President Bush argued in March 2002 that "we fight against poverty because hope is an answer to terror."

However, the initial wave of empirical studies examining this issue in the immediate wake of 9/11 generally found a lack of evidence for the supposition that poverty fostered terrorism.[2] An important question is whether this overall finding still stands. A vast amount of research has accumulated on the potential relationship between wealth and terrorism, and this section will delineate its key takeaways.

One way to conceptualize wealth is to look at the economic profile of individuals. I will not analyze here the research on whether individual wealth influences terrorism since a comprehensive review article by Wolfowicz et al. was published in 2020 that analyzed this issue.[3] Wolfowicz et al. evaluated the results of fifty different studies examining the characteristics of individuals who commit terrorist attacks or become radicalized (that is, develop "attitudes, beliefs, and ideas that justify the use of radical violence to promote change").[4] Looking across these fifty studies, Wolfowicz et al. conclude that socioeconomic status is not significant for radicalization or terrorism.[5] This non-finding conclusion dovetails with that of several other reviews of the terrorism literature undertaken in a similar timeframe.[6]

In this section, I will focus on examining whether the overall wealth of countries—that is, their level of economic development—influences the likelihood of terrorism. A key limitation of the initial wave of empirical work on the influence of a country's wealth on terrorism that emerged immediately after 9/11 is that all of the studies used linear models and did not examine whether a nonlinear relationship might exist.[7]

Starting around a decade after 9/11, a second wave of empirical studies emerged that did seek to examine whether a nonlinear relationship exists between development and terrorism. As Table 5.1 shows, 16 published studies have now investigated this question.

Significantly, all but one of these 16 studies finds that a nonlinear relationship does exist between economic development and terrorism. The one outlier study finds a nonlinear relationship does exist regarding domestic terrorism—but not for transnational terrorism. As Table 5.1 shows, there is significant variation across these 16 studies regarding the years that are analyzed as well as the dependent variable. Considering the differences across these 16 studies, the great overlap regarding their findings is striking.

The clear conclusion thus emerging from this literature is that terrorism is highest at the middle level of development. Terrorism at first is low when countries are poor, it then increases as countries become more developed, but eventually it reaches a peak level and then declines as countries become further developed. Additionally, a recent analysis of an alternative dependent variable (the formation of terrorist groups) also finds that per capita GDP has an inverted U-shaped relationship with the annual number of newly formed terrorist groups in a country.[8] Moreover, one study that examines a related dependent variable—the prevalence of nonterritorial insurgencies—similarly finds that nonterritorial insurgencies are most likely to occur in countries at the middle level of economic development.[9]

What, then, is the theoretical argument for a curvilinear relationship existing between development and terrorism? It is first important to recognize that poor states generally have few security forces that can be used to curb terrorism and also little administrative capacity.[10] In turn, the supply of potential terrorists in poor societies is also generally constrained for two reasons. First, the focus of most individuals in these societies is on subsistence.[11] Second, there are likely few available recruits with sufficient education or other needed characteristics to effectively plan and conduct successful terrorist attacks.[12]

Yet as the wealth of a country rises, changes are likely to occur regarding both the supply of potential terrorists and government capacity such that terrorism is initially likely to increase but eventually will decline. As Enders et al. note:

> For all forms of terrorism, as per capita GDP rises to some middle level in the venue or perpetrators' countries, terrorists and their supporters have greater resources to mount a larger sustained terrorist campaign. However, a threshold per capita GDP will eventually be reached where still higher per capita GDP levels will set in motion terrorism-curbing influences. After some threshold per capita GDP level, terrorists and their supporters must sacrifice much in the way of opportunity cost. Also, potential grievances are apt to dissipate as a perpetrator's economy becomes richer, where government expenditures can serve more varied

Table 5.1. Economic Development and Terrorism

Author(s)	Publish Date	Dependent Variable(s)	Years	Main Finding(s)
Bassetti et al.[1]	2018	Domestic and transnational terrorist attacks	2002–2010	Low-educated middle-income countries experience the highest number of terrorist attacks.
Boehmer/ Daube[2]	2013	Domestic terrorist attacks	1970–2000	Economic development has a curvilinear relationship with domestic terrorism, with intermediate levels of development experiencing the highest frequency of attacks.
Demirkol[3]	2022	Domestic and transnational terrorist attacks	2006–2018	There is an inverted U-shaped relationship between GDP per capita and incidents of terrorism.
Elbakidze/ Jin[4]	2015	Source of transnational terrorism	1980–2000	An inverse U-shaped relationship exists between per capita GDP and frequency of respective nationals acting as perpetrators in transnational terrorism acts.
Enders/ Hoover[5]	2012	Domestic terrorism and international terrorist attacks	1998–2007	GDP per capita has a strong nonlinear effect on both domestic and transnational terrorism.
Enders et al.[6]	2016	Domestic and transnational terrorist attacks	1970–2010	Domestic and transnational terrorist attacks are more concentrated in middle-income countries.
Ezcurra/ Palacios[7]	2016	Domestic terrorist attacks	1990–2010	A non-linear relationship exists between GDP per capita and the incidence of domestic terrorism.
Ezcurra[8]	2017	Domestic terrorist attacks	1972–2010	An inverted U-shaped link exists between domestic terrorism and GDP per capita.
Freytag et al.[9]	2011	Domestic and transnational terrorist attacks	1971–2007	Per capita income is non-linearly related to terrorism; income is negatively related to terrorism only after a certain threshold of income is reached.
Ghatak/ Gold[10]	2017	Domestic terrorist attacks	1970–2007	A curvilinear relationship exists between development and terrorism, with middle-income countries being more vulnerable to homegrown terrorist attacks.
Hou[11]	2021	Source of domestic and transnational terrorism	1970–2016	There is an inverted U-shaped relationship between per capita income and terrorist group formation.
Hunter et al.[12]	2023	Domestic terrorist attacks	2000–2019	GDP per capita has a curvilinear effect on domestic terrorism.
Jones[13]	2023	Domestic and transnational terrorism	1998–2009	There is a statistically significant inverted-U relationship between GDP per capita and domestic, but not transnational, terrorism.

Continued on next page

Table 5.1. (*continued*)

Author(s)	Publish Date	Dependent Variable(s)	Years	Main Finding
Jetter et al.[14]	2024	Domestic and transnational terrorist attacks	1970–2014	There is an inverted U-shaped relationship between GDP/capita and both domestic and transnational terrorism.
Korotayev et al.[15]	2021	Domestic and transnational terrorist attacks	1980–2014	A curvilinear relationship exists between GDP per capita and terrorist activity level.
Lai[16]	2007	Source of transnational terrorism	1968–1998	Middle-income states are most likely to be the originators of terrorism.

[1] Thomas Bassetti, Raul Caruso, and Friedrich Schneider, "The Tree of Political Violence: a GMERT Analysis," *Empirical Economics*, Vol. 54, No. 2 (2018), pp. 839–850.

[2] Charles Boehmer and Mark Daube, "The Curvilinear Effects of Economic Development on Domestic Terrorism," *Peace Economics, Peace Science and Public Policy*, Vol. 19, No. 3 (2013), pp. 359–368.

[3] Atahan Demirkol, "An Empirical Analysis of Securitization Discourse in the European Union," *Migration Letters*, Vol. 19, No. 3 (May 2022), pp. 273–286.

[4] L. Elbakidze and Y. H. Jin, "Are Economic Development and Education Improvement Associated with Participation in Transnational Terrorism?" *Risk Analysis*, Vol. 35, No. 8 (2015), pp. 1520–1535.

[5] Walter Enders and Gary Hoover, "The Nonlinear Relationship Between Terrorism and Poverty," *American Economic Review*, Vol. 102, No. 3 (2012), pp. 267–272.

[6] Enders et al., "The Changing Nonlinear Relationship," pp. 195–225.

[7] Roberto Ezcurra and David Palcios, "Terrorism and Spatial Disparities: Does Interregional Inequality Matter?" *European Journal of Political Economy*, Vol. 42 (2016), pp. 60–74.

[8] Roberto Ezcurra. "Is Government Decentralization Useful in the Fight Against Domestic Terrorism? A Cross-Country Analysis," *Environment and Planning C: Politics and Space*, Vol. 35, No. 5 (2016), pp. 872–897.

[9] Andreas Freytag, Jens J. Krüger, Daniel Meierrieks, Friedrich Schneider, "The Origins of Terrorism: Cross-Country Estimates on Socio-Economic Determinants of Terrorism," *European Journal of Political Economy*, Vol. 27, No. 1 (December 2011), pp. 5–16.

[10] Sambuddha Ghatak and Aaron Gold, "Development, Discrimination, and Domestic Terrorism: Looking Beyond a Linear Relationship," *Conflict Management and Peace Science*, Vol. 34, No. 6 (2017), pp. 618–639.

[11] Dongfang Hou, "The Formation of Terrorist Groups: An Empirical Analysis," *Defence and Peace Economics* (2021).

[12] Lance Y. Hunter, Glen Biglaiser, Ronald McGauvran, and Leann Collins, "The Effects of Social Media on Domestic Terrorism," *Behavioral Sciences of Terrorism and Political Aggression* (2023).

[13] Timothy Lee Jones, "Meta-Analysis and the Integration of Terrorism Event Databases," *International Journal of Cyber Warfare and Terrorism*, Vol. 13, Issue 1 (2023).

[14] Michael Jetter, Rafat Mahmood, and David Stadelmann, "Income and Terrorism: Insights From Subnational Data," *Journal of Conflict Resolution*, Vol. 68 (2024), pp. 509–533.

[15] Andrey Korotayev, Ilya Vaskin, and Sergey Tsirel, "Economic Growth, Education, and Terrorism: A Re-Analysis," *Terrorism and Political Violence*, Vol. 33, No. 3 (2021), pp. 572–595.

[16] Brian Lai, "'Draining the Swamp': An Empirical Examination of the Production of International Terrorism, 1968–1998," *Conflict Management and Peace Science*, Vol. 24, No. 4 (2007), pp. 297–310.

interests. The capacity of the government to quash terrorist groups or to harden potential targets will be formidable at high per capita GDP levels in either the venue or perpetrators' countries. Moreover, education levels, which are positively correlated with per capita GDP, can bolster terrorist attacks at an intermediate income level by providing terrorist groups with operatives with sufficient human capital. But after some per capita GDP, opportunity cost considerations will curb these skilled operatives' enthusiasm in the venue and perpetrators' countries.[13]

An additional consideration is that poor countries are likely to have relatively few attractive targets for terrorists. The number of attractive targets is likely to increase as a country becomes more developed, thereby creating a window of opportunity during the middle stage of development in which a significant number of potential targets will exist but sufficient state capacity for suppressing terrorism is still lacking.[14]

To summarize, the literature provides a very strong empirical basis for concluding that economic development influences terrorism in a nonlinear manner. Specifically, middle-income countries are more likely to be targeted by domestic and transnational terrorism, and such countries are also more likely to be the source of transnational terrorist attacks.

Pathway 13: How Does Economic Globalization Influence Transnational Terrorism?

In the aftermath of 9/11, numerous pundits, policymakers, and scholars posited that economic globalization had played a role in spurring these attacks and was contributing to enhanced international terrorism overall. Summing up this overall perspective, Cronin prominently argued in 2002 that "the current wave of international terrorism, characterized by unpredictable and unprecedented threats from nonstate actors, not only is a reaction to globalization but is facilitated by it."[15]

A core argument made along these lines posits that economic globalization creates disruptions that foster grievances, which in turn lead to international terrorism. For example, Hoffman asserted in 2002 that the rise of transitional terrorism is partly fueled by "a resistance to 'unjust' economic globalization. . . . Insofar as globalization enriches some and uproots many, those who are both poor and uprooted may seek revenge and self-esteem in terrorism."[16] Along similar lines, Baek and Bouzinov noted that "globalization changes the economic structure of a country necessarily producing 'losers' who may fail to adjust, generating grievances among them. Moreover, the modernization that comes with globalization may increase resistance to non-traditional values and ideas, which makes the environment more sympathetic to terror groups."[17] Looking at wider effects, Hess and Blomberg maintained that "if globalization increases world inequality, then it will increase feelings of relative deprivation. These feelings produce political action, some of it violent."[18]

Many also stressed that economic globalization reduces the cost and difficulty of conducting international terrorist operations. Regarding global trade, it was argued that "the same advances in technology that allow for easy access of goods and services also allow for easy access to military hardware and technology" and, in turn, that "the fact that customs agents inspect only a small fraction of goods imported makes the smuggling of terrorist material cheaper."[19] And regarding international finance, Stiglitz and Pagrotsky wrote in 2001, "Terrorism has highlighted the shortcomings of the global financial system in a brutal way. . . . The global financial system makes it too easy to hide money. [The] terrorists are obviously clever and well organized, which means they will find and exploit the many possibilities available to make anonymous transactions."[20]

The frequent assertions linking economic globalization to international terrorism that appeared shortly after 9/11 were made without reference to empirical evidence. In the quarter century following 9/11, a significant number of researchers have empirically analyzed whether economic globalization did, in fact, contribute to an enhanced likelihood of international terrorism as had been frequently hypothesized.

In their prominent examination of the empirical literature on this issue in a 2019 review article, Gaibulloev and Sandler conclude that "there is little convincing evidence supporting globalization as a cause of transnational terrorism."[21] However, in reaching this conclusion, Gaibulloev and Sandler only reference and discuss a small portion of the studies that analyze the relationship between economic globalization and international terrorism. A systematic review of the literature is needed to determine whether their generalization is valid.

Below I analyze the universe of empirical studies that investigate the influence of economic globalization on transnational terrorism. Three critical distinctions were made in undertaking this examination. First, I focus specifically on direct measurements of participation in economic globalization via trade, finance, and production and do not examine other measures of globalization such as WTO membership or the KOF

Globalisation Index (a composite index that combines economic elements of globalization alongside political and social ones). Second, I focus on studies that examine the influence of terrorism generally and not on those that analyze just a particular country or region. Third, I distinguish the effects of economic globalization on target countries (that is, where the terrorist incident occurred) versus source countries (that is, where terrorism originated from).

Having conducted this analysis, I find that Gaibulloev and Sandler's overall contention—namely, that globalization does not appear to be a cause of transnational terrorism—largely stands. As will be seen below, the one seeming exception concerns how trade influences the supply of transnational terrorists.

TRADE AND TRANSNATIONAL TERRORISM

Virtually all research on how trade influences terrorism has specifically focused on transnational terrorism. As shown in Table 5.2, these studies vary in terms of the years analyzed and whether they focus on the source or target of transnational terrorism.

Regarding target countries, no clear overall conclusion emerges across the 11 analyses that examine whether increased trade makes a country more likely to be targeted by transnational terrorism. Four studies find that trade decreases the likelihood of being targeted, three find that trade increases this likelihood, four find no effect, and one shows a mixed effect.

Regarding source countries, however, a clearer pattern emerges. Four of the five source studies find that higher levels of trade reduce the likelihood of a country's citizens engaging in international terrorism, none finds the converse (that trade increases the likelihood of transnational terrorism), and one finds no effect.

While further research would be useful, this initial pattern of findings thus suggests that higher levels of trade by a country reduce the likelihood that its citizens will become transnational terrorists; this runs contrary to the prominent argument after 9/11 that increased exposure to trade would enhance transnational terrorism. As for why enhanced trade may reduce the appeal of terrorism, the main theoretical argument is that openness to trade will spur growth and enhance economic opportunities, thereby reducing economy-driven grievances.[22] As Blomberg and Hess put it, "[I]f terrorism emerges from a sense of relative deprivation, then [trade], insofar that it encourages economic growth, may mitigate terrorist tendencies."[23]

Table 5.2. Trade and Transnational Terrorism

Author(s)	Publish Date	Dependent Variable	Years	Main Finding(s)
Category 1: Trade Has No Effect on Transnational Terrorism				
Baek/Bouzinov[1]	2021	Target	1984–2017	Trade does not have an influence on the likelihood of terrorist attacks.
Braithwaite/Li[2]	2007	Target	1975–1997	Trade does not have a significant effect on transnational terrorist attacks.
Li/Schaub[3]	2004	Target	1975–1997	Trade flows do not influence transnational terrorist attacks.
Robinson et al.[4]	2006	Source	1968–2003	Trade has no effect on transnational terrorism.
Sanso-Navarro/ Vera-Cabello[5]	2018	Target	1990–2014	Trade does not influence transnational terrorist attacks.
Category 2: Trade Lowers the Likelihood of Transnational Terrorism				
Blomberg/Hess[6]	2008	Source	1968–2003	High levels of trade by source countries decreases transnational terrorism.
Blomberg/ Rosendorff[7]	2009	Source	1968–2003	Trade openness in source countries decreases transnational terrorism.
Drakos/Gofas[8]	2006	Target	1985–1998	Trade exerts a negative impact on the occurrence of transnational terrorist attacks.
Elbakidze/Jin[9]	2015	Source	1980–2000	Greater trade openness reduces participation in transnational terrorism.
Kurrild-Klitgaard et al.[10]	2006	Target	1996–2002	High levels of trade are associated with lower levels of transnational terrorist attacks.
Kurrild-Klitgaard et al.[11]	2006	Source	1996–2002	The more trade-oriented a country's economy, the less likely it is to produce transnational terrorists.
Lee [12]	2021	Target	1970–2007	More trade reduces the number of transnational terrorist incidents.
Mascarenhas/ Sandler[13]	2014	Target	1980–2010	Higher trade leads to fewer transnational terrorist attacks.
Category 3: Trade Increases the Likelihood of Transnational Terrorism				
Blomberg/Hess[14]	2008	Target	1968–2003	Trade openness in the target country is associated with increased transnational terrorism.
Blomberg/ Rosendorff[15]	2009	Target	1968–2003	Higher levels of trade exposure in target countries increases transnational terrorism.
Carter/Ying[16]	2021	Target	1970–2014	Country-pairs that trade at higher levels experience more transnational terrorist flows between them.

Table 5.2. (*continued*)

Author(s)	Publish Date	Dependent Variable	Years	Main Finding(s)
Category 4: Trade Has a Mixed Effect on the Likelihood of Transnational Terrorism				
Elbakidze/Jin[17]	2012	Target	1980–2000	Low levels of trade openness decrease the frequency of attacks, but high levels of trade openness are positively associated with transnational terrorist attacks.

[1] Baek and Bouzinov, "Does Democratic Progress Deter Terrorist Incidents?"

[2] Alex Braithwaite and Quan Li, "Transnational Terrorism Hot Spot: Identification and Impact Evaluation," *Conflict Management and Peace Science*, Vol. 24, No. 4 (2007), pp. 281–296

[3] Quan Li and Drew Schaub, "Economic Globalization and Transnational Terrorism: A Pooled Time-Series Analysis," *Journal of Conflict* Resolution, Vol. 48, No. 2 (2004), pp. 230–258.

[4] Kristopher Robinson, Edward Crenshaw, and J. Craig Jenkins, "Ideologies of Violence: The Social Origins of Islamist and Leftist Terrorism," *Social Forces*, Vol. 84, No. 4 (June 2006), pp. 2009–2026.

[5] Marcos Sanso-Navarro and Maria Vera-Cabello, "The Socioeconomic Determinants of Terrorism: A Bayesian Model Averaging Approach," *Defence and Peace Economics*, Vol. 31, Issue 3 (2018), pp. 1–20.

[6] Hess and Blomberg, "The Lexus and the Olive Branch."

[7] S. Brock Blomberg and B. Peter Rosendorff, "A Gravity Model of Globalization, Democracy and Transnational Terrorism," in *Guns and Butter* (Cambridge: MIT Press, 2009), pp. 125–156.

[8] Konstantinos Drakos and Andreas Gofas, "In Search of the Average Transnational Terrorist Attack Venue," *Defence and Peace Economics*, Vol. 17, Issue 2 (2006), pp. 73–93.

[9] Elbakidze and Jin, "Are Economic Development and Education Improvement Associated with Participation in Transnational Terrorism?"

[10] Peter Kurrild-Klitgaard, Mogens K. Justesen, Robert Klemmensen, "The Political Economy of Freedom, Democracy and Transnational Terrorism," *Public Choice*, Vol. 128, No. 1/2 (Jul. 2006), pp. 289–315.

[11] Kurrild-Klitgaard et al., "The Political Economy of Freedom."

[12] Yongjae Lee, "Interstate Wars and Terrorism: The Effect of External Enemies on Domestic and Transnational Terrorism," *The Korean Journal of International Studies*, Vol. 19, No. 1 (April 2021), pp. 73–104.

[13] Raechelle Mascarenhas and Todd Sandler, "Remittances and Terrorism: A Global Analysis," *Defence and Peace Economics*, Vol. 25, No. 4 (2014), pp. 331–347.

[14] Hess and Blomberg, "The Lexus and the Olive Branch."

[15] David B. Carter and Luwei Ying, "The Gravity of Transnational Terrorism," *Journal of Conflict Resolution*, Vol. 65, No. 4 (2021), pp. 1–37.

[16] Blomberg and Rosendorff, "A Gravity Model of Globalization."

[17] L. Elbakidze and Y. H. Jin, "Victims of Transnational Terrorism: An Empirical Characteristics Analysis," *Risk Analysis*, Vol. 32, No. 12 (2012), pp. 2152–2165.

INTERNATIONAL FINANCE AND
TRANSNATIONAL TERRORISM

Research on how international finance influences terrorism is extremely sparse. Concerning source countries, the only study examining whether foreign portfolio investment (FPI) influences the likelihood of terrorism emanating from a country finds that it has no effect.[24]

With respect to target countries, no clear conclusion emerges from the two studies that examine whether a country is more likely to be a target of transnational terrorism if it has high exposure to FPI. One study finds that higher FPI increases the likelihood of being targeted, while the other finds no effect.[25]

As of now, there is no basis for concluding that FPI has an influence on transnational terrorism. More research in this area would clearly be valuable. One question not raised so far in the literature that would be worth exploring is whether the economic shocks associated with international financial crises have an influence on transnational terrorism.[26]

It should also be noted that a study by Mascarenhas and Sandler examines a related variable: remittances, that is, money that is earned by citizens living abroad and is then transferred back to their home country. They find that higher remittances do increase the likelihood of a country being a source of transnational terrorism.[27]

FDI AND TRANSNATIONAL TERRORISM

Very few studies have examined how FDI influences terrorism. As was the case regarding trade, research on the role of FDI has concentrated on examining whether it influences transnational terrorism.[28]

Only two studies analyze whether increased FDI inflows make it more likely that a country's citizens will engage in transnational terrorism. One study finds no effect, while the other finds that FDI reduces the likelihood that a country's citizens will engage in international terrorism.[29]

Four studies examine whether inflows of FDI make a country more likely to be targeted by transnational terrorists. Two find no effect, while two find that FDI reduces the likelihood of being targeted.[30]

We cannot draw clear conclusions from the limited research we have so far regarding whether FDI influences transnational terrorism. More research of this kind would be valuable.

CONCLUSION

Economic globalization was prominently highlighted right after 9/11 as being a key factor contributing to transnational terrorism. However, these claims were made without reference to empirical evidence.

The empirical studies since then have not provided evidence of a relationship existing between economic globalization and transnational terrorism. The one seeming exception concerns the influence of trade on the source of transnational terrorism: the existing findings suggest that higher levels of exposure to trade lower the likelihood that a country's citizens will undertake transnational terrorism.

More research would clearly be valuable to better establish the nature of the relationship between economic globalization and transnational terrorism. In conducting these analyses, researchers should consider that economic globalization may have cross-cutting effects on transnational terrorism—augmenting its prospects in some ways and lessening it in others. After 9/11, numerous analysts were quick to outline reasons why economic globalization could potentially enhance the threat of transnational terrorism. Far less discussed was the opposite dynamic, the ways in which economic globalization might serve to reduce the threat of transnational terrorism. Recall from Chapter 2 that global commerce appears to have a mixed effect on the likelihood of interstate conflict. Along the same lines, there are many reasons to think that "economic globalization is a double-edged sword [that] has the potential both to enhance and to reduce the terrorist threat simultaneously."[31]

Pathway 14: How Does Economic Growth Influence Terrorism?

Changes in a country's level of economic growth is another pathway by which economic factors can potentially influence terrorism. Dozens of scholars have examined whether there is a link between economic growth and terrorism, and they have done so in a variety of ways. For studies that examine transnational terrorism, a key distinction concerns whether scholars examine the level of economic growth in the source country or the target country. While a large number of studies examine the influence of economic growth regarding the target country, only a handful analyze the influence of economic growth concerning the source country.

SOURCE COUNTRY STUDIES

I will first discuss the source country studies. Scholars have outlined various reasons why economic growth may influence the number of transnational terrorist attacks originating from a country. On the one hand, increasing wealth may raise the opportunity cost of engaging in terror and/or reduce certain grievances that might motivate terrorism.[32] On the other hand, terrorism may be enhanced by transformations caused by higher economic growth, such as "a more pronounced clash between secular and sectarian modes of life."[33] In turn, "positive gains in GDP may allow terrorist organizations greater opportunity for material resources to continue engaging in violence."[34]

The four existing source country studies all examine different time periods.[35] Another distinction is that while two of them focus specifically on transnational terrorism, the other two look at transnational terrorism and domestic terrorism in combination. Yet all four studies reach the same overall conclusion: economic growth is not associated with increases in terrorism.

The one asterisk to this overall conclusion is that Kis-Katos et al. do find that economic growth makes one particular form of terrorism—what they term "right-wing terrorism"—more likely. They conceptualize right-wing terrorism as groups "with national-socialist or fascist ideologies, who actively promote racial or national supremacy, hatred, or xenophobic ideas. Moreover, we also classify anti-revolutionary groups as right-wing if they fight left-wing regimes."[36] To explain why only right-wing terrorism becomes more likely when economic growth is higher, Kis-Katos et al. posit that supporters of the extreme right are those that "lose from economic and social transformation of the society bringing about structural change, growing autonomy of the individual, and social differentiation" and that the "intensity of transition processes that create such modernization losers can be approximated by the economy-wide growth rate."[37] Since right-wing terrorism is far less prevalent than terrorism by the other three types of terror groups they identify (left-wing terror groups, ethnic-separatist terror groups, and religious terror groups), Kis-Katos et al. find that the total effect of economic growth on terrorism is not significant.[38]

Overall, it appears that economic growth does not influence the likelihood of terrorism originating from a country. Of course, over significant periods of time, high levels of economic growth can accumulate and eventually can produce changes in a country's overall economic development, a factor that was analyzed in the first section of this chapter.

TARGET COUNTRY STUDIES

There are 35 published studies that examine whether a relationship exists between economic growth and the likelihood of a country being targeted by a terrorist attack. Scholars have outlined various cross-cutting theoretical reasons for why economic growth can potentially influence whether a country is the target of terrorism. On the one hand, if economic growth exacerbates existing inequalities, it can fuel frustration and anger felt by certain individuals and groups that can lead to terrorism.[39] On the other hand, periods of high economic growth will result in more tax revenue for governments, thereby allowing for greater expenditures on counterterrorism measures.[40] In turn, there is a lower opportunity cost for joining a terrorist group when economic growth is constrained, since the economic opportunities foregone are lower than would be the case in periods of high economic growth.[41]

The key findings of the 35 studies on this topic are shown in Table 5.3 (note that there are 40 rows in this table, since five of these studies appear twice because they report findings regarding two different dependent variables). As can be seen, these studies vary across three dimensions: (1) the time period analyzed, (2) the countries studied, and (3) the nature of the terrorism investigated (transnational terrorism, domestic terrorism, or both in combination).

Looking at the results from these studies, no clear overall conclusion emerges. Fifteen of the studies show no effect, ten indicate a negative effect (that is, growth makes a country less likely to be targeted by terrorism), eight suggest a positive effect (that is, growth makes a country more likely to become a target), and seven have mixed results.

Things do not become clearer when we break these studies down into more specific groupings. Of the ten studies that look at targeting by both transnational and domestic terrorism across the entire world, three show no effect, two suggest a positive effect, one indicates a negative effect, and four have mixed results. Of the twelve studies that look at targeting by both transnational and domestic terrorism only within specific regions or countries, two show no effect, three suggest a positive effect, five indicate a negative effect, and two studies have mixed results. Of the eleven studies that analyze targeting just by transnational terrorism, eight show no effect, one shows a positive effect, and two show a negative effect. And of the seven studies that focus on targeting just by domestic terrorism, two show no effect, one indicates a positive effect, three suggest a negative effect, and one has a mixed result.

Table 5.3. Economic Growth and Targeting by Terrorism

Author(s)	Dependent Variable(s)	Publish Date	Countries Studied	Years	Main Finding(s)
Category 1: Economic Growth Does Not Affect Likelihood of Being Targeted by Terrorism					
Baek/ Bouzinov [1]	Transnational and domestic terrorist attacks	2021	Worldwide	1984–2017	Economic growth does not have a statistically significant effect on the likelihood of terrorism.
Campos/ Gassebner [2]	Transnational terrorist attacks	2013	Worldwide	1973–2003	GDP growth has no statistically discernable effect on the likelihood of transnational terrorism.
Drakos/Gofas [3]	Transnational terrorist attacks	2006	Worldwide	1985–1998	GDP growth has an insignificant impact on the likelihood of transnational terrorist activity.
Dreher/ Gassebner [4]	Transnational terrorist attacks	2008	Worldwide	1975–2001	Economic growth does not affect the likelihood of transnational terror events.
Dreher/ Fischer [5]	Transnational terrorist attacks	2010	Worldwide	1976–2000	GDP growth has no statistically significant effect on the likelihood of terrorism in the target countries of transnational terrorism.
Fahey/LaFree [6]	Domestic terrorist attacks	2015	Worldwide	1981–2010	Changes in GDP do not have a statistically significant effect on the incidence of domestic terrorist attacks.
Fahey/LaFree [7]	Transnational terrorist attacks	2015	Worldwide	1981–2010	GDP growth does not have a statistically significant effect on transantional terrorist attacks.
Feldmann/ Perälä [8]	Transnational and domestic terrorist attacks	2004	Latin America	1980–1995	Economic growth does not display a robust relationship to terrorist activity in Latin America.

Table 5.3. (*continued*)

Author(s)	Dependent Variable(s)	Publish Date	Countries Studied	Years	Main Finding(s)
Category 1: Economic Growth Does Not Affect Likelihood of Being Targeted by Terrorism (continued)					
Gassebner/ Luechinger [9]	Transnational and domestic terrorist attacks	2011	Worldwide	1980–2005	GDP growth is not robustly related to transnational terrorism.
Gassebner/ Luechinger [10]	Domestic terrorist attacks	2011	Worldwide	1980–2005	GDP growth is not robustly related to domestic terrorism.
Ismail/Amjad [11]	Transnational and domestic terrorist attacks	2014	Pakistan	1972–2011	GDP growth does not causally affect the risk of terrorism in Pakistan.
Kis-Katos et al. [12]	Transnational terrorist attacks	2011	Worldwide	1970–2007	Higher rates of GDP growth have a non-statistically significant correlation with transnational terrorism.
Krueger/ Laitin [13]	Transnational and domestic terrorist attacks	2008	Worldwide	1980–2002	GDP growth has no statistically discernable effects on transantional terrorism.
Kurrild-Klitgaard et al. [14]	Transnational terrorist attacks	2006	Worldwide	1996–2002	Transnational terrorism is unrelated to economic growth.
Piazza [15]	Transnational and domestic terrorist attacks	2006	Worldwide	1986–2002	GDP growth is unrelated to levels of terrorism.
Category 2: Economic Growth Decreases Likelihood of Being Targeted by Terrorism					
Caruso/ Schneider [16]	Transnational and domestic terrorist attacks	2011	Western Europe	1994–2007	GDP growth decreases the number of terrorist incidents.
Danzell/Zidek [17]	Domestic terrorist attacks	2013	34 Advanced Economies	2000–2009	GDP growth has a small but statistically significant effect in decreasing the likelihood of domestic terrorism.
Danzell et al. [18]	Domestic terrorist attacks	2019	Worldwide	1970–2012	An increase in GDP growth decreases the likelihood of domestic terrorist attacks.

Continued on next page

Table 5.3. (*continued*)

Author(s)	Dependent Variable(s)	Publish Date	Countries Studied	Years	Main Finding(s)
Category 2: Economic Growth Decreases Likelihood of Being Targeted by Terrorism (continued)					
Elmorsy[19]	Transnational and domestic terrorist attacks	2024	North Africa	2011–2023	Increases in GDP growth are associated with decreases in terrorism in North Africa.
Freytag et al.[20]	Transnational and domestic terrorist attacks	2011	Worldwide	1971–2007	Economic growth is negatively related to domestic and transnational terrorism.
Kis-Katos et al.[21]	Domestic terrorist attacks	2011	Worldwide	1970–2007	Higher GDP growth has a small but statistically significant correlation with decreased risk of domestic terrorist attacks.
Li[22]	Transnational terrorist attacks	2005	Worldwide	1975–1997	Growth has a statistically significant and negative effect on the likelihood of transnational terrorism.
Nasir et al.[23]	Transnational and domestic terrorist attacks	2015	Pakistan	2003–2013	There is a significant relationship between increased GDP growth and a decrease in terrorist attacks in Pakistan.
Nurunnabi/ Sghaier[24]	Transnational and domestic terrorist attacks	2018	Tunisia	1979–2015	Growth is negatively correlated with the number of terrorist attacks in Tunisia.
Mohamed et al.[25]	Transnational and domestic terrorist attacks	2019	France	1980–2015	In the long run, increases in GDP reduces terrorism in France.
Category 3: Economic Growth Increases Likelihood of Being Targeted by Terrorism					
Danzell/ Zidek[26]	Transnational terrorist attacks	2013	34 Advanced Economies	2000–2009	GDP growth has a small but statistically significant effect in increasing the likelihood of transnational terrorism.

Table 5.3. (*continued*)

Author(s)	Dependent Variable(s)	Publish Date	Countries Studied	Years	Main Finding(s)
Category 3: Economic Growth Increases Likelihood of Being Targeted by Terrorism (**continued**)					
LaFree et al. [27]	Transnational and domestic terrorist attacks	2024	Worldwide	1970–2019	Increases in GDP increase the number of terrorist attacks in a country.
Mohamed et al. [28]	Transnational and domestic terrorist attacks	2021	Pakistan	1980–2015	An increase in economic growth leads to a significant increase in terror attacks in Pakistan.
Naz et al. [29]	Transnational and domestic terrorist attacks	2022	Pakistan	1972–2019	GDP growth is causally associated with increased terrorism in Pakistan.
Sanso-Navarro/ Vera-Cabello [30]	Domestic terrorist attacks	2018	Worldwide	1970–2014	An increase in economic growth is positively correlated with terrorism.
Sanso-Navarro/ Vera-Cabello [31]	Transnational terrorist attacks	2018	Worldwide	1970–2014	An increase in economic growth is positively correlated with terrorism.
Shahbaz et al. [32]	Transnational and domestic terrorist attacks	2013	Pakistan	1973–2010	Economic growth Granger causes terrorism in Pakistan.
Tavares [33]	Transnational and domestic terrorist attacks	2004	Worldwide	1987–2001	Growth is weakly but statistically correlated with an increase in the incidence of terrorism.
Category 4: Economic Growth Has a Mixed Effect on Likelihood of Being Targeted by Terrorism					
Bayar/ Gavriletea [34]	Transnational and domestic terrorist attacks	2018	Middle East & North Africa	2008–2014	Economic growth is a significant determinant of terrorism in all of the countries examined except Algeria, Djibouti, Iraq, Israel, Libya, and Oman.
Blomberg et al. [35]	Transnational terrorist attacks	2004	Worldwide	1968–1991	For high-income countries, economic contractions significantly increase the risk of terrorism. There is no effect for low-income countries.

Continued on next page

Table 5.3. (*continued*)

Author(s)	Dependent Variable(s)	Publish Date	Countries Studied	Years	Main Finding(s)
Category 4: Economic Growth Has a Mixed Effect on Likelihood of Being Targeted by Terrorism (continued)					
Choi[36]	Transnational and domestic terrorist attacks	2015	Worldwide	1970–2007	When countries sustain higher levels of industrial growth rather than agricultural growth, they are less likely to experience international and domestic terrorism.
Gries et al.[37]	Domestic terrorist attacks	2011	7 Western European Countries	1951–2004	Economic growth in Germany, Portugal, and Spain is causally associated with a decrease in domestic terrorism, but the relationship does not hold for France, Greece, Italy, or the UK.
Korotayev et al.[38]	Transnational and domestic terrorist attacks	2021	Worldwide	1980–2014	GDP growth only decreases terrorist activity if accompanied by increases in economic equality, education, and employment; otherwise, GDP growth increases terrorist activity.
Lassoued et al.[39]	Transnational and domestic terrorist attacks	2018	Worldwide	2008–2015	Economic growth has a negative effect on terrorism in developing countries, but a positive effect on terrorism in developed countries.
Meierrieks/ Gries[40]	Transnational and domestic terrorist attacks	2012	Latin America	1970–2007	Economic growth decreases domestic and transnational terrorism in lower middle-income Latin American countries, but has no effect in upper middle-income Latin American countries.

Table 5.3. (*continued*)

Author(s)	Dependent Variable(s)	Publish Date	Countries Studied	Years	Main Finding(s)
Category 4: Economic Growth Has a Mixed Effect on Likelihood of Being Targeted by Terrorism (continued)					
Meierrieks/ Gries [41]	Transnational and domestic terrorist attacks	2013	Worldwide	1970–2007	Economic growth exerts a causal effect on the incidence of terrorism during the Cold War era, but not during the post-Cold War era.

[1] Baek and Bouzinov, "Does Democratic Progress Deter Terrorist Incidents?"

[2] Nauro Campos and Martin Gassebner, "International Terrorism, Domestic Political Instability, and the Escalation Effect," *Economics & Politics*, Vol. 25, No. 1 (March 2013), pp. 27–47.

[3] Drakos and Gofas, "In Search of the Average Transnational Terrorist Venue."

[4] Axel Dreher and Martin Gassebner, "Does Political Proximity to the U.S. Cause Terror?" *Economics Letters*, Vol. 99 (2008), pp. 27–29.

[5] Axel Dreher and Justina A. V. Fischer, "Government Decentralization as a Disincentive for Transnational Terror? An Empirical Analysis," *International Economic Review*, Vol. 51, No. 4 (November 2010), pp. 981–1002.

[6] Susan Fahey and Gary LaFree, "Does Country-Level Social Disorganization Increase Terrorist Attacks?" *Terrorism and Political Violence*, Vol. 27, No. 1 (2015), pp. 81–111.

[7] Fahey and LaFree, "Does Country-Level Social Disorganization Increase Terrorist Attacks?"

[8] Andreas E. Feldmann and Maiju Perälä, "Reassessing the Causes of Nongovernmental Terrorism in Latin America," *Latin American Politics and Society* Vol. 46, No. 2 (2004), pp. 101–132.

[9] Gassebner and Luechinger, "Lock, Stock, and Barrel."

[10] Gassebner and Luechinger, "Lock, Stock, and Barrel."

[11] Aisha Ismail and Shehla Amjad, "Cointegration-Causality Analysis between Terrorism and Key Macroeconomic Indicators: Evidence from Pakistan," *International Journal of Social Economics*, Vol. 41, No. 8 (2014), pp. 664–82.

[12] Krisztina Kis-Katos, Helge Liebert, and Günther G. Schulze, "On the Origin of Domestic and International Terrorism," *European Journal of Political Economy*, Vol. 27, Supp. 1 (2011), pp. S17–S36.

[13] Krueger and Laitin, "Kto Kogo? A Cross-Country Study."

[14] Kurrild-Klitgaard et al., "The Political Economy of Freedom."

[15] James Piazza, "Rooted in Poverty?: Terrorism, Poor Economic Development, and Social Cleavages." *Terrorism and Political Violence*, Vol. 18 (2006), pp. 159–177.

[16] Raul Caruso and Friedrich Schneider, "The Socio-Economic Determinants of Terrorism and Political Violence in Western Europe (1994–2007)," *European Journal of Political Economy*, Vol. 27, Supp. 1 (2011), pp. S37–S49.

[17] Orlandrew Danzell and Steve Zidek, "Does Counterterrorism Spending Reduce the Incidence and Lethality of Terrorism? A Quantitative Analysis of 34 Countries," *Defense & Security Analysis*, Vol. 29, No. 3 (2013), pp. 218–233.

[18] Danzell et al., "Determinants of Domestic Terrorism," pp. 536–558.

Continued on next page

Table 5.3. (*continued*)

[19] Samah Elmorsy, "Determinants and Economic Impacts Of Terrorism And Conflicts On North African Countries Compared To Middle East Countries: Panel Data Approach (2011–2023)," *MSA-Managemen Sciences Journal*, Vol. 3, Issue 4 (2024), pp. 28–83.

[20] Freytag et al., "The Origins of Terrorism."

[21] Kis-Katos et al., "On the Origin of Domestic and International Terrorism."

[22] Quan Li, "Does Democracy Promote or Reduce Transnational Terrorist Incidents?" *Journal of Conflict Resolution*, Vol. 49, Issue 2 (2005), pp. 278–297.

[23] Saad Nasir, Rab Nawaz Lodhi, Kiran Farooq, and M. Qatadah Idrees, "Exploring the Nexus: Terrorism and Economic Growth in Pakistan," *Journal of Independent Studies and Research-Management, Social Sciences and Economics*, Vol. 13, No. 2 (July 2015), pp. 99–111.

[24] Mohammad Nurunnabi and Asma Sghaier, "Socioeconomic Determinants of Terrorism," *Digest of Middle East Studies*, Vol. 27, No. 2 (2018), pp. 278–302.

[25] Hassen Mohamed, Mehdi Ben Jebli, and Slim Ben Youssef, "Renewable and Fossil Energy, Terrorism, Economic Growth, and Trade: Evidence from France," *Renewable Energy*, Vol. 139 (Aug. 2019), pp. 459–467.

[26] Danzell and Zidek, "Does Counterterrorism Spending Reduce the Incidence and Lethality of Terrorism?"

[27] Gary LaFree, Bo Jiang, Yesenia Yanez, "Comparing the Determinants of Worldwide Homicide and Terrorism," *Journal of Contemporary Criminal Justice*, Vol. 40, No. 1 (2024), pp. 172–196.

[28] Hassen Mohamed, Mohsen Alimi, Slim Ben Youssef, "The Role of Renewable Energy in Reducing Terrorism: Evidence from Pakistan," *Renewable Energy*, Vol. 175 (Sep. 2021), pp. 1088–1100.

[29] Ayesha Naz, Zubaria Andlib, Azra Nasir, "Relationship among Globalization, Terrorism, and Economic Growth in Pakistan," *Nust Journal of Social Sciences and Humanities*, Vol. 8, No. 1 (Jan–Jun 2022), pp. 37–59.

[30] Sanso-Navarro and Vera-Cabello, "The Socioeconomic Determinants of Terrorism."

[31] Ibid.

[32] Shahbaz et al., "An Analysis of a Causal Relationship."

[33] José Tavares, "The Open Society Assesses its Enemies: Shocks, Disasters and Terrorist Attacks," *Journal of Monetary Economics*, Vol. 5, Issue 5 (2004), pp. 1039–1070.

[34] Yilmaz Bayar and Marius Dan Gavriletea, "Peace, Terrorism and Economic Growth in Middle East and North African Countries," *Quality and Quantity*, Vol. 52, Iss. 5 (2018), pp. 2373–2392.

[35] S. Brock Blomberg, Gregory D. Hess, Akila Weerapana, "Economic Conditions and Terrorism." *European Journal of Political Economy*, Vol. 20 (2004): 463–478.

[36] Choi, "Economic Growth and Terrorism."

[37] Thomas Gries, Tim Krieger, Daniel Meierrieks, "Causal Linkages Between Domestic Terrorism and Economic Growth," *Defence and Peace Economics*, Vol. 22, No. 5 (2011), pp. 493–508.

[38] Korotayev et al., "Economic Growth, Education, and Terrorism."

[39] Tahar Lassoued, Arafet Hamida, and Zouhaier Hadhek, "Terrorism and Economic Growth," *International Journal of Economics and Financial Issues*, Vol. 8, Iss. 1 (2018), pp. 175–178.

[40] Daniel Meierrieks and Thomas Gries, "Economic Performance And Terrorist Activity In Latin America," *Defence and Peace Economics*, Vol. 23, No. 5 (2012), pp. 447–470.

[41] Daniel Meierrieks and Thomas Gries, "Causality Between Terrorism and Economic Growth," *Journal of Peace Research*, Vol. 50, No. 1 (2013), pp. 91–104.

Inconclusive results also emerge when we look at studies that focus on particular countries or regions. Two studies look at targeting in Latin America by transnational and domestic terrorism, one of which shows no effect while the other produces a mixed result. In turn, four studies look at targeting in Pakistan by transnational and domestic terrorism, and one finds no effect, two indicate a positive effect, and one suggests a negative effect.

Overall, the literature does not provide a basis for concluding that economic growth influences the likelihood of a country being targeted by terrorism. The analysis here thus buttresses Krueger and Laitin's conclusion from 2008 that "macroeconomic shifts generally fail to map on to changes in terrorist activity."[42]

Pathway 15: Wealth and Civil Peace Theory

The massive literature on the causes of civil war frequently emphasizes that a link exists between a country's level of wealth and the likelihood of internal conflicts. Unrecognized in this literature is that Smith developed an argument along these lines stretching back hundreds of years.

In the section of *The Wealth of Nations* where Smith analyzes this issue (Book 3, Chapter 4), he emphasizes that internal security and stability were lacking during the period in which feudalism flourished. As he underscores, the king was "incapable of restraining the violence of the great lords. . . . They . . . continued to make war according to their own discretion, almost continually upon one another, and very frequently upon the king; and the open country still continued to be a scene of violence, rapine, and disorder."[43]

After feudalism ended, internal stability and security greatly improved, as "the great proprietors were no longer capable of interrupting the regular execution of justice, or of disturbing the peace of the country."[44] Smith highlights the role of commerce in promoting the end of feudalism. However, he makes clear that once the move away from feudalism did begin to occur, its eventual transformation into a more centralized political structure—one in which much more political authority was concentrated in the hands of the king—was not something that commercial interests had pushed for or even wanted. As Smith underscores, commerce played an indirect and non-intentional role in promoting this shift: "The merchants and artificers . . . acted merely from a view to their own interest, and in pursuit of their own pedlar principle of turning a penny wherever a penny was to be got" and had no "knowledge or foresight of that great revolution which [their industry] was gradually bringing about."[45]

The nature of Smith's formulation was of course specific to the era in which he wrote (feudalism was officially abolished in England in 1660, just a little more than a hundred years before *The Wealth of Nations* was published). But his particular line of argument matches up with a general one of great prominence: that economic development reduces the likelihood of internal conflict, which can be termed "wealth and civil peace theory."

The existing civil war literature outlines three core mechanisms by which economic development is likely to reduce the prospects for internal conflict. First, economic development is seen as reducing the scope and intensity of grievances from the population, thereby leading to a lower willingness to engage in revolts. Second, economic development increases state capacity, including the resources needed to provide internal stability. That is, richer states can have larger police and military forces as well as greater administrative capacity, all of which make it harder for rebel groups to be successful. Finally, by increasing the income that citizens can earn in the labor force, economic development increases the opportunity cost of engaging in rebellion; in this view, poverty enhances the prospects for rebellion because "rebel leaders can easily recruit [the poor] compared with what governments will be able to offer through the regular economy."[46]

Prior to a pathbreaking 2010 article by Ward, Greenhill, and Bakke, analysts had found that higher levels of wealth lower the likelihood of civil war but wealth was regarded as being just one influence among many.[47] In their article, Ward, Greenhill, and Bakke persuasively critique the literature on civil conflict on the basis that it devotes "too much attention to finding statistically significant relationships, while too little attention has been paid to finding variables that improve our ability to predict civil wars."[48] What their examination reveals is that out of all variables, wealth (as measured by GDP per capita) is the one that makes the largest contribution to predicting the onset of civil war.[49]

The empirical literature has of course evolved further since the Ward, Greenhill, and Bakke article was published. But their underlying finding remains unchallenged. A review of the nearly five hundred analyses citing their article that were published in the decade after it was written reveals that none of them presents any systematic critique of their finding concerning the key influence of wealth on civil war onset.[50] A subsequent article employing an alternative statistical method for making predictions validates their core finding: "The best predictor of civil war onset is national poverty as measured by both the growth rate of national gross domestic product (GDP) and GDP per capita. This reinforces the results of nearly every examination into the causes of civil war onset published in the past decade."[51] And the article that arguably provides the most comprehensive examination of the link between economic development and civil conflict also confirms their core finding, underscoring that "[t]he wealth dimension is . . . shown to be the most important underlying cause of civil war."[52]

Pathway 16: How Does Economic Globalization Influence Civil Conflict?

With the marked increase in civil wars in the final portion of the twentieth century coinciding to a significant extent with a dramatic expansion in economic globalization, many have wondered whether the two developments are related. A significant literature emerged that empirically examines how economic globalization influences the likelihood of civil conflict. Analysts focused on four different elements of the global economy, each of will be reviewed below: trade, commodities trading, FDI, and international finance.

The theoretical arguments in the literature on globalization and civil war can be broadly grouped into two camps—one optimistic, the other pessimistic.[53] The pessimistic school of thought sees globalization as a disruptive force that undermines domestic stability. In this perspective, globalization increases the vulnerability of countries to powerful short-term crises or economic shocks that can exacerbate domestic social tensions that can spur conflict. Economic globalization is also seen as increasing economic inequality—across individuals, geographic regions, or ethnic groups—which fosters greater social cleavages and grievances and thereby promotes civil war. Moreover, analysts stress that the opportunity cost of engaging in violence is reduced for those within a country that has been harmed by globalization.

In contrast, the optimistic school of thought sees globalization as a source of greater economic opportunities that reduce the prospects for civil conflict. Some within this perspective maintain that by creating new economic opportunities, globalization will augment earning capacity and thereby increase the opportunity cost of individuals engaging in armed violence. Others stress that augmented ties to the global economy will increase the overall resources available to governments for deterring or suppressing activity by rebel groups. And some argue that significant links to the global economy create a stronger incentive for governments to minimize domestic conflict, since the maintenance of these economic links would be placed at risk by unrest.

Significant theoretical arguments thus point in both directions. What does empirical research say about the nature of the relationship between economic globalization and civil conflict? The discussion below reviews the range of studies that have analyzed whether specific elements of economic globalization influence the likelihood of civil conflict, beginning with trade.

TRADE

The most notable way to analyze how economic globalization influences the likelihood of civil conflict is through a focus on trade, with eleven studies taking this approach. Blanton and Apodaca (2007) focus on just exports, while the other ten studies in this literature measure a country's trade openness through its total imports and exports as a share of its GDP.

The findings from these eleven studies are summarized in Table 5.4. Overall, these analyses point in the direction of the optimistic perspective regarding globalization and civil conflict. Seven out of eleven studies find that trade reduces the likelihood of conflict, and no studies find the opposite, that trade exacerbates civil conflict. Moreover, the one study with a mixed effect notably shows that trade deters the most severe civil wars. Additionally, one of the three studies concluding that trade has no direct effect does find that it has an indirect positive effect: trade-induced economic growth reduces the likelihood of civil conflict.

However, two studies that examine not just the level of trade but also the *process* of trade liberalization provide a cautionary note. The 2007 study by Bussmann and Schneider finds that although higher trade is associated with a lower risk of civil war, the initial process of becoming open to global trade does create economic disruptions that can increase the likelihood of armed conflict. The 2005 analysis by Bussmann et al. reaches this same conclusion.

COMMODITIES TRADE

Looking beyond overall trade, it is also important specifically to examine the effects of trade in commodities. This is because a very large number of countries are "commodity export dependent"—that is, commodities comprise 60 percent or more of their total exports. A total of 101 countries now meet this criterion, of which 38 rely on agricultural exports, 32 on mining exports, and 31 on fuel exports. Notably, the vast bulk of

Table 5.4. Trade and Civil Conflict

Author(s)	Publish Date	Main Finding(s)
Category 1: Trade Has No Effect on Civil Conflict		
Elbadawi/Hegre [1]	2008	Although trade has little direct effect, trade-induced economic growth reduces the long-term likelihood of domestic conflict.
Ezcurra/Manotas [2]	2017	Trade has no significant effect on the incidence of civil conflict.
Magee/Massoud [3]	2011	Trade openness does not influence internal conflict.
Category 2: Trade Reduces Likelihood of Civil Conflict		
Barbieri/Reuveny [4]	2005	Trade reduces likelihood of civil war.
Blanton/Apodaca [5]	2007	Trade increase incentives to resolve civil conflicts.
Bussmann/Schneider [6]	2007	Trade is associated with a lower risk of civil war.
Bussmann et al. [7]	2005	Trade reduces the onset of civil conflict.
De Soysa [8]	2002	Trade significantly reduces the risk of civil conflict.
Krause/Suzuki [9]	2005	Trade reduces the risk of civil war.
Sorens/Ruger [10]	2014	Trade lowers the risk of civil war.
Category 3: Trade Increases Likelihood of Civil Conflict		
No studies		
Category 4: Trade Has Mixed Effect on Civil Conflict		
Martin et al. [11]	2008	Trade deters the most severe civil wars, but increases the risk of lower-scale conflicts.

[1] Ibrahim Elbadawi and Håvard Hegre, "Globalization, Economic Shocks, and Internal Armed Conflict," *Defence and Peace Economics,* Vol. 19, No. 1 (2008), pp. 37–60.

[2] Roberto Ezcurra and Beatriz Manotas, "Is There a Link Between Globalisation and Civil Conflict?" *The World Economy,* Vol. 40 (2017), pp. 2592–2610.

[3] Magee and Massoud, "Openness and Internal Conflict."

[4] Barbieri and Reuveny, "Economic Globalization and Civil War."

Continued on next page

Table 5.4. (*continued*)

5 Robert Blanton and Clair Apodaca, "Economic Globalization and Violent Civil Conflict: Is Openness a Pathway to Peace?" *The Social Science Journal*, Vol. 44, No. 4 (2007), pp 599–619.

6 Margit Bussmann and Gerald Schneider, "When Globalization Discontent Turns Violent: Foreign Economic Liberalization and Internal War," *International Studies Quarterly*, Vol. 51, No. 1 (2007), pp. 79–97.

7 Margit Bussmann, Gerald Schneider, and Nina Wiesehomeier, "Foreign Economic Liberalization and Peace: The Case of Sub-Saharan Africa," *European Journal of International Relations*, Vol. 11 (2005), pp. 551–579.

8 Indra De Soysa, "Paradise is a Bazaar? Greed, Creed, and Governance in Civil War, 1989–99," *Journal of Peace Research*, Vol. 39, No. 4 (2002), pp. 395–416.

9 Volker Krause and Susumu Suzuki, "Causes of Civil War in Asia and Sub-Saharan Africa: A Comparison," *Social Science Quarterly*, Vol. 86, No. 1 (2005), pp. 160–177.

10 Jason Sorens and William Ruger, "Globalisation and Intrastate Conflict: An Empirical Analysis," *Civil Wars*, Vol. 16 (2014), pp. 381–401.

11 Philipe Martin, Thierry Mayer, and Mathias Thoenig, "Civil Wars and International Trade," *Journal of the European Economic Association*, Vol. 6, No. 3 (2008), pp. 541–550.

commodity-export-dependent countries (87 out of 101) are developing countries; this includes all countries in South America and more than three-quarters of the countries in Africa.[54]

Analysts articulate various reasons regarding why being dependent on commodities for exports is likely to enhance the prospects for civil war. Most notably, when a dramatic reduction in commodity export prices occurs, this can lead to significant economic distress and instability.

As Table 5.5 shows, the eight studies that have examined the potential effect of commodities trade on civil conflict have examined three different independent variables: five examine changes in commodity prices, two analyze the extent of commodity exports in the economy, and one analyzes commodity terms of trade shocks (that is, shocks to the ratio of commodity export prices to commodity import prices). Despite this significant variation across these studies, there is broad overlap regarding their findings: six out of eight studies find that commodities trade makes civil wars more likely. This includes four out of five studies that examine commodity prices and both of the analyses that examine commodity exports as a percentage of the economy.

FDI

Another core element of economic globalization is FDI. Six studies in total examine the influence of FDI on civil conflict.

Table 5.5. Commodities Trade and Civil Conflict

Author(s)	Publish Date	Independent Variable(s)	Main Finding(s)
Category 1: Commodities Trade Has No Effect on Civil Conflict			
Caruso[1]	2011	World prices of commodities	No evidence of a relationship between commodity prices and the probability of civil war.
Category 2: Commodities Trade Reduces Likelihood of Civil Conflict			
No studies			
Category 3: Commodities Trade Increases Likelihood of Civil Conflict			
Amo-Yartey[2]	2004	Primary commodity exports as a fraction of GDP	Reliance on primary commodity exports increases the risk of civil war.
Berman/ Couttenier[3]	2015	Shocks to global agricultural commodity prices	Shocks to global agriculture demand increase conflict intensity and size.
Brückner/ Ciccone[4]	2010	Shocks to export commodity prices	Downturns in the price of a countries' main export commodity increase civil war likelihood.
Cali/Mulabdic[5]	2017	International commodity prices and country-specific trade shares	Increases in the price of a state's exported commodities raises the risk of civil conflict and its duration.
Collier/ Hoeffler[6]	2004	Primary commodity exports as a fraction of GDP	A greater amount of primary commodity exports as a fraction of GDP increases the risk of conflict.
O'Trakoun[7]	2015	Shocks to global food commodity prices	Shocks to export prices faced by food commodity exporters increases civil conflict.
Category 4: Commodities Trade Has a Mixed Effect on Civil Conflict			
Janus/ Riera-Crichton[8]	2015	Commodity terms of trade declines	Commodity terms of trade declines cause civil war in countries with intermediate ethnic diversity, while the effects on highly diverse or homogenous societies are insignificant.

Continued on next page

Table 5.5. (*continued*)

---

[1] Raul Caruso, "Continuing Conflict and International Prices of Commodities: Theory and Empirical Evidence from Sub-Saharan Africa," *Ethnic Conflict, Civil War and Cost of Conflict* (2011), pp. 23–49.

[2] Charles Amo-Yartey, "The economics of civil war in Sub-Saharan Africa," *Postconflict Economics in Sub-Saharan Africa: Lessons from the Democratic Republic of the Congo* (USA: International Monetary Fund, 2004), pp. 87–128.

[3] Nicolas Berman and Mathieu Couttenier, "External Shocks, Internal Shocks: The Geography of Civil Conflicts," *The Review of Economics and Statistics*, Vol. 97, No. 4 (October 2015), pp. 758–776.

[4] Markus Brückner and Antonio Ciccone, "International Commodity Prices, Growth and the Outbreak of Civil War in Sub-Saharan Africa," *Economic Journal*, Vol. 120, No. 544 (May 2010), pp. 519–534.

[5] Massimiliano Cali and Alen Mulabdic. "Trade and civil conflict: Revisiting the cross-country evidence," *Review of International Economics*, Vol. 25, No. 1 (2017), pp. 195–232.

[6] Paul Collier and Anke Hoeffler, "Greed and Grievance in Civil War," *Oxford Economic Papers*, Vol. 56, No. 4 (Oct. 2004), pp. 563–595.

[7] John O'Trakoun, "Food Price Uncertainty and Political Conflict," *International Finance*, Vol. 18, Issue 3 (2015), pp. 299–320.

[8] Thorsten Janus and Daniel Riera-Crichton, "Economic Shocks, Civil War and Ethnicity," *Journal of Development Economics*, Vol. 115 (2015), pp. 32–44.

Half of the six studies in this literature find that FDI reduces civil conflict. Barbieri and Reuveny conclude that FDI generally reduces the likelihood of civil war.[55] In turn, Bussmann and Schneider find that FDI reduces the overall risk of civil conflict onset.[56] And Blanton and Apodaca conclude that FDI reduces the risk of escalation from minor civil conflicts to large-scale civil war.[57]

Of the remaining three studies, the Sorens and Ruger analysis finds that FDI does not influence civil conflict,[58] and the other two produce mixed findings. Mihalache-O'Keef finds that raw materials FDI undermines the prospects for civil peace, whereas other forms of FDI decrease the risk of civil conflict.[59] And Kibria et al. conclude that FDI reduces the risk of civil conflict in countries that are rich in fuel-related natural resources (oil and gas), whereas FDI increases the likelihood of conflict for countries that are rich in nonfuel natural resources (such as minerals and ores).[60]

In sum, out of the six studies examining how FDI influences civil conflict, three find that FDI generally promotes civil peace, two find that it does so under certain conditions, and one finds no effect. Significantly, no study finds that FDI augments civil conflict. From these findings, it is reasonable to conclude that FDI does not harm the prospects for civil peace, as the pessimistic perspective on the link between globalization and civil conflict would expect. But we lack clarity as to whether FDI generally promotes civil peace, as appears to be the case with trade. The influence of FDI related to raw materials extraction is a key question at issue that should be researched further.

INTERNATIONAL FINANCE

A final element of economic globalization is international finance. Within the literature on civil war, scholars have focused on FPI—the international purchase of stocks and bonds.

The research on how FPI influences the prospects for civil conflict is extremely limited, with just three studies examining this relationship. Two of these three studies find that FPI has no effect on civil conflict.[61] The third analysis concludes that FPI reduces the likelihood of civil war.[62]

Regarding FPI, the only conclusion we can draw at this point is that there no evidence in support of the pessimistic perspective on the link between globalization and civil conflict. Further research on the link between international finance and civil war would clearly be valuable.

CONCLUSION

Analysts have advanced both a pessimistic and optimistic set of theoretical arguments regarding how the global economy can influence civil conflict. Regarding FDI and FPI, there is a lack of evidence in support of either perspective. Regarding overall trade, the initial evidence points in the direction of the optimistic perspective. Yet when we look at the element of trade that is most consequential for many developing countries—trade in commodities—we see support for the pessimistic perspective.

PART II

Theoretical Examination of the Economics-Security Interaction

CHAPTER SIX

Comparing Liberal Political Economy and Mercantilist/ Realist Political Economy

IDENTIFYING THE THREE KEY CONCEPTUAL DISTINCTIONS

THIS CHAPTER BEGINS the effort to lay the foundation for more productive future theorizing about the influence of economic factors on security affairs. The surveyed range of sixteen pathways we now have is obviously extensive, but they will not be sufficient: as the world changes and as the role of economic factors shifts within it, novel theories regarding the economics-security interaction will be needed. Moreover, there will be a need for new understandings of how economic factors are influencing, or are likely to influence, the security behavior of particular states or groups of them.

As noted in Chapter 1, this new thinking about the economics-security interaction will not emerge from nowhere; rather, it will be shaped by our deeper conceptual understanding. The better our underlying conceptual understanding, the more likely it is that our new theories and understandings of specific cases will be useful.

Our current conceptual understanding of the economics-security interaction has been deeply influenced by two canonical frameworks in political economy, which for clarity are labeled here as "liberal political economy" and "realist political economy." The latter, alternatively called "mercantilism," "statism," "realism," or "economic nationalism," has been propounded over the centuries by figures such as Alexander Hamilton and

Friedrich List; the former, which is also labeled "liberalism," "free trade liberalism," "economic liberalism," or "commercial liberalism," includes proponents such as David Ricardo and Richard Cobden.

All would agree that these two political economy frameworks are very different. It is certainly easy enough to see that the policies emerging from them contrast starkly: no one would confuse the policy prescriptions emerging from Hamilton or List with those emanating from Cobden or Ricardo. It is also certainly easy enough to see how the overall worldview of politicians contrastingly resonates with one of these approaches versus the other: for example, Donald Trump's worldview strongly corresponds with mercantilism/realism, whereas Barack Obama's matches up with liberalism.

But the question at issue in this chapter is not differing policy prescriptions or the overall worldviews of politicians. It is something more fundamental: at root, exactly how do these political economy frameworks contrast in terms of how they conceptualize the role of economics in world politics? Answering this question is not straightforward. Indeed, our current guides to this question actually lead scholars and students astray. Recognizing why this is the case—and delineating a more productive means of conceptually distinguishing these theoretical frameworks—is the purpose of this chapter.

Following the line of argument in this chapter—which involves pulling apart and critiquing the two most significant categorization schemes for distinguishing these two political economy frameworks—is something that scholars who are familiar with these frameworks will be well prepared for. But for students or others who are first being introduced to these political economy frameworks, following this discussion will be more difficult. In turn, those scholars who are acquainted with these frameworks but have little interest in grand theory or intellectual history may find it unwieldy.

For the various readers with less connection to the kinds of theoretical issues analyzed in this chapter, it is hardly crucial to digest its details. In the end, this chapter is ultimately a "set-up" chapter that lays the groundwork for the theoretical analysis in chapters 7 through 10. There are just two key takeaways that emerge from this chapter that are vital for understanding the discussion in that follows in chapters 7 through 10. They can be stated simply.

The first is that we need to move beyond the most systematic existing categorization schemes for distinguishing realist and liberal political economy, which have respectively been outlined by Robert Gilpin and

Jonathan Kirshner. As the analysis in this chapter will show, each of their categorization schemes is problematic. Of particular note, each fails to capture the subtleties and range of liberal political economy; this is most apparent and most consequential with respect to Adam Smith, who is grossly caricatured by their formulations. Kirshner's analysis is nevertheless helpful in some respects; I build upon some elements of his analysis. In contrast, understanding Gilpin's formulation is useful primarily to comprehend the manner and degree to which liberal political economy, and Adam Smith in particular, has been misunderstood by analysts of world politics. Due to its great prominence, Gilpin's analysis has been extremely influential in this regard.

The second key takeaway from this chapter is that to productively contrast realist and liberal political economy as well as to unpack the inherent tension that exists within the latter theory itself, it is necessary to focus on distinctions between them regarding their answers to three key conceptual questions. First, how do economic goals relate to security goals? Second, what kinds of economic factors are important to study when analyzing world politics? And third, how and how much do economic actors and other societal interests influence policies regarding security affairs? In my view, these are the most significant conceptual questions that future analysts must consider when theorizing about the economics-security interaction; they will, respectively, be the focus of the next three chapters.

Robert Gilpin's Approach to Distinguishing Political Economy Frameworks

Gilpin provides by far the most prominent and influential understanding of how realist and liberal political economy compare and contrast with each other conceptually. Cohen underscores that Gilpin's taxonomy of these two political economy frameworks (along with Marxism) is "still regarded as the logical starting point for most serious discussion" within the field of international political economy. Indeed, as Cohen stresses, Gilpin's understanding has been so prominent for so long that it has "become an unexamined part of every specialist's toolkit."[1]

While it is not necessary to understand why Gilpin designed his categorization scheme as he did, his decision to develop a tripartite coding scheme (that is, not merely to distinguish realist and liberal political economy from each other but also to contrast each of them with Marxism) is likely a key reason why he ultimately created categories that are not especially well equipped to make a proper distinction between realist and liberal political economy, the task that both Kirshner and I focus on. It is in part for this reason that I do not include an analysis of Marxism in this chapter; I discuss Marxism at the start of Chapter 8 and also in one section of Chapter 11.

Gilpin's two explorations of how to conceptually distinguish realist and liberal political economy—in his 1975 book and his 1987 book—reach the same conclusions, but the earlier book is more helpful since it lays out his coding procedure in a very explicit manner. In his 1975 book, Gilpin outlines a five-pronged categorization scheme, differentiating these political economy frameworks on the basis of:

(1) the relationship between economics and politics;
(2) the nature of economic relations;
(3) the nature of the actors;
(4) the goal of economic activity; and
(5) theory of change.

Before proceeding to examine Gilpin's categorization of realist and liberal political economy on the basis of these categories, it should be noted that Gilpin uses the term *mercantilism* to describe the former theory in his 1975 book; I will sometimes do so as well in this section to keep the discussion clear, since I often quote from his analysis.[2]

CATEGORY 1: RELATIONSHIP BETWEEN ECONOMICS AND POLITICS

The first category in Gilpin's categorization scheme is the relationship between economics and politics. Regarding liberal political economy, Gilpin argues:

> Although the liberal ideal is the separation of economics from politics in the interest of maximizing world welfare, the fulfillment of this ideal would have important political implications. The classical statement of these implications was that of Adam Smith in *The Wealth of Nations.* . . . [H]e attacked the barriers erected by feudal principalities and mercantilistic states against the exchange of goods and the enlargement of markets. If men were to multiply their wealth, Smith argued, the contradiction between political organization and economic rationality had to be resolved in favor of the latter. That is, the pursuit of wealth should determine the nature of the political order.[3]

According to Gilpin, the liberal view is that "the requirements of economic rationality *ought* to determine political relations," while "[m]ercantilist writers . . . have emphasized the primacy of politics; politics in this view determines economic organization. Whereas . . . liberals have pointed to the production of wealth as the basic determinant of social and political organization, the mercantilists of the German historical school, for example, stressed the primacy of national security, industrial development, and national sentiment in international political and economic dynamics."[4]

A key conceptual problem with this element of Gilpin's categorization framework is that he is comparing apples and oranges: he contrasts what liberals think ought to happen (economics *should* determine politics) with what a mercantilist believes does happen (politics *does* determine economics). To provide an accurate comparative coding scheme, the theories cannot be on different conceptual playing fields.[5]

This element of Gilpin's framework also does not allow Smith's views to be captured accurately. Gilpin argues, "Smith and other proponents of the market system have tended to deemphasize the security and other costs of the market system."[6] This is simply inaccurate: Smith accords great significance to military security, arguing in fact that "defence . . . is of much more importance than opulence."[7] At the same time, Smith also places great value on economic capacity, which should alert us to the fact that it will ultimately be most valuable to focus on the nature of the *trade-off* made between economic goals and security goals.

In the end, this first general category of Gilpin's is not helpful for parsing the frameworks and also has the unfortunate result of mischaracterizing Smith.

CATEGORY 2: NATURE OF ECONOMIC RELATIONS

The second category in Gilpin's categorization scheme is the nature of economic relations. Gilpin argues, "Following Smith, liberalism assumes that there is a basic harmony between the true national interest and the cosmopolitan economic interest. . . . Liberals argue that, given this underlying identity of national and cosmopolitan interests, the state should not interfere with economic transactions. . . . Mercantilists . . . on the other hand, begin with the premise that the essence of economic relations is conflictual."[8]

The key problem with this coding category is that it only becomes usable if each of the theoretical frameworks is caricatured. In fact, liberal political economy hardly sees international relations as consistently harmonious, and realist political economy likewise does not always see it as always conflictual. Consider the prospects for cooperation: realists are not always pessimistic that it will eventuate, while liberals hardly see cooperation as always easy or always stable.[9]

Consider also the issue of protectionism. Smith and mercantilist political economists such as List are not nearly as far apart on this dimension as Gilpin portrays them to be.[10] As was discussed in Chapter 2, Smith argues that it is sometimes necessary to pursue protectionism precisely because he sees international relations as being a very competitive realm. Although Smith sought to outline as strong a critique as possible against Britain's mercantilist policy of his own time, he never expected, nor wanted, a full elimination of protectionist barriers in part because he saw some of them as being necessary to sustain adequate defensive capacity.[11] Gilpin entirely misses this perspective and instead caricatures all liberals as always unwaveringly favoring free trade and as being unaware, or unconcerned, about the fact that free trade can have negative effects for countries and that some states will gain more relative to others from economic exchange.[12]

Gilpin is also simply incorrect in coding all liberals as favoring a cosmopolitan conception of interests that center on the promotion of the welfare of humanity; some liberals, such as David Ricardo and John Stuart Mill, did adopt this viewpoint, but this was certainly not the perspective that was propounded by Smith. As Walter underscores, Smith did not "hold to a harmony-of-interests doctrine" but instead argues "that the mutual interests of states are limited."[13]

Ultimately, this second coding category of Gilpin's is not useful. It obscures more than it clarifies, and it does a particular disservice in mischaracterizing the perspective of Smith.

CATEGORY 3: GOAL OF ECONOMIC ACTIVITY

The third category in Gilpin's categorization scheme is the goal of economic activity. Gilpin argues: "For the liberal, the goal of economic activity is the optimum or efficient use of the world's scarce resources and the maximization of world welfare." In contrast, he maintains that "the goal of economic (and political) activity for . . . mercantilists is the redistribution of wealth and power" to the best advantage of the national interest.[14]

Gilpin is incorrect in arguing that mercantilism is the only theory that places an emphasis on the nations' pursuit of wealth and power. As

Baldwin, Kirshner, and others have aptly noted, there is, in fact, agreement among liberal and realist political economy on this point over the long term (more on this point below).[15] Gilpin also errs in asserting that all liberals focus on the world's interest instead of being focused on the interests of the state. As noted above, this is simply not the case for Smith.

Ultimately, Gilpin is correct that state preferences have to be part of any categorization scheme for distinguishing realist political economy from liberal political economy, but his particular coding scheme is not clarifying. More specificity is needed to accurately contrast these political economy frameworks and also to capture the views of Smith.

CATEGORY 4: NATURE OF THE ACTORS

The fourth category in Gilpin's categorization scheme is the nature of the actors. Gilpin argues: "For liberals, the state represents an aggregation of private interests: public policy is but the outcome of a pluralistic struggle among interest groups. . . . Mercantilists, however, regard the state as an organic unit in its own right: the whole is greater than the sum of its parts. Public policy, therefore, embodies the national interest."[16] Ultimately, Gilpin codes liberalism as seeing households and firms as the main actors, while mercantilists see nation-states as the main actor.

Gilpin's "all or nothing" formulation regarding the role of societal actors is too stark. Nevertheless, this coding category of Gilpin's is on to something and captures realist political economy quite well. It is not, however, nuanced enough to capture the full range of thought within liberal political economy.

As the analysis in Chapter 9 will emphasize, although liberal theorists typically do subscribe to a "bottom-up" conceptualization of policy formation, not all do. Smith certainly does not: he felt that state leaders could sometimes act independently of societal interests.[17] Using the coding category of Gilpin's, we would thus have to conclude that Smith accords with realist political economy on this dimension.[18] And yet Smith, contra realism, also sees concentrated societal interests as frequently being important shapers of policy. Smith's middle ground conception simply cannot be captured by Gilpin's stark "all or nothing" formulation.

In sum, Gilpin is heading in the right direction with this coding category, but a modified, more nuanced version is needed for distinguishing liberal political economy from its realist counterpart.

CATEGORY 5: UNDERSTANDING
OF INTERNATIONAL CHANGE

The final category in Gilpin's categorization scheme is the understanding of international change that each political economy framework offers. Gilpin posits that mercantilism "sees change as taking place owing to shifts in the balance of power."[19] In contrast, he contends that liberal political economy emphasizes "the tendency towards equilibrium; liberalism takes for granted the existing social order and given institutions. Change is assumed to be gradual and adaptive—a continuous process of dynamic equilibrium. There is no necessary connection between such political phenomena as war and revolution in the international system and the evolution of the economic system."[20]

At a conceptual level, Gilpin's coding of the theories inappropriately mixes two different questions: (1) does the theory see change as prevalent? and (2) how does the theory see change as occurring? For liberal political economy, he addresses only the first question (stressing that it sees a tendency toward equilibrium), whereas for mercantilism he focuses on the second question (noting that it explains change as occurring in response to shifts in the distribution of power).

Moreover, liberal political economy is not nearly as static as Gilpin portrays it to be: it does see change as sometimes occurring and does have a theory of how this happens. Specifically, the drivers of change are economic shifts and institutional shifts (both domestic and international); if some, or especially all, of the core institutional and economic variables that liberalism highlights move significantly, then it expects change to occur.

Since both liberal and realist political economy actually do see change as occurring, this general category is not useful. A more productive route is needed to show how they differ regarding the interaction of the political and economic realms. As will be discussed subsequently, the key issue to focus on in this regard is the role of economic factors in the system.

OVERALL ASSESSMENT

Gilpin deserves great credit for highlighting the need to conceptually distinguish realist and liberal political economy in a systematic manner and for outlining an explicit coding scheme for doing so; in this regard, I will build on his approach. But as a concrete guide for accurately portraying how these conceptions of political economy compare and contrast with each other, Gilpin's analysis clearly falls short.[21]

A particularly unfortunate consequence of Gilpin's formulation is that it has corrupted how liberal political economy is understood due to the great prominence of his analysis. According to Gilpin, "from Adam Smith to [liberalism's] contemporary proponents, liberal thinkers have shared a coherent set of assumptions and beliefs about the nature of human beings, society, and economic activities."[22] It is no wonder that Gilpin finds liberal political economy to be so unsatisfying given that he sees its understanding as being one in which: (a) there is a harmony between that national interest and the global interest; (b) the state should never interfere with economic transactions; (c) the state is not the main actor in international affairs; (d) public policy never reflects the national interest but is instead is always completely determined by the struggle of interest groups; (e) the goal of economic activity is the maximization of world welfare; and (f) economics should be separated from politics. Of all liberals, it is Smith—held up by Gilpin as the exemplar liberal political economist that holds these views—who is the most wronged by this treatment. Smith would roll over in his grave to learn that he was ever characterized in this way: his thinking does not correspond with *any* of the views that Gilpin attributes to liberal political economy.

An alternative categorization scheme is clearly needed to correctly understand the conceptual contrast between liberal political economy and realist political economy as well as to properly appreciate that Smith's theoretical formulation stands apart from both. In the next section, I analyze Jonathan Kirshner's more useful approach. While Kirshner's overall framework is also inadequate, it does help in some ways to lay the foundation for productively differentiating these political economy frameworks.

Jonathan Kirshner's Approach to Distinguishing Political Economy Frameworks

Jonathan Kirshner provides the best current framework for understanding how realist and liberal political economy differ conceptually. He compares and contrasts them across the following six categories:

(1) underlying state preferences;
(2) the economic-security trade-off in the short and medium term;
(3) the conception of the security environment;
(4) the degree of state autonomy;
(5) the difficulty of cooperation; and
(6) the concern about dependency on other states for defense capabilities.

Kirshner's analysis is thoughtful and makes useful points; I profited from reading it. That being said, his overall framework is insufficient and, as with Gilpin's framework, it fails to sufficiently capture the nuance of liberal political economy. Once again, Smith's views end up being especially miscast: as with Gilpin, Kirshner uses Smith as the key exemplar of liberal political economy and in the process greatly mischaracterizes his views.

CATEGORY 1: UNDERLYING STATE PREFERENCES

Kirshner begins his discussion by usefully stressing that there is an important theoretical feature common to both realist and liberal political economy: "Power flows from productive capability and productive capability from economic growth. . . . Economic growth and capacity are the underlying source of power; economic and political goals are complementary in the long run." As he stresses, "these are core assumptions upon which realism draws, but they are not uniquely realist positions, and should be considered part of a common foundation shared with liberalism."[23]

I agree with this assessment; David Baldwin and others do as well.[24] Of course, if this understanding is held in common by realist and liberal political economy, then we cannot use this coding category as a means of differentiating them.

CATEGORY 2: THE ECONOMIC-SECURITY TRADE-OFF IN THE SHORT AND MEDIUM TERM

Regarding state preferences, Kirshner correctly notes that we can and should differentiate realist from liberal political economy concerning a specific issue: how states manage the trade-off in the short and medium term between economic gains and military security.[25] He maintains that "one of the most distinctive aspects of the realist vision of states' search for security is the willingness of states to make economic sacrifices in order to achieve political gains. In this respect realism diverges from liberalism, which tends to emphasize economic ends."[26]

To explain why these frameworks see the economic-security trade-off as they do, Kirshner points toward the notion that the theories regard these priorities as being ordered differently, with security being the highest end for realism, and economic gain being the highest end for liberalism.[27] Such a formulation fits realist political economy well, but more nuance is needed to capture the full range of liberal political economy; as noted earlier, Smith's famous statement that "defence . . . is of much more importance than opulence" does not fit with Kirshner's portrayal of liberalism.[28]

Ultimately, Kirshner is correct that it is vital to focus on how states make trade-offs between military security and economic capacity in the short and medium term, and his depiction of the realist understanding of this question is accurate. However, more work is needed to properly understand the full nature of what liberal political economy has to say about this issue.

CATEGORY 3: CONCEPTION OF THE SECURITY ENVIRONMENT

A third coding category Kirshner identifies to differentiate realist from liberal political economy concerns the conception of the security environment. Kirshner quotes Carr as observing that "Potential war . . . is a dominant factor in international politics" and argues that, in the eyes of realists, "states must anticipate the possibility of war."[29] Kirshner then clarifies this stance further, noting, "Realists do not see a constant 'state of war,' nor do liberals consider war impossible. . . . What distinguishes realists is that they can be placed on that end of a continuum which stresses the likelihood of war, threats of war, and the need for states to shape their policies in light of this consideration."[30]

Kirshner's only basis for his characterization of liberal political economy as being relatively unconcerned about the threat of war are some quotes he draws from List about Adam Smith. Kirshner first quotes List as noting that "Adam Smith's doctrine presupposes the existence of a state of perpetual peace and of universal union."[31] Kirshner then quotes the following characterization of Smith by List: "Although here and there he speaks of wars, this occurs only incidentally. The idea of a perpetual state of peace forms the foundation of all his arguments."[32] However, List cannot be cited as an authority on Smith's views—period. As Earle stresses, List fundamentally misrepresents Smith: "Smith's bitter opponent List missed the truth . . . he mistook the views of Smith's followers as those from Smith himself."[33] Whether this was done deliberately or was the product of List merely relying on the interpretations of Smith by others is unclear. Either way, List's characterization of Smith is simply wrong and should never be used.

Missed by Kirshner is that there is significant variation within liberal political economy regarding how the security environment is conceived. In his theorizing, Smith sees states focusing on the "shadow of war" to a much greater degree than, for example, John Stuart Mill, who comes much closer to fitting the "optimistic" label that liberals are typically tagged with.[34]

A bigger conceptual problem is that deriving an overall characterization of the realist and liberal conceptions on states' responsiveness to the fear of conflict becomes impossible once we recognize that each sees the prospects for conflict as varying across time and space according to a series of independent variables (such as international institutions, domestic political structures, the distribution of power, and the nature of military technology). From this perspective, when asking about the threat of war, the ultimate answer from each perspective is that "it depends"—which makes it unhelpful as a coding category.

CATEGORY 4: DEGREE OF STATE AUTONOMY

The fourth category in Kirshner's categorization scheme is the degree of state autonomy. Kirshner posits that "from the realist view the state is a distinct actor with its own interests. . . . Realists stress the state as a distinct entity from the sum of particular interests; as an entity with the capability and inclination to pursue its own agenda; and as the principal actor in international relations."[35] His characterization of liberal political economy is less precise: he notes that "liberals are more likely to see harmony between the interests of the state and the sum of particular interests. . . . Realists, on the other hand, anticipate that divergences of interest will often arise and that the state will intervene when necessary to defend its interests."[36]

Kirshner's analysis heads in the direction of identifying a core distinction that can and should be made between these political economy frameworks. However, his focus on the overall degree of state autonomy is not precise enough. We need to focus on a more specific issue: these frameworks have contrasting views of the significance and role of societal interests in the formation of policy. As it turns out, this is not merely a clarifying distinction between realist and liberal political economy; it is also possible and necessary to differentiate within liberal political economy on this basis. As I will show in Chapter 9, there are two distinct understandings within liberal political economy on this matter, one of which occupies a middle-ground space between realist political economy and the conventional liberal formulation.

As Chapter 9 will show, Smith clearly resides within this middle-ground space. He firmly disagrees with the view that there is harmony between the interests of the state and those of commercial interest groups. And although he maintains that societal interests will often shape policy, he underscores that the government under some circumstances can act on preferences that are distinct from such interests. Smith's perspective is thus neither bottom-up nor top-down; it is in between.

CATEGORY 5: THE DIFFICULTY OF COOPERATION

The fifth element in Kirshner's categorization scheme concerns the difficulty of international cooperation. Kirshner posits that the understanding within realist political economy is that "international economic cooperation will be difficult to establish and maintain. . . . With economic growth underlying long-run military capability, and given concerns for the possibility of war, states will find it difficult to cooperate."[37] He notes that this perspective is not restricted to international economic cooperation but extends generally: Kirshner maintains that realist political economy "expects cooperation to founder over the distribution of gains."[38]

Kirshner does not explicitly discuss the understanding of cooperation that exists within liberal political economy, and it would be unsound to portray it as adopting the converse view—that cooperation is easy to establish and maintain. This reveals an underlying conceptual problem with this coding category: it becomes usable only if we caricature the frameworks. As was noted above, just as liberal political economy does not always think that it will be easy to establish cooperation, realist political economy is not always pessimistic that cooperation will eventuate; both theories see the prospects for cooperation as varying in response to specific variables. As a result, it is not helpful to differentiate the theoretical frameworks on this basis.

CATEGORY 6: CONCERN ABOUT DEPENDENCY ON OTHER STATES FOR DEFENSE-RELATED CAPABILITIES

The sixth and final element in Kirshner's categorization scheme concerns whether states are willing to be dependent on other states for defense-related capabilities. The realist political economy perspective, Kirshner maintains, is that "states cannot simply allow the market to dictate that they specialize in a production portfolio which does not provide for the domestic manufacture of goods vital for the provision of national defense."[39] Kirshner notes further: "Given the possibility of war, states will strive for national self-sufficiency in order to assure the ability to produce the means to fight, as well as to reduce vulnerabilities that would result from the disruption of peacetime patterns of international economic flows. This is an important reason why realists tend to be skeptical of arguments touting the benefits of interdependence."[40]

Kirshner does not specifically mention how liberal political economy assesses this issue, and it seems unreasonable to assert that it adopts the opposite position: that states will *prefer* to be dependent on others for defense capabilities. This reveals a conceptual problem with this coding category of Kirshner's: it is one-dimensional. The real issue is not whether states have a preference for autonomy in the defense realm but rather what priority they place on it in relation to economic efficiency. In other words, how much are states willing to pay in order to have an autonomous defense base? This issue was the specific focus of the "weapons autonomy trade-off theory" that was delineated and evaluated in Chapter 4.

OVERALL ASSESSMENT

Kirshner's categorization scheme for distinguishing realist and liberal political economy is much more useful than Gilpin's; I will build on two of his categories in my own analysis. That being said, Kirshner's framework ultimately presents a distorted view of liberal political economy as being a theory that (a) sees decision-makers as always emphasizing economic ends; (b) does not see the state as the principal actor in international relations; (c) tends to see harmony between the interests of the state and the sum of societal interests; and (d) does not see states as shaping policies in light of the likelihood of war and threats of war.[41] Like Gilpin, Kirshner also holds up Smith as the key exemplar of liberal political economy and then proceeds to misrepresent his views: there is a marked lack of correspondence between the various positions Kirshner attributes to liberal political economy and Smith's actual thinking. In the end, we need to move beyond Kirshner's analysis in order to properly distinguish between liberal political economy and realist political economy and also to accurately understand Smith's views.

Conclusion: Identifying the Three
Key Conceptual Distinctions

The analysis of economic factors in world politics has been significantly influenced by realist and liberal political economy. This chapter has sought to better understand how they can best be distinguished conceptually. In developing this argument, I was critical of the most systematic previous efforts to conceptually distinguish these frameworks, which were respectively undertaken by Gilpin and Kirshner. However, Kirshner's analysis does lay the groundwork for recognizing two of the three conceptual distinctions that can profitably be used to distinguish these frameworks, which will respectively be examined in the next three chapters.

First, Kirshner properly recognizes that while liberal and realist political economy cannot be distinguished regarding the relationship between military security and economic capacity in the long term, they can be productively differentiated regarding how these goals trade off in the short and medium term. While Kirshner accurately captures how realist political economy understands this trade-off, more work is needed to grasp what liberal political economy has to say on the question; this analysis is undertaken in Chapter 7. As I will show, there are two distinct understandings within liberal political economy on this matter, with the one flowing from Smith occupying a middle-ground space between realist political economy and conventional liberal political economy.

Kirshner's analysis points us in the direction of another core conceptual distinction that should be drawn between realist and liberal political economy. His argument, that these frameworks should be distinguished regarding the degree of state autonomy, is not precise enough, but there is a related, more specific issue on which they can and should be conceptually differentiated: their contrasting views regarding the role of economic actors and other societal interests in the formation of policy. As I will show in Chapter 9, there are once again two distinct understandings within liberal political economy on this issue, with the Smithian conception residing between the top-down understanding of realist political economy and bottom-up formulation of conventional liberal political economy.

Beyond these two just-noted conceptual distinctions, there is a third that needs to be drawn between realist and liberal political economy that Kirshner's analysis does not in any way address. This third distinction, the subject of Chapter 8, concerns the role that economic factors play in world politics. There are multiple economic factors that analysts could potentially focus on, and it is important to have a proper understanding of their range when making this analytical choice. As I will show in Chapter 8, analysts have been unfortunately directed away from examining the kinds of structural economic factors that Smith focuses on.

To summarize, when distinguishing realist and liberal political economy, these are the three conceptual distinctions that are critical to focus on. As the next three chapters will show, by taking this approach we will be able to properly understand the unique and valuable perspective that Smith offers regarding the role of economics in world politics. Gilpin and Kirshner ultimately both follow in the footsteps of List and many other earlier realist/mercantilist analysts in setting up liberal political economy as taking on an unreasonable set of propositions, as identifying Smith as being the key exemplar liberal theorist who takes such unreasonable positions, and then as forwarding realist political economy as a "realistic" alternative.[42] As the next three chapters will show in detail, Smith is hardly unrealistic about world politics, and his underlying theoretical conception actually competes with—rather than is representative of—conventional liberal political economy.

CHAPTER SEVEN

How Do Economic Goals Relate to Security Goals?

TO DEVELOP A useful future understanding of how economic factors influence security affairs, it will be important for analysts to grapple with the complex, dynamic nature of the trade-off between economic goals and security goals. This trade-off has all too frequently been set aside or overly simplified by analysts of security affairs, which is highly problematic since it lies at the heart of many essential decisions in world politics.[1] As I have argued elsewhere, our understanding of vital issues such as the level of spending on national defense, investment in military technologies, alliance formation, and the nature of the cooperative agreements states pursue with others all depend significantly on this trade-off.[2]

The insufficient consideration of the economic-security trade-off by analysts of security affairs is undoubtedly due in part to the understandings of it that flow from realist political economy and conventional liberal political economy. Each of these theoretical traditions regard this trade-off as being simple (not complex) and as being static (not dynamic); as such, the implicit takeaway from these theoretical frameworks is that this trade-off need not be analyzed in detail.

Recall from Chapter 6 that Jonathan Kirshner emphasizes that realist and liberal political economy are unified in viewing economic capacity as the underlying source of state power in the long run and, in turn, that they cannot be distinguished regarding their understanding of the relationship between military security and economic capacity in the long term. Where these two frameworks diverge and should be differentiated, he correctly argues, concerns their understanding of the short- and medium-term trade-off between military security and economic capacity.[3]

What, then, is the understanding of the short- and medium-term trade-off between military security and economic capacity within realist political economy and conventional liberal political economy? Kirshner's characterization of how this trade-off is understood within realist political economy is valid: it sees military security as the core priority, which trumps economic capacity in the short and medium term.[4]

As for conventional liberal political economy, Kirshner is correct that it regards economic wealth as the core priority of the economic actors and other societal interests who are seen as driving policy.[5] In this regard, Zacher and Matthew note that "liberals accept that state survival and autonomy are important . . . but they are viewed as secondary interests to the primary interests of individuals."[6] As Moravcsik maintains, "[P]ressure from economic special interests tends to dominate security concerns, even in 'least likely' cases like military procurement."[7]

As we shall see, Smith ultimately offers an understanding of the short- and medium-term trade-off between economic capacity and military security that occupies a middle-ground space between the conceptions of realist political economy and conventional liberal political economy. If we were to represent Smith's conception of this trade-off in a single sentence, we would say that he views states as seeking to maximize the economic resources under their control subject to the constraint of providing for short-term military security. Understanding why this sentence is the best characterization of Smith's understanding will require some detailed exploration, which I undertake below.

Smith's Conception of State Preferences

Because Smith's critique of mercantilism is so well known and so persuasive, he is often understood as having a markedly different conception of state preferences from the mercantilist one. This is not correct.

Smith agreed with mercantilism that maximizing the economic resources the state could deploy in a competitive world was of paramount importance. As Smith notes, "The riches, and so far as power depends upon riches, the power of every country, must always be in proportion to the value of its annual produce, the fund from which all taxes must ultimately be paid. But the great object of the political economy of every country, is to increase the riches and power of that country."[8] Hont helpfully underscores that "Smith's critique of the 'mercantile system' did not imply the abandonment of defensible reason of state, the unending quest of states to survive and flourish. Instead it suggested that reason of state required adaptation to the competitive pattern of economic modernity. Smith's advocacy of winning the international price competition by outpacing all other nations in terms of productivity growth was also his answer to the problem of modern war finance."[9]

Smith clearly saw the world as being fiercely competitive and stressed the overriding importance of a country's firms being economically strong and in advancing economic productivity to survive and thrive in such a world. As Hont notes in this regard, "Smith did not lose sight of the core of the original Machiavellian idea that only growing communities could genuinely flourish. He insisted it was not the richest nation that flourished most, but the one that grew fastest." Smith accordingly counseled pursuing "productivity growth relentlessly" and was "a forceful advocate of vigorous economic growth who encouraged the full political and economic conversion . . . to aggressively competitive trade."[10]

Ultimately, Smith is best understood as differing sharply from mercantilism not on the overall goals of states in the system but on how best to achieve them. As Prasch underlines, "Smith never raises issue with the mercantilists' policy goals, only with their attempts to achieve them. He attributes to the mercantilists the related policies of creating a favorable balance of trade and the consequent hoarding of precious metals. While he disagrees with their method, he does propose his system of free trade and natural liberty as a means to promote the greatness of England, both in its economic strength and in its ability to sustain an army overseas."[11]

It is important to recognize that Smith devoted much attention in his writings to the issue of Britain developing the necessary military capacity to ensure its safety in a conflictual world.[12] As Harlen maintains, "Smith believed . . . that a nation that was unable to protect itself would lack the security necessary to develop politically and economically."[13] The extent of Smith's attention to military capacity has been largely missed over the centuries: as Winch underscores, the "significant, military themes that run through his writings" have received little notice, which "could be the result of these themes becoming obscured by the nineteenth-century association of economic liberalism with pacific sympathies."[14]

Regarding the best means for promoting military capacity, one topic Smith discussed at length is why having a professional army becomes more necessary as the use of military force becomes more complicated. In this regard, Smith's famous argument regarding the division of labor provides the basis for his assertion that having a standing army had become preferable for economically modern states:

In the republicks of antient Greece and Rome, during the whole period of their existence, and under the feudal governments for a considerable time after their first establishment, the trade of a soldier was not a separate, distinct trade, which constituted the sole or principal occupation of a particular class of citizens. . . . The art of war, however, as it is certainly the noblest of all arts, so in the progress of improvement it necessarily becomes one of the most complicated among them. The state of the mechanical, as well as some other arts, with which it is necessarily connected, determines the degree of perfection to which it is capable of being carried at any particular time. But in order to carry it to this degree of perfection, it is necessary that it should become the sole or principal occupation of a particular class of citizens, and the division of labour is as necessary for the improvement of this, as of every other art.[15]

Smith's Understanding of the Pursuit of Autonomy in Defense-Related Production

In a competitive world, Smith was thus keenly aware of the critical value of economic productivity as well as the vital need to safeguard a country's military security. But then how did Smith understand the short- and medium-term trade-off between military security and economic capacity? Smith's overall conception of this trade-off can best be understood by examining his assessment of the willingness of governments to be dependent on others for defense-related capabilities.

In some circumstances where Smith did see an economic-security trade-off regarding defense-related production, he prioritized military security goals over economic capacity. The most notable example in this regard is Britain's passage of the Navigation Acts restricting the use of foreign shipping; in this case, Smith thought it was wise to engage in protectionism in order to enhance the British merchant fleet and thereby augment Britain's security. As Smith notes,

> The defence of Great Britain . . . depends very much on the number of its sailors and shipping. The act of navigation, therefore, very properly endeavors to give the sailors and shipping of Great Britain the monopoly of the trade of their own country. . . . The act of navigation is not favourable to foreign commerce, or to the growth of that opulence which can arise from it. . . . As defence, however, is of much more importance than opulence, the act of navigation is, perhaps, the wisest of all the commercial regulations of England.[16]

Smith's perspective regarding the Navigation Acts would seem in line with the realist political economy conception of states as being averse to dependency in defense-related production and thus as showing a willingness to sacrifice economic efficiency to safeguard autonomy in this area.[17] Yet Smith's endorsement of protectionism in this instance hardly means that he strongly favored or expected governments to generally subjugate economic efficiency to military security if the two priorities conflicted regarding defense production. Smith is clear in noting that that he did *not* generally see it as being "advantageous to lay some burden on foreign, for the encouragement of domestick industry." He was only willing to do so under certain specific conditions: when "a particular sort of industry is necessary for the defence of the country."[18]

Ultimately, Smith's conception of when governments should and would promote autonomy in defense-related production at the expense of overall economic efficiency is much more circumscribed than the realist/mercantilist understanding. As Harlen notes in this regard, "Hamilton and List felt that Smith was correct in noting that national defense was a solid justification for protectionism, but that he had not gone far enough in applying this rationale. Smith had restricted the national defense argument to commodities of direct relevance to the military. In contrast, List and Hamilton argued that national security generally required the development of a manufacturing base."[19]

Smith, supremely aware of the opportunity cost of pursuing autonomy —a more persuasive articulation of this line of argument has never been written—not surprisingly advocates paying those costs only when it is especially necessary to do so to advance a country's miliary security. In his view, to adopt a broader range of protectionist policies would be too costly for productivity, and thus would harm—not help—a country's long-term security. As was discussed in Chapter 2 and will be delineated further in Chapter 8, this line of argument of Smith's has only become more pertinent and more persuasive over time as the difficulty of being closed off from the global economy has increased.

Smith's Conception of Risk Aversion

In sum, we can see from Smith's discussion of the scope of autonomy in defense production that his understanding of the economic-security trade-off only overlaps sometimes with that of realist political economy. This, then, raises a question: how close is Smith's conception of this trade-off to the one forwarded by conventional liberal political economy? The most accurate answer that Smith's understanding of this trade-off is significantly removed from the conventional liberal political economy formulation. To understand why this is the case, we need to get a sense of Smith's conception of the security environment facing states.

I believe the cleanest, most theoretically tractable approach for contrasting political economy frameworks regarding their conceptions of the security environment is to regard them as generally viewing statesmen as having different approaches to decision-making. So how can we best do this? In my assessment, the most useful way is to differentiate them on the basis of their conception of risk aversion.

Risk aversion has long been employed by analysts of world politics, but O'Neill correctly points out that theorists have been imprecise in terms of their understanding of it.[20] O'Neill carefully and persuasively outlines the basis for a useful approach to risk aversion—one that I will follow here—which defines "risk aversion comparatively, in the sense that it ranks decision-makers by degree of aversion but does not label them as risk-averse or -acceptant relative to a zero point."[21] He stresses that "the comparative notion by its definition asks about different individuals' choices in the same situation, and with context held constant risk attitude will depend on the decision maker. . . . Instead of absolute statements about one person's risk attitude, the definition produces a comparison of risk attitudes."[22] O'Neill notes that although risk aversion does not seem to be invariant across all contexts, it does appear to be consistent within a given context and across a common type of risky decisions; accordingly, he maintains leaders are likely to approach decisions regarding world politics with a certain underlying risk aversion.[23]

O'Neill's discussion underscores that specifying an interval scale for risk aversion in international affairs is problematic.[24] Although it does not make sense to provide a specific point estimate of risk aversion for realist and liberal political economy, we can compare them; here, the simple point is that the former sees state leaders as being comparatively more risk-averse than does the latter. Regarding the core issues in world politics that generate concerns among states—most notably, the degree to which a state should take precautionary measures to ensure its survival—realist political economy sees state leaders as being less willing to tolerate the risk of losses than does liberal political economy. As a result, realists expect that states will be relatively more willing to pay the costs of undertaking precautionary measures than liberals do.

But what is Smith's conception of risk aversion? The standard interpretation among international relations scholars is that Smith did not see statesmen as being very risk-averse since he viewed states as naturally having a solidarity of interest.[25] For example, Wight interprets Smith as someone who did not subscribe to "a doctrine of national interest [that] starts from the premise of a conflict of interests, and asserts the autonomy of the national interest" but instead as someone who subscribed to the "opposite premise, of an international community and solidarity of interest."[26] Similarly, Rosecrance emphasizes, "There are two polar forms of international reality. Hobbes, Machiavelli, and Rousseau sketched one version for us. It is a world in which the interests of nations are put ahead of the interests of the collectivity of states. . . . Adam Smith, however, envisioned another kind of world. It is a system [with] an international harmony of interests."[27]

This frequently expressed understanding of Smith seeing states as having a solidarity of interests is simply wrong. The mistake that Wight, Rosecrance, and other analysts make is to see "Smith's thought . . . as prefiguring that of lateral liberals"—many of whom directly expressed their admiration for Smith.[28] As Helleiner underscores, many prominent liberals writing *after* Smith in the nineteenth century—such as David Ricardo, John Stuart Mill, and Richard Cobden—*did* favor a cosmopolitan conception of interests that centered on solidarity and the promotion of the welfare of humanity; however, this was decidedly not true of Smith: "Adam Smith was . . . not at all typical of the cosmopolitan liberals that followed him."[29]

Across Smith's writings, what emerges clearly is a view of states as being comparatively more risk-averse than in the conventional liberal formulation. The general view Smith outlines is one in which states are very concerned about the power of other states and take extensive precautions to advance their security, sometimes to the point of being willing undermine their economic capacity in order to do so. As Walter emphasizes, "the international realm for Smith is unpredictable and dangerous," and he therefore feels it was unwise for a state to "neglect its defense" and adopts the position that "the only secure way to preserve civilization and liberty is to prepare for war."[30] In turn, Hont emphasizes that Smith was not at all hopeful that the political causes of war would ever be eliminated.[31]

In *The Theory of Moral Sentiments*, Smith highlights the two key factors—each of which is easily recognizable to contemporary scholars—that undergird his understanding of why states needed to be wary and take extensive precautions to ensure their security: nationalism and the lack of a hierarchical authority. Regarding nationalism, Smith notes:

> Every individual is naturally more attached to his own particular order or society, than to any other. . . . The love of our country seems, in ordinary cases, to involve in it two different principles: first, a certain respect and reverence for that constitution or form of government which is actually established; and secondly, an earnest desire to render the condition of our fellows-citizens as safe, respectable, and happy as we can. . . . The love of our country seems not to be derived from the love of mankind. . . . France may contain, perhaps, near three times the number of inhabitants which Great Britain contains. In the great society of mankind, therefore, the prosperity of France should appear to be an object of much greater importance than that of Great Britain. The British subject, however, who upon that account, should prefer upon all occasions the prosperity of the former to that of the latter country, would not be thought to be a good citizen of Great Britain. We do not love our country merely as a part of the great society of mankind; we love it for its own sake, and independently of any such consideration.[32]

In Smith's eyes, the key problem is the unsettling combination of nationalism and the lack of a hierarchical authority:

> The love of our own country often disposes us to view, with the most malignant jealousy and envy, the prosperity and aggrandisement of any other neighbouring nation. Independent and neighbouring nations, having no common superior to decide their disputes, all live in continual dread and suspicion of one another. Each sovereign, expecting little justice from his neighbours, is disposed to treat them with as little as he expects from them. . . . Each nation foresees, or imagines it foresees, its own subjugation in the increasing power and aggrandizement of any of its neighbours.[33]

Yet if nationalism could be superseded by some other more powerful force, then this dangerous combination of nationalism and a lack of hierarchical authority could be diluted. On this point, Smith differs in an important respect from the standard liberal understanding in that he did *not* think that the passions of nationalism could ever be superseded by economic interests. As Walter underscores:

> In contrast to Montesquieu and the liberal internationalists of a later time . . . for Smith, the passions of men could not be overcome by mere

economic interest. . . . Smith, unlike these writers, sees people as motivated by a more complex and powerful set of passions than simply economic self-interest. And if this is true for individuals, it is even more true for nations, whose behavior is so often dominated by the passion of national sentiment. For Montesquieu, however, human character was more simple: "it is fortunate for men to be in a situation in which, though their passions may prompt them to be wicked, they have nevertheless an [economic] interest in not being so." This was the basis for his belief that the growth of commerce might constrain the tendency to war. For Smith, even if the irrational mercantilist pursuit of national economic advantage could be prevented from further disrupting international relations, this would hardly be sufficient to enable the elimination of conflict in human affairs.[34]

Moreover, compared to Kant and many other liberal writers, Smith was also less inclined to conclude that international institutions could have a powerful restraining influence on international security affairs. To be clear, Smith does clearly recognize the significance of international institutions in world politics. As van de Haar notes, Smith did recognize that there were "a number of rules and regulations for interstate regulations" that created "some order in international relations."[35] Yet although Smith saw international institutions as being more significant than realists, he was also no Kantian on this front.

Smith's position regarding the restraining influence of international institutions is most apparent when we examine his general attitude toward international law. He did recognize the significance of international law, yet, as Walter concludes, "international law . . . is dismissed [by Smith] as a fairly weak rod with which to constrain the passions and interests of powerful nation."[36] In *Lectures on Jurisprudence*, Smith stresses that the force of international law was, and always would be, constrained due to the lack of a hierarchical authority:

> It is to be observed that the rules which nations ought to observe, or do observe with one another, cannot be treated so accurately as private or public law. . . . With respect to the laws of nations, we can scarce mention any one regulation which is established with the common consent of all nations, and observed as such at all times. This must necessarily be the case, for where there is no supreme legislative power nor judge to settle differences, we may always expect uncertainty and irregularity.[37]

In *The Wealth of Nations*, Smith notes further: "The regard for the laws of nations, or for those rules which independent states profess or pretend to think themselves bound to observe in their dealings with one another, is often very little more than mere pretense or profession. From the smallest interest, upon the slightest provocation, we see those rules violated every day, either evaded or directly violated without shame or remorse."[38]

Smith repeatedly emphasizes the critical importance of "protecting the society from the violence and invasion of other independent societies," which he felt "can be performed only by means of a military force."[39] Of course, alliances are one way that states can pursue to defend themselves, but Smith was, as Walter emphasizes, "skeptical of the equilibrating role of the balance of power" because he saw states as overwhelmingly being focused on their own particular interests and not that of the larger alliance.[40] As Smith maintains in this regard, statesmen "project and form alliances among neighbouring or not very distant nations, for the preservation either of, what is called, the balance of power, or of the general peace and tranquility of states with the circle of their negotiations. The statesmen, however, who plan and execute such treaties, have seldom anything in view, but the interest of their respective countries."[41]

In Smith's understanding, the wariness of leaders also influenced the degree to which states pursued free trade. As Baldwin notes, "Smith saw clearly that what was mutually beneficial from an economic standpoint might not be so from a political standpoint when he observed that the 'wealth of a neighbouring country' might be 'dangerous in war and politics' even though 'certainly advantageous in trade.'"[42] Walter emphasizes further that for Smith, "the contradiction between national economic and political interests is particularly acute for neighboring countries" since they have a greater opportunity to use force against each other due to their proximity.[43]

That Smith saw neighboring states as being particularly wary of each other is what caused him to view them to actually be less likely to pursue free trade with each other. As Smith notes in this regard: "The wealth of a neighbouring nation . . . may enable our enemies to maintain fleets and armies superior to our own. . . . [T]he very same circumstances which would have rendered an open and free commerce between the two countries so advantageous to both, have occasioned the principal obstructions to that commerce."[44]

Ultimately, Smith's understanding of the security environment leads him to have a conception of states being comparatively more risk-averse than in conventional liberal political economy. The lack of precision regarding exactly how far apart they are in terms of their conception of risk aversion will likely strike many as frustrating. If we could establish an interval scale, then we would be able to specify the distance between the theories in a non-arbitrary way. But as O'Neill correctly underscores, we can't do this. What we can say is that the difference in risk attitude is substantial enough that it leads to a meaningfully different understanding of state behavior.

Conclusion: A Middle-Ground Conception of the Economic-Security Trade-Off

Smith's underlying conception of risk aversion leads him to see the pursuit of military security as having a higher priority for states than within conventional liberal political economy. At the same time, he places a great priority on enhancing a country's productivity and does not see governments as privileging military security over economic capacity in the short or medium term when a trade-off exists between them in the manner that realist political economy does. Instead, Smith sees states as privileging military security at the expense of economic efficiency only when it is especially necessary to do so for the country's protection from military threats. In the end, Smith ultimately occupies a middle-ground position between realist and conventional liberal political economy regarding the short- and medium-term trade-off between economic capacity and military security.

For future research, Smith's analysis leads to a clear lesson to bear in mind regarding the economic-security trade-off: that this trade-off is important; that it is complex and dynamic; and that it should be carefully analyzed. As I will demonstrate in Chapter 10, this lesson is very pertinent regarding the end of the Cold War case.

As valuable as this lesson is, the reach of Smith's understanding has been constrained because he does not provide a succinct, generalized statement that accurately captures his overall conception of how states manage the economic-security trade-off.[45] It then becomes sensible to ask: what would such a statement look like? Considering the great importance Smith places on augmenting economic productivity alongside his conception of risk aversion, it is appropriate to characterize Smith as viewing states as seeking to maximize the economic resources under their control—and thus their long-term power and security, given that wealth is a necessary means to power—subject to the constraint of providing for short-term military security.

CHAPTER EIGHT

The Role of Economic Factors in World Politics

A VITAL CONCEPTUAL question for future analysts to consider concerns what economic factor(s) to focus on when examining world politics. As Chapter 1 noted, a key role for grand theory is to direct us to choose certain variables for investigation. In this regard, Smith's theoretical analysis highlights the crucial need to investigate how economic structure, both domestic and international, can influence world politics.

Concerning the influence of economic structure, Marxist theory will undoubtedly leap to mind for many. Marx's conception of economic structure includes technology, machines, and materials (which he called "the material forces of production") as well as the social arrangements that regulate how products are created and distributed (which he called "the relations of production"). In turn, Marx notes that an ideological "superstructure" exists above this economic structural base, and that the base and superstructure mutually influence each other.

Marxism was once very significant within the field of international relations, but it shrank drastically in prominence following the end of the Cold War for, in my own view, a set of reasonable reasons. In my assessment, the Marxist understanding has numerous flaws that impair its usefulness for understanding world politics, including: (a) it has a complicated and overly broad conception of economic structure; (b) relatively few propositions flow from its conception of economic structure regarding world politics; (c) it sees economic structure as having deterministic (and not probabilistic) effects on world politics; and (d) its few propositions regarding world politics have lacked empirical support.[1]

Smith's conception of economic structure—which stands apart from that of Marxism—has unfortunately so far not been prominent among analysts of world politics. So, what exactly is Smith's conception of economic structure? At the domestic level, it is what a society's economy is geared toward producing and not its overall level of wealth. And at the global level, it is the overall structure of the global economy that a state exists within and not dyadic economic linkages between states.

Smith sees changing economic structure as having the potential to have a significant, direct influence on world politics. This general conception of the role of economic factors stands in contrast to that of realist political economy and conventional liberal political economy. Within realist political economy, economic factors are not understood to have a significant, direct influence on security affairs. Rather, the core influence of economic factors is seen as being an indirect one: growth influences the distribution of power, which, in turn, alters security dynamics.[2]

The contrasting conventional liberal view is, as underscored previously, that economic factors—principally trade linkages—have a pacifying effect on international security affairs. For example, John Stuart Mill noted in 1848 that "it may be said without exaggeration that the great extent and rapid increase in international trade, in being the principal guarantee of the peace of the world, is the great permanent security for the uninterrupted progress of the ideas, the institutions, and the character of the human race."[3] This general line of thinking continues to strongly resonate today: analyses of how the global economy influences security affairs overwhelmingly center on trade linkages and are frequently based on the theoretical expectation that higher dyadic trade flows will reduce the likelihood of conflict.[4]

The next two sections of this chapter will respectively delineate Smith's conception of domestic and global economic structure and will update them to account for recent economic transformations. Following this discussion, I will then contrast the kind of structural approach to the global economy that Smith takes with the dyadic approach that is featured in conventional liberal political economy. The last section of the chapter will then clarify two key elements of Smith's approach that are vital to bear in mind: that it is probabilistic, not deterministic, and that economic factors are seen as having a mixed effect on world politics.

Domestic Economic Structure

Regarding domestic economic structure, Smith influentially argued that societies pass through different economic stages and that this has a great influence on both international and domestic behavior. As he notes, "There are four distinct stages that mankind pass: 1st, the Age of Hunters; 2dly, the Age of Shepherds; 3dly, the Age of Agriculture; and 4thly, the Age of Commerce."[5]

Smith underscores that the age of hunters is characterized by a focus on providing sustenance "by the wild fruits and wild animalls which the country afforded. Their sole business would be hunting the wild beasts or catching the fishes. . . . The only thing amongst them which deserved the appellation of a business would be the chase."[6]

Next is the age of shepherds, which is characterized by the herding of animals: "In the process of time, as their numbers multiplied, they would find the chase too precarious for their support. They would be necessitated to contrive some other method whereby to support themselves. . . . The most natural contrivance they would think of, would be to tame some of those wild animals they caught. . . . Hence would arise the age of shepherds."[7]

Next up is the age of agriculture, which would emerge to meet the sustenance demands of a more significant population. As Smith notes, "when a society becomes numerous they would find difficulty in supporting themselves by herds and flocks. Then they would naturally turn themselves the cultivation of land and the raising of such plants and trees as produced nourishment fit for them."[8]

Finally would be the age of commerce, which Smith argued would arise in response to increases in agricultural productivity as well as the pursuit of specialization and would be characterized by an exchange of goods:

> As society was farther improved, the severall arts, which at first would be separated; some persons would cultivate one and others others, as they severally inclined. They would exchange with one another what they produced more than was necessary for their support, and get in exchange for them the commodities they stood in need of and did not produce themselves. This exchange of commodities extends in time not only betwixt the individuals of the same society but betwixt those of different nations. Thus we send to France our cloths, iron work, and other trinkets and get in exchange their wines. . . . Thus at last the age of commerce arises.[9]

In short, Smith sees it as crucial to recognize—and to analytically examine—how societies undergo qualitative economic changes as they become larger and more economically sophisticated, and what matters in this regard is what they generally produce.

DISTINGUISHING THREE KINDS OF DOMESTIC ECONOMIC STRUCTURES

Smith's four-part differentiation of economic structure was accurate and useful during his time. Yet much has obviously changed economically since then. As a result, it is necessary to update the economic structure categories that Smith used.

The same principal force that Smith saw as propelling the emergence of the age of commerce—the pursuit of specialization—has led the most advanced states of today to shift toward having economies that are largely based around the production of knowledge—so-called "knowledge-based economies." The rise of knowledge-based economies is a post–World War II phenomenon. Consider the experience in the United States: "whereas in the 1950s, 80 per cent of the value added in US manufacturing industry represented primary or processed foodstuffs, materials or mineral products, and 20 per cent knowledge, by 1995, these proportions had changed to 30 and 70 per cent respectively."[10]

One needed update to Smith's underlying conception of economic structure is thus to divide commercial societies into two types. The first type—industrial economies—are those commercial societies that primarily focus on the production of goods, as was the case with all commercial societies in Smith's time and for about a century and half afterward.

The second type of commercial societies—knowledge-based economies—are those where industries based around knowledge have achieved central significance; these are the kind of economies that the most advanced states have transformed into during the post–World War II period. A variety of measurement techniques can be used to code exactly which societies have economies concentrated around knowledge.[11]

Smith's underlying conception of economic structure also needs to be updated in another respect. We lack economies today that can generally be characterized as being based around hunting or shepherding. And while many societies today nicely fit Smith's conception of agricultural economies, there are of course now also a significant number of countries that concentrate on the cultivation of the land where the focus is on the extraction of natural resources. Jonathan Markowitz helpfully aggregates economies based around agriculture and those based around natural resources into a single overall category: "land-oriented states."[12] With his coauthors, he has created a dataset that precisely distinguishes from 1816 to 2015 exactly which countries have land-oriented economies.[13] Markowitz and his coauthors specifically define a state as agricultural-dependent if its share of agriculture as a percentage of GDP is 15 percent or higher. In turn, they "consider a state resource-dependent if resource rents exceed 7.5% of GDP."[14]

In sum, Smith usefully conceptualizes domestic economic structure in terms of what a society focuses on producing, and he lays out a series of categories in this regard that were appropriate for his time. If we update this approach to reflect the economic conditions of today, we are left with three different kinds of domestic economic structures that need to be distinguished: (1) land-oriented economies, (2) industrial economies, and (3) knowledge-based economies.

Global Economic Structure

At the heart of Smith's argument about global economic structure is that there is an opportunity cost to being closed off from international commerce. *The Wealth of Nations* argues persuasively that a choice to avoid participation in the global economy comes at the cost of lost efficiency. For Smith, the key advantage of economic openness is that it allows for increased specialization: he argues that a more extensive division of labor becomes possible if a state participates in trade than if it closes itself off from trade. Hence, a state that does not participate in international trade will not be able to maximize its economic productivity. As he notes in this regard:

> By means of it, the narrowness of the home market does not hinder the division of labour in any particular branch of art or manufacture from being carried to the highest perfection. By opening a more extensive market for whatever part of the produce of their labour may exceed the home consumption, it encourages them to improve its productive powers, and to augment its annual produce to the utmost, and thereby to increase the real revenue and wealth of the society.[15]

What is often missed is that Smith underscores that states also benefit from economic openness in a second way: by gaining access to more advanced technologies and knowhow. Smith emphasized that for a very large state, such as China, that has a very substantial, diverse domestic market (and thus contains within its borders substantial capacity for specialization) it is this latter benefit of economic openness that is most consequential. As Smith reviews, "the great extent of the empire of China, the vast multitude of its inhabitants, the variety of climate, and consequently of productions in its different provinces, and the easy communication by means of water carriage between the greater part of them, render the home market of that country of so great extent, as to be alone sufficient to support very great manufactures, and to admit of very considerable subdivisions of labour." He then goes on to argue that by engaging "more extensive foreign trade . . . the Chinese would naturally learn the art of using and constructing themselves all the different machines used in other countries, as well as the all the other improvements of art and industry which are practised in all the different parts of the world. Upon the present plan they have little opportunity of improving themselves by the example of any other nation; except that of the Japanese."[16]

At the time Smith was writing and for about two centuries afterward, trade was the core integrating force in global commerce; this is why Smith focused on appealing to the leaders of the United Kingdom to make the country open to trade. At the heart of Smith's appeal in this regard was the idea that opening to trade was essential to ensure the country had a competitive advantage over other countries in a dangerous, competitive world.[17] As Hont notes in this regard, "Smith's support for free trade was . . . part and parcel of his proposed modernization of war finance. In his view a combination of financial revolution and the rise of ultraproductive export industries was sufficient to generate the income needs that could meet modern military needs flexibly, if and when national security required it. This strategy, however, was viable only if access to world markets was unimpeded at all times."[18]

In short, Smith saw pursuing specialization as necessary for maximizing productivity, which in turn was key for ensuring a state's long-term security. Even centuries later, many leaders seem to not understand this argument and instead are prone to excessively insulate their countries from the global economy because they misperceive this route as being the best one for enhancing long-term security. It is not, as Smith showed centuries ago—and his line of argument has only become stronger over time. As was discussed in Chapter 7, Smith argued persuasively that protectionism was only warranted in very specific circumstances—namely, when a particular industry was vitally significant for defense.

Smith thus emphasizes the significance of the opportunity cost of closure. Trade dominated global commerce in Smith's time, and the extent to which a country engaged in trade is thus what mattered. But today's global economy is fundamentally different: trade now has a secondary status as a driver of global commerce due to the onset of the "globalization of production." Smith's trade-focused conception of global economic structure consequently needs to be updated.

FACTORING IN THE GLOBALIZATION OF PRODUCTION

The globalization of production is a qualitative change in the commercial activities of MNCs in which their production activities have become more geographically dispersed.[19] More specifically, in recent decades MNCs have sought to reap various locational efficiencies by slicing up the value-added chain (that is, dividing up the production sequence of a product) and locating different aspects of production in those countries that are most advantageous.

While firms have always engaged in subcontracting (that is, turning to other firms to supply certain elements of the production process), it was only in the final decades of the twentieth century that we truly saw the emergence of international subcontracting as an important global activity; before then, subcontracting had largely been focused domestically. During this same period, MNCs simultaneously moved strongly toward having their foreign affiliates carry out different parts of the production process as part of a global production strategy. This is a marked shift from the predominant pattern prior to the 1970s, when the foreign affiliates of MNCs were predominantly "stand-alone" affiliates focused on serving the local market and were not oriented toward participating in a geographically dispersed production chain. Moreover, at the same time that MNCs were geographically dispersing their production activities, they were also simultaneously moving toward a much greater dispersion of technological development via a dramatic increase in the number international inter-firm alliances and augmented research and development (R&D) undertaken by foreign affiliates.

To be clear, we do not live in an age of truly globaliz*ed* production. For one thing, the globalization of production is not occurring equally across all industries: production has been geographically dispersed to the greatest extent in high-technology sectors and those sectors of manufacturing characterized by high levels of R&D and significant economies of scale, such as machinery, electronic components, transportation equipment, and computers.[20] Moreover, the geographic dispersion of production does not encompass the entire world: the "fragmentation of production . . . is a phenomenon largely confined to developed countries and the East Asian region."[21] This is because only the economically most advanced countries have a significant number of MNCs that are able to geographically disperse their production and, in turn, only a relatively small number of less advanced economies possess the kinds of locational advantages that MNCs seek to tap when they slice up the value chain.

With respect to global economic structure, the onset of the globalization of production reveals the critical need for analysts of world politics to make two distinctions. The first is that global commerce was once dominated by trade, but this is no longer the case: now, it is primarily shaped by the global production decisions of MNCs. Indeed, much of trade today is merely a byproduct of the globalization of production: by the end of the twentieth century, the combined significance of international subcontracting and intra-firm trade (that is, transactions across borders within a single firm) were estimated to account for around two-thirds of world trade.[22]

Second, it is important to recognize that the opportunity cost of closure can vary over time—not simply what drives it but also how strong it is. There is always an opportunity cost of closure, as Smith so tellingly argued, but today it is extremely high—far more so than ever before in history. Put another way, there are long-standing handicaps associated with international economic isolation; yet, as underscored in Chapter 2, in recent decades these handicaps were dramatically augmented as production became increasingly globalized and the cost, difficulty, and importance of technological development concomitantly rose.[23]

Dyadic Approach vs. Structural Approach

Dyadic economic linkages—that is, economic ties between pairs of states—are important. But the more extensive the level of internationalization in the global economy and the more significant the opportunity cost of closure, the more important it becomes to pay attention to global economic structure and not exclusively focus on dyadic economic linkages. In these circumstances, Snyder correctly underscores that "a dyadic approach is insufficient" since competitive pressures increase "in proportion to the number of actors participating and the extent of the commercial interaction among them." He emphasizes that when global economic integration is high, "the reason why a [structural] perspective, as opposed to a dyadic logic, is necessary is that systems of multiple actors create 'network externalities.' Network externalities are incentives and disincentives produced, at times unintentionally, as a by-product of the interactions of multiple actors." He notes further that "[m]ultiple actors create a reality that cannot be reduced to any single actor or dyad. It is the totality that conditions the behavior of the part; understanding this requires a [structural] perspective."[24]

In my view, both global economic structure and dyadic economic linkages are worthy of attention; whether one chooses to concentrate on examining one or the other is a theoretical choice that an analyst makes. In theory an analyst could simultaneously focus on the effects of economic structure and dyadic linkages; in practice, however, analysts tend to focus on one or the other.[25]

In recent decades, it has been the dyadic approach that has most captured the attention of analysts of security affairs; in comparison, there has been a dearth of scholarly attention to the influence of global economic structure. On the one hand, this lopsided focus is somewhat surprising given the significance and novelty of the globalization of production. On the other hand, theory guides what elements of the world analysts chose to analyze, and we have lacked a general theoretical framework that highlights the importance of examining global economic structure.

Yet even though analysts are prone to specialize, one might question whether this is useful: if dyadic linkages and global economic structure both matter, can the latter be productively examined separately? Yes. Although dyadic linkages and economic structure are both important, the latter certainly has the potential to have important effects on international affairs on its own (as will be concretely shown in the analysis of the end of Cold War case in Chapter 10). Devoting more attention to such direct effects in the future seems worthwhile in light of recent changes in the global economy.

Two Clarifications about Smith's Structural Approach

Smith directs analysts to examine the significance of economic structure, both domestic and global. Because structural analyses are often seen as having certain theoretical connotations, let me outline two clarifications to regarding the kind of approach Smith has in mind.

The first is that Smith did not see economic factors as having a unidirectional effect on world politics. Smith has very frequently been portrayed as someone who saw economic factors generally, and commerce specifically, as being pacifying, but this is simply not the case, as the discussion in Chapter 2 noted. Smith saw economic factors as making the world more conflictual in some ways and more peaceful in others.

The second clarification is that although Smith was firmly of the view that economics and world politics were directly linked in important ways, he was not an "economic determinist": he clearly did not see economic factors as always having a decisive influence. As Walter notes in this regard, Smith was "far from the view, common to both liberal utopians and Marxists, that economic forces would ultimately triumph over politics. . . . The importance of Smith's thinking, particularly that about political economy, is that a central role for the economic in human affairs need not marginalize the importance of institutions nor trivialize the political."[26]

One can highlight a variable as being valuable to examine without making a claim that it is the only significant one or even the most important one. Indeed, this is the only reasonable scientific position to adopt: the importance of a variable is ultimately an empirical question, not something to be established by theoretical fiat.

Conclusion

Smith's conception of the role of economic factors in world politics has not been properly understood or appreciated over the centuries. Smith directs us to concentrate on the influence of economic structure—both domestic and global—on world politics.

Updating Smith's conception of domestic structure to the present day, three kinds of economies now need to be distinguished: (1) industrial economies; (2) knowledge-based economies; and (3) land-oriented economies. This is the conceptualization that analysts should use in the future when analyzing the influence of domestic economic structure on security affairs.

Regarding global economic structure, two key points need to be recognized. The first is that international commerce today is now driven primarily by the global production decisions of MNCs and not by trade. The takeaway for upcoming research is straightforward: being overwhelmingly focused on the security ramifications of trade may have once made sense, but it no longer does.

The second critical point about global economic structure is that the opportunity cost of closure is now significantly higher than in past eras. Future theorizing about the economics-security interaction would be wise to pay careful attention to the fact that the costs of isolation from the global economy have ascended to a historically unprecedented level.

Finally, it is crucial to understand that although Smith highlighted the significance of economic structure, he was no economic determinist and also did not see it as having a unidirectional effect on world politics. Ultimately, the core takeaway that emerges from this chapter for future analyses is not that economic structure is some sort of master variable, but rather that it is potentially important and that analysts would thus be wise to pay careful attention to it. The significance of this point was demonstrated in Chapters 2 and 4 and will also be underlined clearly in the analysis of the end of the Cold War case in Chapter 10.

CHAPTER NINE

How Do Economic Actors
Affect Security Policy?

HOW DO ECONOMIC actors influence security policy? This is a vital conceptual question confronting future analysts of the economics-security interaction. As noted in Chapter 6, realist and liberal political economy can be usefully differentiated regarding the degree to which government leaders form policy distinct from pressures from economic actors and other societal interests. On this key issue, they thus provide very different understandings and guidance for analysts.

Regarding realist political economy, Jonathan Kirshner presents a valid assessment that it sees the government as an actor that (1) has its own interests; (2) is distinct from the sum of societal interests; (3) has the ability and desire to further its own agenda; and (4) is willing and able to defend its interests when there is a divergence between the interests of the government and those of societal interests.[1] In this view, external incentives have a direct influence on international behavior by altering the decision calculus facing policymakers.

Below I outline two conceptions of the role played by societal interests within liberal political economy that contrast both with realist political economy and with each other: the typical one, which is represented in conventional liberal political economy, and an alternative one, which is grounded in Smith's understanding. In this discussion, I will focus on the role of economic actors because they are typically better positioned to influence policymaking than other societal interests due to their extensive resources and because Smith devotes so much attention to the political activities of—in his words—"merchants and manufacturers."

The Role of Economic Actors and Societal Interests
in Conventional Liberal Political Economy

Conventional liberal political economy "rests on a 'bottom-up' or plu-
ralist view of politics."[2] In this view, political changes reflect what economic actors and other societal interests want. As Zacher and Matthew
note in this regard, "liberals view states . . . as pluralistic actors whose
interests and policies are determined by bargaining among groups and
elections. . . . The interests of states . . . are viewed as changing because
liberals see individuals' values and the power relations among interest
groups evolving over time."[3] As Moravcsik puts it, the liberal view is that
the state "is constantly subject to capture and recapture, construction and
reconstruction, by coalitions of social interests. It constitutes the critical
'transmission belt' by which the preferences and social power of individuals and groups are translated into foreign policy."[4]

To be clear, the conventional liberal formulation is not a purely "domestic" understanding of international behavior. Within conventional liberal
political economy, international factors are important; however, the point
is that they exercise their influence on foreign policy behavior *indirectly*
by changing what economic actors and other societal interests want and/
or how powerful they are. In this regard, government policy is seen as
ultimately being "determined by bargaining power among interest groups,
but these groups' definitions of their interests are affected by a host of
factors . . . [A]t the international level, there are technological capabilities
that allow states to affect each other in different ways, patterns of interactions and interdependencies, transnational sociological patterns, knowledge, and international institutions."[5]

Regarding security affairs, there are two analytical concerns worth
noting about the conventional liberal conception of political change. For
one thing, economic actors and other societal interests do not always
know what to prefer in the security realm. Many key societal interests do
not have a clear stake regarding many security policy issues. As I have
emphasized elsewhere, many economic actors are so marginally affected
by security policy issues that they either do not follow them or do not
undertake political actions based on them.[6] The same appears true of
the public: research indicates that much of the public is poorly informed
about foreign policy issues and is greatly influenced by elite framing.[7]

Second, the conventional liberal understanding tacitly assumes that
if there are recognizable gains to be accrued from policy change, then
economic actors and other societal interests will organize to secure these

gains and/or that politicians have the capacity to determine what these groups want and to respond accordingly. Yet even among those economic actors and societal interests that do have firm security policy preferences, many of them may not organize effectively to promote political change. And even in the event that groups are, in fact, organized effectively, there is still no guarantee that anything will happen—it will ultimately depend on whether politicians choose to respond to them. Moreover, there may be groups on both sides of an issue whose lobbying efforts will offset each other.

Does this mean that the conventional liberal conception of policy change is wrong? No. Not useful? Hardly. I raise these analytical concerns merely to indicate that there is intellectual space for an alternative liberal formulation to be considered alongside it.

Smith's Understanding of the Role of Economic Actors and Societal Interests

As noted in Chapter 6, Smith has been frequently misunderstood, by Gilpin and many others, as having a bottom-up conception of politics. This is simply wrong. As Baldwin helpfully underscores:

> According to Gilpin, the mercantilists view nation-states as "the real actors in international economic relations . . . [and] national interest determines foreign policy." He contrasts this view with the liberal emphasis "on the individual consumer, firm, or entrepreneur." This characterization flows from Gilpin's contention that mercantilist goals were defined in terms of national interest while liberal goals were defined in terms of global welfare. If Adam Smith's book had been entitled "An Inquiry into the Nature and Causes of the Wealth of Consumers, Firms, and Entrepreneurs," of course, Gilpin's point would be strengthened. The actual title, however, is difficult to reconcile with Gilpin's description.[8]

As Skinner maintains, Smith's conception of the government was based on the view that it can sometimes "act with an eye to the good of the whole" and also that it "can acquire the necessary knowledge before it acts."[9] At the same time, in keeping with "his role as a *political* economist . . . [Smith] did not merely postulate the existence of government, but also sought to explain its probable structure, and the way in which that structure might impinge on the manner in which the necessary functions are performed." Smith also recognized "that the Commons was an important focus for pressure groups whose objectives were partial, that is, not necessarily connected with the public interest, and even opposed to it."[10]

Walter underlines that Smith makes "a clear distinction between . . . the partial interests of 'rapacious merchants and manufacturers' . . . on the one hand and national interests on the other."[11] Smith did not see much in the way of harmony between the national interest and the political behavior of economic actors; a great deal of *The Wealth of Nations* is devoted to arguing that that "the general interest of society" was *not* being promoted by the political actions of merchants and manufacturers.[12] For Smith, the political order that he observed was characterized by policies that were overly influenced by concentrated economic interests and thereby excessively benefited them at the public's expense.

Smith saw not only that the political interests of clamoring merchants and manufacturers frequently departed from the general interest of society but also that these economic actors often sought to deceive the public: "the interested sophistry of merchants and manufacturers confounded the common sense of mankind. Their interest is, in this respect, directly opposite to that of the great body of the people."[13] At another point, Smith further argues that merchants and manufacturers "have generally an interest to deceive and even to oppress the publick, and who accordingly have, upon many occasions, both deceived and oppressed it."[14]

Given the strong political influence of economic actors on policy that he observed, Smith hardly thought the government would consistently act in favor of promoting the overall national interest. In turn, Smith is clear in arguing that if a move toward enacting policies—like free trade— that will advance the common good of society ever occurs, this would not likely be due to the political actions of merchants and manufacturers: "it is the interest of the merchants and manufacturers of every country to secure to themselves the monopoly of the home market. Hence in Great Britain, and in most other European countries, the extraordinary duties upon almost all goods imported by alien merchants."[15] More generally, Smith was clear in noting that any policy proposals advocated by merchants and manufacturers "ought always to be listened to with great precaution, and ought never to be adopted till after having been long and carefully examined, not only with the most scrupulous, but with the most suspicious attention."[16]

Smith thus saw the state as the actor most likely to act to advance the public good, and it is certainly clear that much of *The Wealth of Nations* can be viewed as a long memo to policymakers on what they should do to advance this objective.[17] In this regard, McNally notes that in Smith's view:

> it is the role of the state to initiate those policies which will correct the defects of commercial society. Smith's undertaking is thus *political economy* in the fullest sense of the term—advice to legislators on the political policies they ought to follow in the pursuit of national wealth and power. . . . Smith saw his task as contributing to the "the science of the legislator, whose deliberations ought to be governed by general principles which are always the same." . . . Thus, *The Wealth of Nations* can be seen as a piece of scientific counsel addressed to the legislator, the "prudent lawgiver," who attempts . . . to frame the best laws that the people will accept.[18]

What specific principles did Smith recommend to legislators? At a procedural level, Smith advocated that they should rise above the demands of economic actors and other concentrated societal interests and promote the national interest; as he puts it, they should conduct their deliberations "not by the clamorous importunity of partial interests, but by an extensive view of the general good."[19] Smith certainly felt that this was possible: as he maintains, "merchants and manufacturers . . . neither are, nor ought to be the rulers of mankind."[20] As Skinner emphasizes: "while it is true that Smith made much of the part played by sectional economic interest in government, he was very far from suggesting that the Commons was a kind of clearing house for such interests. . . . He was also alive to the existence of the statesmen governed by an extensive view of the general good."[21] This point will be discussed more extensively in the next section.

A more specific piece of procedural advice Smith offered was to constantly scrutinize existing policies to see if they continued to be worthwhile for promoting the common good of society. Smith was well aware that policies often stay in place long after their usefulness because of what is now termed "path dependency." As Smith notes: "Laws frequently continue in force long after the circumstances, which first gave occasion to them, and which could alone render them reasonable, are no more."[22] Smith saw such path dependency as potentially being very harmful; as Skinner emphasizes, Smith argued that "arrangements which were once appropriate, but are now no longer so should be removed. . . . Smith calls for the abolition of institutions and customs which are remnants of the past; for the abolition of positions of monopoly and privilege, and, finally, for a major reform of national policy."[23]

But Smith obviously went much further than offering procedural advice; he also offered specific guidance on which policies should be followed to best promote the national interest. Most famously, he argued that governments should recognize the critical need to move away from protectionism. In Smith's eyes, there were strong external competitive pressures to move away from protectionism; if Britain failed to do so, he felt its economy would be weakened and its security would be endangered.[24]

The Role of Political Entrepreneurs
in Overcoming Concentrated Interests

Smith's view that the government could act to further the public good can easily be misinterpreted. This does not mean that Smith views all, or even most, politicians as being capable of doing this. For Smith, the point is that some politicians were sometimes able to do so.

Smith did not have a positive view of most politicians; he was scornful of them as generally being "spendthrifts" and saw them as being prone to "extravagance" and "the greatest errors of administration."[25] Put simply, Smith did not feel that the average politician was up to the job of promoting the best interests of society. As one explanation for why, he suggests that the average politician is too intimidated by societal interests. Regarding the special interests that fight against free trade, for example, Smith highlights the

> zeal and unanimity . . . with which master manufacturers set themselves against every law that is likely to increase the number of their rivals in the home market. . . . This monopoly has so much increased the number of some particular tribes of them, that, like an overgrown standing army, they have become formidable to the government, and upon many occasions intimidate the legislature. The member of parliament who supports every proposal for strengthening this monopoly, is sure to acquire . . . great popularity and influence with an order of men whose numbers and wealth render them of great importance. If he opposes them, on the contrary, and still more if he has authority enough to be able to thwart them, neither the most acknowledged probity, nor the highest rank, nor the greatest publick services can protect him from the most infamous abuse and detraction, from personal insults, nor sometimes from real danger, arising from the insolent outrage of furious and disappointed monopolists.[26]

Although Smith did not have a positive view of most politicians, as a class he did view them as being relatively less harmful than the kinds of clamoring economic actors he saw as having long had an overly strong political influence: "The capricious ambition of kings and ministers has not, during the present and the preceding century, been more fatal to the repose of Europe, than the impertinent jealousy of merchants and manufacturers."[27] The more important point is that Smith did not pin his hopes for the development of societally efficient policies on the actions of average politicians; key in this regard was the emergence of what economists and political scientists now call "political entrepreneurs."[28]

Political entrepreneurs do not take the existing domestic political constraints that favor a continuation of the status quo as a given; instead, they actively seek to break free of these constraints by reshaping public opinion and/or changing political institutions and/or by empowering or creating interest groups that favor a change in policy. As Sheingate emphasizes, political entrepreneurs are "creative, resourceful, and opportunistic leaders whose skillful manipulation of politics somehow results in the creation of a new policy . . . or a new institution, or transforms an existing one. . . . [They] shape the terms of political debate: they frame issues, define problems, and influence agendas."[29] Joskow and Noll note that political entrepreneurs have the capacity to be effective because they are in a position to "package a message in an attractive and comprehensible way and thereby convince some unorganized voters" or interest groups that a shift away from a status quo is desirable.[30]

To be clear, a political entrepreneur is hardly boundless in their powers of persuasion; as Riker emphasizes, such an agent "can neither create preferences nor hypnotize. What he can do is probe until he finds some new alternative, some new dimension, that strikes a spark in the preferences of others."[31] In turn, Dahl underscores that although political entrepreneurs can be powerful agents of change, their emergence is episodic: "majorities, parties, interest groups, elites, even political systems are all to some extent pliable; a leader who knows how to use his resources to the maximum is not so much the agent of others as others are his agents. Although a gifted political entrepreneur might not exist in every political system, wherever he appeared he would make himself felt."[32]

Smith highly lauds those politicians who see an opportunity for improving societal welfare and seek to move beyond the constraints of concentrated interests who favor maintaining a political status quo that excessively benefits them. In *The Theory of Moral Sentiments*, Smith points to "the greatest and noblest of all characters, that of the reformer and legislator of a great state" and highlights that the key characteristic of good leadership is "to promote, by every means in his power, the welfare of the whole society of his fellow-citizens."[33] As noted above, much of *The Wealth of Nations* can be read as advice to potential political entrepreneurs as to why Britain would best be served by breaking free of the existing domestic constraints fostered by the political actions of concentrated economic actors and instead adopting new policies that better advanced its overall national interest.

This perspective is clearest with respect to free trade, where Smith appeals to "the wisdom of future statesmen and legislators to determine" the best means of overcoming political opposition to open markets.[34] In Smith's eyes, the promotion of protectionism was due to a lack of a proper understanding of how governments could best advance their economic and security interests; his motivation was to correct this deficiency.[35]

It is important to recognize that although Smith clearly wants and expects political entrepreneurs to sometimes emerge and move beyond policies that cater to societal interests, he also counsels that it is unwise to make fast, dramatic policy shifts and to push for change without any regard to political opposition.[36] In this regard, Smith holds in great disrepute what he calls "the man of system," which is a political leader who:

> is apt to be very wise in his own conceit; and is often so enamoured with the supposed beauty of his own ideal plan of government, that he cannot suffer even the slightest deviation from it. . . . Some general, and even systematical, idea of the perfection of policy and law, may no doubt be necessary for directing the views of the statesman. But to insist upon establishing, and upon establishing all at once, and in spite of all opposition, every thing which that idea may seem to require, must often be the highest degree of arrogance. It is to erect his own judgment into the supreme standard of right and wrong. It is to fancy himself the only wise and worthy man in the commonwealth, and that his fellow-citizens should accommodate themselves to him and not he to them.[37]

In Smith's view, a wise political entrepreneur will act with moderation when seeking to reshape the political environment and should "accommodate, as well as he can, his public arrangements to the confirmed habits and prejudices of the people. . . . [W]hen he cannot establish the best system of laws, he will endeavor to establish the best that the people can bear."[38] Smith advances this general line of argument with respect to ending protectionism, arguing that it would be both unrealistic and unwise to push for free trade either too quickly or too comprehensively. As Smith notes, to expect that

> freedom of trade should ever be entirely restored in Great Britain, is as absurd as to expect that an Oceana or Utopia should ever be established in it. . . . The undertaker of a great manufacture who, by the home markets being suddenly laid open to the competition of foreigners, should be obliged to abandon his trade, would no doubt suffer very considerably. . . . The equitable regard, therefore, to his interest requires that changes of this kind should never be introduced suddenly, but slowly, gradually, and after very long warning.[39]

External Competitive Pressures and Political Entrepreneurship

In sum, Smith underscores the value of political entrepreneurs who work to implement policy changes that promote societal efficiency and do so in an assertive, but not revolutionary, manner. This brings up a crucial question: what motivates political entrepreneurship? Smith hardly has a conclusive answer; what he highlights is the significance of external competitive pressures.

North argues that the opportunities perceived by political entrepreneurs can arise from "external changes in the environment (technological or political changes, for example)."[40] More specifically, he emphasizes, "external sources of change . . . may weaken the power of existing organizations, strengthen or give rise to organizations with different interests and change the path. The critical actor(s) in such situations will be political entrepreneurs whose degree of freedom will increase in such situations and, on the basis of their perceptions of the issues, give them the ability to induce the growth of organizations with different interests."[41]

Smith's perspective aligns with North's argument. In Smith's discussion of how external competitive pressures can spur political entrepreneurship, economic considerations manifest themselves in two different ways. For the first consideration, a topic of Chapter 8, Smith emphasizes that a competitive global security environment spurred the need to augment economic productivity in order to advance the long-term economic capacity of a country, which is the ultimate foundation of a country's security from external threats. In turn, Smith also viewed states as being keenly focused on economic competitiveness *even if* security tensions ever came to be lessened. As Hont emphasizes in this regard, Smith felt that the global economy would always "continue to exhibit warlike ruthlessness."[42]

Yet Smith was keenly aware that an intense focus on competing with other countries in the economic realm could easily be taken too far and could cause states to "look with an invidious eye upon the prosperity of all the nations with which it trades, and to consider their gain as its own loss."[43] Smith, believing that falling prey to such "commercial jealousy"— as has occurred with many leaders over the centuries, right up until the present day—was a terrible mistake, argued strongly for adopting another way of thinking about international economic competition—one in which nations competed intensely but at the same time did not focus on "beggaring all their neighbours."[44]

As Hont emphasizes: "Smith searched for an alternative to commercial jealousy that maximized both national pride and economic growth, while eliminating the detrimental consequences of national prejudice and envy. This alternative was 'national emulation,' the competitive pursuit of national economic excellence." Hont goes on to note that in Smith's view, "emulation was the positive counterpart of envy. . . . [E]mulation was 'an anxious desire that we ourselves should excel' and it was 'originally founded in our admiration of the excellence of others.' An envious man felt pain at seeing others excel. An emulous man, in contrast, felt aggrieved because he himself had failed to match the achievements of others. . . . Envy created hatred, and emulation produced zeal, striving, activity, and progress."[45] This matches up with North's argument that poor relative growth rates can be a key factor that promotes political entrepreneurship: "poor economic performance in the context of low information costs about contrasting performance elsewhere will undermine the influence and political clout of existing organizations and will sometimes give political entrepreneurs sufficient freedom to initiate productive rule changes."[46]

In sum, Smith's understanding is that external competitive pressures can sometimes create both the incentive and the opportunity for political entrepreneurs to push for appropriate policies and institutions such that they can remain competitive with other countries militarily and/or economically. There are certainly many cases in which this kind of external competitive dynamic has spurred political entrepreneurship that enhanced societal efficiency. A famous example of this type is Japan's effort to overhaul its entire political and economic structure along Western lines during the Meiji period following Commodore Perry's 1854 "opening" of Japan. More recently, one of the most persuasively documented cases of this dynamic is Kang's analysis of Taiwan and South Korea, in which he stresses that a key reason for their dramatic developmental success during the post–World War II period was a strong motivation on the part of the leaders of these countries to rapidly build themselves up economically due to very significant external security threats they respectively faced.[47]

Of course, external competitive pressures will not always be sufficiently strong to spur efforts by political entrepreneurs to enhance efficiency. Moreover, the domestic institutional context is clearly also crucial: inefficient policies and institutions will often have significant path dependency because, as North puts it, "the political and economic organizations that have come into existence in consequence of the institutional matrix typically have a stake in perpetuating the existing framework."[48] Although the pressures of international competition can sometimes overcome this path dependency by undermining the viability of the policy status quo and spurring political entrepreneurship, this will hardly always be the case.

Conclusion: A Middle-Ground Conception of the Role of Economic Actors

Smith's understanding of the role of economic actors and other societal interests in the polity ultimately occupies a theoretical space in between that of realist political economy and conventional liberal political economy. Whereas realist political economy sees the government as always being willing and able to defend its interests when there is a divergence between what it wants and what societal interests want, Smith does not. In Smith's view, there will frequently be no political force to counteract the influence of societal interests; he stresses that policies often have significant path dependency exactly because some societal interest will benefit from the policy status quo and will fight to retain it. At the same time, Smith underscores that external competitive pressures can sometimes spur political entrepreneurship; when this happens, the government can be in a position to act on preferences that are distinct from societal interests. In the end, Smith thus offers a contingent perspective that is neither bottom-up nor top-down.

Smith's argument about how external competitive pressures can act as a spur for policy change is a mechanism that has of late been underappreciated.[49] In much contemporary scholarship, the overriding focus regarding the political significance of external competitive pressures has been on how they lead to changes in the power and/or preferences of economic actors and other societal interests and how they, in turn, create pressure on policymakers to act in response. This is the bottom-up dynamic that conventional liberal political economy centers on; although it is often very important, it is far from the complete story. What Smith long ago pointed us to, and what contemporary analysts too frequently neglect, is that policy changes can also sometimes be prompted by political entrepreneurship that occurs directly in response to external competitive pressures.

For future analyses, a core lesson that flows from Smith's theoretical conception is that competitive external pressures can sometimes spur political entrepreneurship. As we will see in the next chapter, Smith's conception of the role of political entrepreneurs in pushing for policy change in response to changing competitive pressures is very helpful for understanding the case of the end of the Cold War.

CHAPTER TEN

The Significance
of the Theoretical Analysis

THE END OF THE COLD WAR

THE ANALYSIS OF the sixteen pathways examined in the first part of the book provides a rich empirical portrait of how economic factors influence security affairs. But they do not tell us everything we need to know. Additional pathways and theories will need to be delineated. Moreover, it will also be necessary to develop new explanations and predictions about the influence of economic factors on particular states.

As was underscored in Chapter 1, theory helps to guide analysts regarding "where to look" when analyzing world politics. The previous three chapters outlined the key elements of what a Smithian theoretical understanding of the role of economic factors in world politics looks like. This chapter uses the case of the end of the Cold War as a means of demonstrating in practice what this theoretical understanding can do.

The previous chapters pointed to three general lessons flowing from Smith concerning the role of economic factors that future analysts should bear in mind. The first lesson (noted in Chapter 7) is that the trade-off between economics and security cannot be neglected since it is neither simple nor static; it must be examined since it is complex and dynamic. The second lesson (Chapter 8) is that analysts need to pay more attention to the influence of economic structure—both domestic and global—on security affairs, but in doing so they should not conceive of it as having either a deterministic or a unidirectional effect. Finally, the third lesson (Chapter 9) is that an important potential pathway to consider by which economic factors can influence policy is the promotion of action by political entrepreneurs in response to changes in external competitive pressures.

As this chapter will show, the end of the Cold War reveals that there is a concrete need for analysts to pay heed to these three lessons. My assessment is that if a Smithian theoretical framework had been readily available as a guide to thinking regarding the role of economic factors in world politics, then the end of the Cold War would have been far less shocking and might even have been foreseen. Some decisive features of this case were missed, and the most likely reason for this is that the existing theoretical frameworks did not highlight them as warranting attention.

The chapter begins by delineating why the end of the Cold War is valuable to examine. I then discuss the critical role played by changing economic structure in this case. The next two sections then use this case to illustrate, respectively, the importance of considering the economic-security trade-off in dynamic terms and the significance of political entrepreneurship in response to external competitive pressures.

Why Focus on the End of the Cold War?

There are five reasons the end of the Cold War is valuable for demonstrating why future analysts should pay heed to the lessons that flow from a Smithian understanding of the role of economic factors in world politics. First, the end of the Cold War is the most substantively important change in security affairs since 1945. Second, the failure of leading theories to predict this event beforehand—or, seemingly, to explain it afterward—was seen within the academy and beyond as a glaring failure of the scientific study of international relations. Third, more so than any other event in recent decades, this case and the manner in which analysts tried to explain it promoted dramatic theoretical shifts regarding the study of world politics—most notably, the rise of constructivism as a major theory.[1] Fourth, it is a case for which scholars now know a crucial role was played by economic factors, generally, and structural economic factors, in particular—one that was insufficiently recognized by scholars for almost a decade afterward. Fifth and finally, the literature on this event is truly massive—through 2000, there were 719 analyses with the phrase "end of the Cold War" in the title; the total number of such analyses in the present day has reached 2,210.[2]

The combination of points 4 and 5 is truly damning and truly telling: it is almost unfathomable that such a massive number of analysts could so neglect the role of structural economic factors in this case before 2001 (which is when the first systematic analysis of how they influenced this case—by William Wohlforth and myself—was published).[3] To explain this neglect of structural economic factors by hundreds and hundreds of analysts over a decade, the only conceivable explanation is that we lacked a general theoretical framework in the field that pointed analysts toward this research task.[4]

As I will discuss below, analysts failed to appreciate how structural economic changes in the latter part of the Cold War were systematically undermining the ability of the Soviet Union to maintain its long-term foreign policy stance. Furthermore, they missed how the economic costs of the Soviet Union's foreign policy were escalating in ways that made it likely the country's leadership would be willing to make trade-offs with the pursuit of security to put the country on an economic path that was more sustainable. And finally, they did not properly appreciate the key role of external competitive economic pressures in propelling the political entrepreneurship of Mikhail Gorbachev.

Before proceeding, let me note that the end of Cold War is a very complex case and that the analysis below hardly does justice to the role of economic factors within it, nor certainly to the range of other variables that were significant. My goal here is merely to briefly outline the essential details of this case that are necessary for understanding the significance of the three lessons noted above that flow from Smith's theoretical framework (a more complete discussion of the role of economic factors is available in other publications of mine).[5]

Economic Structure and the End of the Cold War

By the final phase of the Cold War, two significant structural economic shifts had occurred among the world's leading economies—all of which were arrayed against the Soviet Union. Analysts at the time failed to recognize how these two structural changes systematically undermined the position of the Soviet Union. This oversight is arguably the most significant reason why scholars were so dramatically caught off guard by the Cold War's end.

The first structural economic shift was that the United States and the other most advanced states had undergone a transformation toward knowledge-based economies. By the 1980s, the Soviet Union had not yet undergone a transformation to this kind of economy; it could most accurately be described as having begun the initial steps of such a transition and as having bleak prospects for successfully completing it. The Soviet Union's centralized command economy was generally incompatible with the proper functioning of a knowledge-based economy: command economies can function fairly well in a world with slow rates of innovation and simple technologies, but they do poorly when the pace of innovation becomes rapid and crucial technologies are highly complex—as had become the case in the final phase of the Cold War. The Soviets dubbed this the "scientific and technological revolution," and there was little doubt that it was leaving them behind. As Valery Boldin, Gorbachev's chief of staff who joined the anti-Gorbachev coup in August 1991, acknowledged, "In the US a truly colossal development took place . . . in a word, the USA's development had entered the stage of the real technological revolution."[6]

The second structural economic shift was the emergence of the "globalization of production" due to the rapid onset of the geographic dispersion strategies by MNCs. As was discussed in Chapter 8, the globalization of production is a historically unprecedented change in the international economy that features efforts by MNCs to geographically disperse production into those countries that offer the greatest locational advantages. The globalization of production had a crucial effect on the Soviet Union's ability to sustain the Cold War competition for two simple reasons: it and its allies were isolated from this global production shift, and this change in the global economy achieved its greatest salience among the Soviets' international competitors, that is, the United States and its allies.

These two interrelated[7] structural economic shifts made it fundamentally harder for the Soviet Union to remain competitive with the United States and the alliance it led. By the early 1980s, a systemic shift—for the worse—had occurred in the Soviet Union's underlying economic and technological capacity. Although Soviet growth rates declined steadily for twenty-five years after 1960, there is an important break-point beginning roughly in the mid-1970s, when Soviet economic performance took a sudden turn for the worse. Rates of return on capital investment and expenditures on R&D and, critically, the rate of technological innovation all slowed measurably after the mid-1970s. In turn, comparisons on the basis of modern forms of technological competitiveness—as opposed to older indicators that focused on raw industrial output, such as steel production—revealed that the Soviets were rapidly falling behind the United States and the West; Soviet trade statistics told a similar story.

Reflecting on these dismal trends, Gorbachev pointedly noted soon after assuming power that "in our country, scientific and technical progress is slowing down,"[8] and he sternly criticized his predecessors "for failing to keep abreast of the faster-paced West in the scientific and technological revolution."[9] Concerns about rapidly declining technological competitiveness were widespread in the Soviet military as well. As

William Odom recounts, "It was becoming clear to Soviet military leaders that they were facing a third wave of new military technologies. The developments in micro-electronics, the semiconductor revolution and its impact on computers, distributed processing, and digital communications were affecting many aspects of military equipment and weaponry. . . . [The] new revolution in military affairs was demanding forces and weapons that the Soviet scientific-technological and industrial bases could not provide."[10] On this score, General M. A. Gareev, who during the 1980s had been the deputy chief of the General Staff in charge of military-scientific work, pointedly noted: "Our inferiority in this area was manifest in our reconnaissance technologies, navigation equipment, target identification systems, electronic countermeasures, computers—all the equipment which uses electronics."[11] Many Soviet military leaders were particularly concerned about what would happen when the next generation of U.S. high-technology conventional weapons being developed in the 1980s that truly took advantage of the microelectronics revolution was deployed. As Colonel General Mikhail Moiseev noted, the United States was moving toward equipping "their armed forces with the kinds of weapons systems for which the search for countermeasures will demand many times more time and resources from the Soviet Union."[12]

The problem was that by this time, Moscow had essentially reached the limit of its ability to match the sophistication of U.S. weaponry by employing its time-honored "hunkering down" strategy of concentrating resources on the development of weaponry and militarily significant technology. Given the punishingly high degree to which the Soviets were already pouring scarce economic resources—especially R&D and engineering talent—into the military, the possibility that this burden might increase even further was truly a daunting prospect for Gorbachev and many other Soviet policymakers. Two factors are of key importance here: (1) the long-standing inefficiencies associated with the Soviet command economy were greatly magnified in this new technological environment; and (2) the Soviets were now dealing with a new handicap, namely, the onset of the globalization of production and Soviet isolation from it. The point is that even before the 1980s, the Soviets were already running uphill in the arms race because of their inefficient command economy; the new technological nature of weapons development and the onset of the globalization of production then shifted the incline of the hill up even higher and would have continued to do so to a progressively greater extent over time, had the Cold War continued.

It is easy enough to understand how isolation from the globalization of production increased the Soviet difficulty of keeping up with the West in terms of general economic and technological productivity. Less obvious is why Soviet isolation simultaneously made it so much more difficult to remain technologically competitive in the arms race. What is crucial to understand in this regard is that during the 1970s and 1980s, U.S. and Soviet firms involved in defense-related production took diametrically opposite paths concerning the globalization of production. As was outlined in Chapter 2, the sectors that were becoming most globalized in the last portion of the Cold War were those dual-use industries that provide much of the foundation for military power in the modern era.

While U.S. firms were able to adapt successfully to the microelectronics revolution and the rapid general change in the parameters of technological development during the final phase of the Cold War by engaging in increased global collaboration, Soviet firms did not have this strategy available to them. Instead of being able to disperse production throughout the world to reap various efficiencies, as firms from the United States and its main allies—Japan, West Germany, South Korea, France, and Britain— were able to do, the Soviets were forced to make almost all of their key components and perform nearly all of their production within the Eastern bloc. Even a hard-line conservative such as Valery Boldin clearly recognized that the Soviets were falling behind technologically in the 1980s and that this was in significant part due to "our lack of world experience, our country's lack of access to world markets. . . . We stewed in our own juices for the simple reason that most of our electronics went to defense purposes, and defense was a completely closed sector."[13]

That contemporary analysts failed to appreciate the significance of these two structural economic shifts for Soviet foreign policy is one thing. What is even more notable is that they were neglected for a decade after the Cold War ended. This underscores the value of a Smithian theoretical framework that points analysts to carefully examine economic structure. In the absence of this theoretical perspective, analysts were not directed to analyze how structural economic changes created strong pressures on the Soviet Union to dramatically alter its foreign policy.

The Economic-Security Trade-Off
and the End of the Cold War

Both during the final phase of the Cold War and in the massive discussion of the case during the 1990s of why it ended, there was little discussion of the changing nature of the economic-security trade-off for the Soviet leadership. Had the Soviet leadership inflexibly placed security at the top of their priorities, they would have never backed off from the pursuit of military preparedness no matter how high the economic costs. And had the Soviet leadership placed economic gains at the top of their priorities, they would have backed away from the Cold War confrontation long before the late 1980s given that the pursuit of this foreign policy had long incurred great costs on Soviet consumers and the civilian economy. Instead, as a Smithian understanding makes clear, the Soviet approach to the economic-security trade-off shifted dynamically over time: once maintaining the Cold War competition became extremely costly in economic terms, the Soviet leadership became more willing to take a risk on the security front by shifting toward a more accommodating foreign policy stance. The essential details of the Soviet economic-security trade-off during the final phase of the Cold War are briefly delineated below.

By the early 1980s, defense spending in the Soviet Union had certainly reached a punishingly high level: 40 percent of the budget and 15–20 percent of GDP—at least four times the U.S. level. Not only was the defense burden high and rising, but Moscow's international position imposed other economic costs that were also increasing in this period; in particular, subsidies to its allies in Eastern Europe were a large and growing burden. Overall, the CIA estimated that the economic costs of the Soviet Union's global position more than doubled between 1970 and 1982.

Internal documents reveal that Gorbachev was well informed about these rapidly rising economic burdens associated with the Cold War competition. In one Politburo session, for example, Gorbachev stressed: "Our goal is to prevent the next round of the arms race. If we do not accomplish it, the threat to us will only grow. We will be pulled into another round of the arms race that is beyond our capabilities, and we will lose it, because we are already at the limit of our capabilities. . . . If the new round begins, the pressure on our economy will be unbelievable."[14]

Of great concern was the opportunity cost of attempting to continue to find stopgap remedies to match U.S. high-technology weaponry. A key reason the Soviet Union had been able to sustain competitiveness in military technology throughout much of the Cold War was by draining the commercial economy in service of the military sector. As a result, a huge portion of the country's resources in R&D and technological development were already being channeled into the military. The possibility that further increases would be necessary to remain technologically competitive in the arms race was a truly ominous prospect that was well recognized by Soviet policymakers in the 1980s. As Odom reports, "a surprisingly broad consensus existed among most of the Soviet elite that the Soviet economy was in serious trouble and that the burden of military expenditures was much to blame."[15]

For this reason, many Soviet policymakers shared Gorbachev's assessment concerning, as he put it, "the need to drastically reduce our defense budget—an indispensable condition for improving the economy."[16] This is true even of many within the Soviet military. As Odom notes, "In interviews and in their memoirs senior former Soviet military officers uniformly cited the burden of military spending as more than the Soviet economy could bear."[17] As Marshal Yazov, a key participant in the August 1991 coup, recalled: "There was nothing left for investment in the economy. It was necessary to think about reducing defense expenditures. It was necessary to think about more advanced technologies and about science-intensive production processes, etc."[18] Similarly, another key participant in the coup, Marshal Akhromeev, wrote shortly before he committed suicide that "all who knew the real situation in our state and economy in the mid-1980s understood that Soviet foreign policy had to be changed. The Soviet Union could no longer continue a policy of military confrontation with the United States and NATO after 1985. The economic possibilities for such a policy had been exhausted."[19]

What about the other side of economic-security trade-off—the security side? Nothing appreciably changed regarding nuclear weapons during this period and they did not propel the new Soviet interest in pulling back from the Cold War competition; what these weapons certainly did provide was a margin of safety that made lowering defense expenditures and pursuing foreign policy retrenchment easier for many to swallow. Of notable importance is that the value of Eastern Europe as a "buffer zone"—which Soviet leaders had initially seen as having paramount importance given the devastation of World War II—faded in importance once the Soviets had an assured "second strike" capability that established mutual nuclear deterrence. Of course, nuclear deterrence had diminished the Soviets' security rationale for the East European empires since at least the mid-1960s. Why, then, did the Soviets not move to pull back from the East European empire earlier? The key point here is that the Soviets had little need to systematically question their Cold War foreign policy commitments until these commitments became unbearably costly in economic terms.

Ultimately, it is unfortunate that analysts were not directed to consider the economic-security trade-off in the dynamic, flexible manner that Smith points to. This led analysts to miss that a move by Moscow to rein in military spending and pull back from the Cold War competition might occur once the economic costs of maintaining the Soviet foreign policy status quo was producing dramatic and systemic effects on the country's overall economic capacity and competitiveness. Had analysts of world politics been directed to pay careful attention to the possibility of a shift in the Soviet approach to the economic-security trade-off, they probably would not have been caught so off guard by the dramatic change in Soviet foreign policy that transpired.

Competitive Economic Pressures, Political Entrepreneurship, and the End of the Cold War

As the above discussion makes clear, there were strong economic pressures on the Soviet Union in the final phase of Cold War. Of course, leaders do not respond to economic pressures with automaton-like efficiency. Individual leaders matter; they will not all make the same choices. By seeking to head off the economic pressures facing the Soviet Union through decisive action at this time, Gorbachev truly was a political entrepreneur—a highly unsuccessful one, as it turns out: his ill-fated attempt to put the Soviet Union on a more sustainable economic trajectory had the effect of greatly worsening the country's economic straits.

It is important to understand that it was not just Gorbachev who saw and responded to the growing economic pressures on the Soviet Union; he just did so in a more dramatic way than his predecessors. It was Leonid Brezhnev who first gathered his military leaders in 1982 to lecture them about keeping defense expenditures under control. It was Brezhnev, Yuri Andropov, and Konstantin Chernenko who actually capped the growth in Soviet military spending. And it was Brezhnev, Andropov, and Ideology Czar Mikhail Suslov who privately revoked the Brezhnev Doctrine in 1980–81 when they ruled out direct intervention in Poland as beyond Soviet capabilities. But these leaders were reluctant to move away from the old precepts of Soviet foreign policy. Instead, they tried to cling to the status quo while struggling to contain its escalating economic costs.

Gorbachev took a different approach. He opted to put in place a number of significant economic reforms in order to produce an "accelerated" Soviet economy. By 1988, however, it had become apparent that this policy of "acceleration" was doomed to failure. Gorbachev's efforts to jump-start the economy not only did not improve the Soviet Union's overall economic performance, it made things worse in various ways: producing a budget deficit, higher inflation, a ballooning internal debt, a growing foreign exchange shortage, and a rising defense burden as a share of GDP.

These fiscal and financial imbalances on top of the underlying systemic decline propelled the economy into a tailspin. And that led to dramatically increased pressure on the Soviets' traditional foreign policy. It was only in this period that Gorbachev's foreign policy proposals truly began to move in a more radical direction that involved redefining Soviet foreign policy practices and decisively pulling back from the Cold War competition.

In seeking to respond to the growing economic pressures on the Soviet Union, what was Gorbachev's underlying motivation? The most common interpretation in the literature that emerged in the decade after the end of the Cold War is just what a conventional liberal understanding would expect: that Gorbachev was "consumerist" in his motivations for reform— that is, with a primary interest in improving consumer welfare.[20] Is this right? Or, as Smith's theoretical perspective would lead us to expect, was the key motivating force a desire to reverse the declining overall competitiveness of the Soviet Union to improve its long-term position on the world stage?

The evidence clearly favors the latter perspective. The notion that Gorbachev was driven primarily by consumerist motivations is belied by (1) his actions (rhetoric aside, he made no effort to increase outlays for consumer welfare in this period); (2) his public statements (three months before assuming power in 1985, for example, Gorbachev stressed that "only an intensive economy which is developed on the most modern scientific-technical basis can . . . safeguard the strength of the country's position in the international arena and allow it deservedly to enter the twenty-first century a great and prospering power");[21] and (3) internal deliberations within the Politburo (Politburo notes from 1985–87 clearly show that Gorbachev wanted to shift the Cold War into a framework more favorable to the Soviet Union and believed he would have the resources to do this without placing traditional Soviet foreign policy interests at risk).

But what about the efforts to increase Soviet openness to the global economy at this time, which was arguably the most revolutionary element of Gorbachev's entire economic reform package? The notion that these policy moves can be traced to a consumerist motivation is undercut by the significant efforts to push for increased international economic openness even on the part of officials with strong defense-industrial credentials who had little concern for the plight of consumers or civilian firms—most significantly, Prime Minister Ryzhkov and Lev Zaikov, the chairman of the Military-Industrial Commission. What these two men shared, beyond a strong commitment to Soviet power, was concrete experience running large defense plants, and thus firsthand knowledge of the real capacities and needs of the military-industrial sector. Both were overwhelmingly focused on the need for technological upgrading in order to maintain Soviet relative power—viewing it as essential, in Zaikov's words, to have "the production of machines, instruments and equipment . . . correspond to the world level."[22] Significantly, Ryzhkov and Zaikov not only spoke of the need for increased international economic openness but also undertook important steps in implementing policies to this effect.

In many cases, bottom-up pressures from economic actors or other societal interests will be the key motivating force leading to policy change. But political entrepreneurs sometimes will act in direct response to changing external competitive pressures. That is the dynamic that occurred in the end of the Cold War case. Had Smith's theoretical perspective on how competitive external economic pressures can act a spur for political entrepreneurship been prominent, then scholars would have been more likely to recognize, and to do so quickly, how the rapidly shifting economic terrain facing the Soviet Union might serve to prompt the dramatic policy changes by Gorbachev.

Conclusion: Paying Heed to Three Lessons from Smith's Framework

The end of the Cold War case clearly reveals the value of paying heed to the lessons illuminated by a Smithian theoretical framework regarding (1) the importance of examining economic structure; (2) the dynamic nature of the economic-security trade-off; and (3) the potential significance of political entrepreneurs who act in response to competitive external pressures.

In the absence of an appropriate theoretical guide, analysts will be skewed away from examining what needs to be examined. This is not to say that we should expect a Smithian theoretical framework to be as relevant for understanding other cases and phenomena as with the end of the Cold War case. The key point is simply that this perspective can potentially be very helpful: analysts may miss important things about how the world works if they are not directed to consider the role of economic factors in this fashion.

PART III

Conclusion

CHAPTER ELEVEN

Looking Forward

THIS BOOK BEGAN by noting that the premium on thinking carefully about how economic factors influence world politics has never been greater. Although it has become ever more important to carefully analyze the role of economics in world politics, our theoretical and empirical understanding has not kept pace. The aim of this book was to help address this analytical problem by undertaking a systematic theoretical and empirical analysis of the influence of economic factors on a particular domain of world politics—security affairs.

Yet, helping to address a problem is not the same as fully solving it. Much work still needs to be done to improve our understanding of the economics-security interaction. In this concluding chapter, I reflect on the analysis in the book with an eye toward identifying the issues that deserve more attention in the future.

Expanding the Pathways Analysis

The empirical portion of this book evaluated sixteen pathways by which economic factors can influence security affairs. For many of these pathways, I reached conclusions by undertaking a systematic review of a large number of existing empirical studies. But for other pathways, there was only a small number of relevant empirical studies. And in some cases, there were either no extant studies or the existing ones were not adequately directed to the relevant issue, in which case I undertook new empirical evaluations. More empirical research on these less thoroughly examined pathways would be valuable. Ultimately, social science must be social: we can only have high confidence in a finding after it has been extensively vetted by a range of researchers.

My focus here was on evaluating these pathways on their own. But they of course interact; as such, another vital issue for future research will be to analyze how these pathways work together. For centuries, numerous analysts have argued that economic factors can generally pull states in a specific overall security direction. Most notably, many theorists have long prominently argued that enhanced global commerce would foster peaceful relations: this was an expectation, for example, for Montesquieu in the eighteenth century, for John Stuart Mill in the nineteenth century, for Richard Rosecrance in the twentieth century, and for proponents of the "capitalist peace" in this century.

What Smith believed—a perspective the empirical analysis in this book clearly validates—is that economic factors generally, and global commerce specifically, will not produce a unidirectional effect in the security realm. Having identified and assessed these pathways, I see no reason to expect that either economic factors, generally, or commerce, specifically, will ever be shown to net out in one general direction, either toward peace or toward conflict.

What is more plausible is that a certain net effect could potentially emerge in certain contexts—say, in a region or among a certain set of countries. Specifying in detail the directional effects and weights of the relevant pathways in different contexts—geographic, temporal, and so on—will be a vital area for future research. Identifying which pathways exist and evaluating how they work, as this book has done, was a necessary prelude to this critical task, which researchers should now undertake.

It should also be noted that future analytical attention need not be restricted to these sixteen pathways. Recall that eight of these pathways have links to *The Wealth of Nations* and that the other eight were selected for examination following consultations I had with a range of other analysts who also focus on the economics-security interaction. While these sixteen pathways cover a great deal of ground, there are others that can potentially be added to the list. Future researchers can and should make the case for the inclusion of additional pathways that merit consideration alongside the sixteen pathways delineated here when analyzing whether economic factors have any net effects in specific contexts.

We should also not forget that my focus here was specifically on evaluating pathways by which economic factors can *directly* influence security affairs:

Economic Factors → Security Affairs

Yet as numerous analyses in the literature make clear, economic factors can also influence security affairs *indirectly* by producing changes in a different "intermediate" independent variable, which then produces shifts in security dynamics:

Economic Factors → Δ in Intermediate Variable → Security Affairs

As just one example, consider that the level of a state's economic development will have some influence on its degree of democratization, which will then alter its security dynamics with other states, depending on their levels of democratization.

It would also be worthwhile in the future to undertake the same kind of approach regarding indirect pathways that this book took concerning direct pathways. That is, it would be useful to identify the key indirect pathways of this kind and then bring to bear the necessary empirical evidence to evaluate them.

Economic Statecraft

In focusing on pathways by which economic factors can directly influence security affairs, this book set aside the examination of "economic statecraft" in which specific policies are implemented that are designed to shift the economic conditions facing another state and thereby produce alterations in its behavior.[1] In these circumstances, economic factors are not operating as they typically would; they are instead being deliberately manipulated by political policies to produce political effects:

Economic Statecraft Policies → Δ in Economic Conditions
→ Security Affairs

Economic statecraft policies, which states can either implement on their own or alongside others, can aim to alter either the actual economic conditions of the target state in the short term or its expected economic conditions in the future, or both. Sanctions—for which the aim is to reduce the access of the targeted state to some forms of economic activity—are the most obvious form of economic statecraft. But economic statecraft also encompasses the positive use of economic inducements—providing greater market access, granting access to technology, and so on—to induce changes in foreign policy behavior.

Evaluating economic statecraft is not a straightforward exercise. In part, this is due to the vast number of studies on this topic: a recent search for articles that contain the phrase "economic sanctions" in the title produced more than four thousand results.[2] Moreover, I fully agree with David Baldwin that evaluating the effectiveness of economic statecraft requires nuance: we must use multidimensional standards; we must examine gradations of success; we must consider economic statecraft in comparison to alternative policy instruments like the use of military force; and in comparing economic statecraft to other policy tools, we must look at both their benefits and their costs.[3] Baldwin's logic on all of these points is unassailable, but recognizing them does mean that the task facing researchers who evaluate economic statecraft is greatly complicated. Further adding to this complexity is the high degree of variance in the targets of economic statecraft (consider the vast differences between, say, the economies of North Korea, Iran, Russia, and China) as well as the changes in the global economy over time that alter both the availability and utility of various forms of economic statecraft.

At this point, we are woefully lacking in cumulative knowledge regarding the influence of economic statecraft. Efforts to bring order to the large number of existing empirical studies on this topic would therefore be welcomed, but this will be a very difficult task.

Economic-Security Trade-Off and Theories of Decision-Making

Smith underscores that there is no simple relationship between economic goals and security goals, that the trade-off between these two goals is instead complex and dynamic, and that this trade-off should be analyzed in detail. All of these analytical points are valuable. And in the context of the analysis of individual cases, recognizing these insights may well be sufficient as a guide for researchers—as was shown in the analysis of the end of the Cold War in Chapter 10.

But is it possible to say anything more than this? Can we develop an overall theoretical understanding of the economic-security trade-off? Smith's thinking does point to an overall view, but it is one that can only be stated in an extremely general form: that states will seek to maximize the economic resources under their control subject to the constraint of providing for short-term military security.

Yet it is easy enough to identify examples in which states manage the economic-security trade-off over the long term in ways that run contrary to this general understanding. Consider North Korea. For decades, it placed an overriding priority on promoting its security, with military spending consuming roughly a quarter of its economic wealth.

Following this course contributed to it becoming one of the very poorest countries on the planet, with a GDP per capita that is only around 5 percent of the level of South Korea (significantly, prior to the second half of the twentieth century, North Korea had historically been the richer part of Korea).

And while North Korea long placed an extreme emphasis on the pursuit of security at the expense of economic goals, other states have taken essentially the opposite approach. Consider the experience of Germany in the first three decades after the end of the Cold War. During this period, Germany consistently ignored the risk that Russia might deprive it of natural resources for security reasons—as eventually occurred in 2022. In turn, Germany's military spending plummeted so much that, in a 2020 report issued by the German Parliamentary Commissioner for the Armed Forces, the German military was described as woefully undersized and the readiness of its weapons systems (already on the small side) as "dramatically low."[4]

The experiences of Germany and North Korea raise a key question regarding the economic-security trade-off that future research should investigate: why do countries sometimes adopt extreme approaches to the economic-security trade-off? The more general question of interest for future research is: what are the factors that influence how decision-makers approach the economic-security trade-off? Time horizons, risk aversion, and leadership perceptions of the potential for gains are some of the factors that readily come to mind here. And to understand considerations such as these, we must look to theories of decision-making.

On this front, what is fascinating and little known is that Smith developed an understanding of decision-making that presaged—by hundreds of years—the development of what is now called "behavioral economics." As Ashraf, Camerer, and Lowenstein emphasize, Smith's understanding of decision-making "is remarkably similar to 'dual-process' frameworks advanced . . . by behavioral economists. . . . [Smith] also anticipates a wide range of insights regarding phenomena such as loss aversion, willpower and fairness that have been the focus of modern behavioral economics."[5]

Of course, there are multiple theories of decision-making that can and should be examined when analyzing the economic-security trade-off. In turn, these varying theories of decision-making have relevance for how we understand the role of economic factors in ways that go beyond this trade-off; exploring this general issue would certainly be a very fruitful area of future research.

Security Pressures and Political Entrepreneurship

As discussed in Chapter 9, Smith underscored the importance of political entrepreneurs as a source of policy changes that promote overall societal welfare. Smith highlighted the significance of external competitive pressures in motivating political entrepreneurship. Although Smith did outline some ideas as to how such pressures can prompt political entrepreneurship, these lines of argument were all very general ones.

In the centuries after the publication of Smith's works, a large literature has developed on political entrepreneurs that includes works by a wide range of prominent scholars. However, we are still far from having an adequate understanding of the conditions under which political entrepreneurship occurs. A number of authors—most notably, Douglass North—have also emphasized the significance of competitive external pressures as a spur for political entrepreneurship that advances a country's economic capacity.[6] But much of the focus of these authors has been on the economic and technological pressures that states face, with relatively few analysts highlighting the role of a state's security environment in prompting such political entrepreneurship. As such, an area ripe for more work concerns how variation in a state's security environment influences the emergence of political entrepreneurs.

How Much Should We Focus on Economic Structure?

Smith emphasized the critical importance of focusing on economic structure when analyzing world politics. I fully agree with this argument and have been strongly influenced by it. As I look across the field, it is easy enough for me to conclude that there should be a greater focus on how economic structure influences security affairs.

What is less clear is the overall balance that should exist between analyses that focus on the security effects of global economic structure versus those that focus on dyadic economic linkages between states. I see no reason to focus on global economic structure at the expense of dyadic analyses. To date, the inverse has occurred to a very significant extent, which I do think is a mistake. But it would be ironic and unfortunate to "over-correct" and focus too much on global economic structure and, in so doing, not devote enough attention to dyadic analyses. Across the field, having a rough balance between these two kinds of approaches seems prudent.

A related question is the extent to which we can focus on economic structure using a "decision theoretic" approach (where the focus is on how one decision-maker responds to their environment, in this case the economic environment) independently from a "game theoretic" approach (where the focus is on how multiple actors engage in strategic interaction with each other). My view here accords with that of David Lake, who argues that taking a decision theoretic approach to world politics will only rarely be a limitation that requires supplementation by a game theoretic approach.[7] Given that so little recent work has been done on economic structure, undertaking more such research ought to be first order of business and, when doing so, initially adopting a decision theoretic approach seems reasonable. Other scholars may disagree; if so, they are welcome to challenge this argument.

Globalization and the Political Order

What we now call globalization did not exist in Smith's time. Yes, there was some international trade, but not much—in significant part due to the high protectionist barriers at the time, which Smith excoriated and argued should be lowered. Yes, there were some multinational corporations, but not many—and most of those that did exist focused largely on securing natural resources and did not engage in anything like the geographic slicing up of the value chain that has occurred in recent decades. And yes, there were some financial transactions across borders, but relatively little compared to today and without anything like the incredible variety and speed we see now.

Smith thus had no reason consider how or whether a highly globalized economy depends on features of the political world. With respect to the economics-security interaction, two vital questions along these lines are: (1) whether and to what extent a highly globalized world economy is dependent on there being a leading state that seeks to sustain international stability; and (2) whether and to what extent a leading state can leverage its provision of security to others in ways that allow it to shape globalization and thereby help sustain its position of leadership. Reflecting on these questions, I have elsewhere posited that there seems to exist a crucial feedback loop between (a) actions taken by the United States to foster stability in the regions that are most crucial to the global economy; and (b) the ability of the United States to use its provision of security to its allies to shape the contours of economic globalization in ways that help maintain its economic preeminence.[8]

Regarding this potential feedback loop, a key question is what would happen to America's economic gains from the global economy if it were to completely abandon some or all of its overseas security commitments: would they be diminished and, if so, by how much? It would be profitable for readers to engage this question as well as the more general one concerning the extent to which America's current leadership position is sustained by global economic openness.

Factoring in Additional General Theoretical Frameworks

The theoretical portion of this book was deliberately limited to a focus on mercantilist/realist political economy and liberal political economy for four reasons. First, they are by far the most prominent general theoretical approaches for thinking about the role of economic factors in world politics—something that has been true for centuries. Second, a key theoretical priority of mine was to show that a middle-ground space exists between these two frameworks that analysts have missed. Third, previous analysts had been led astray in their understandings of mercantilist/realist and liberal political economy in part because they set up categorization schemes that sought to analyze additional frameworks beyond these two.[9] Fourth, I did not want the theoretical portion of this book to become unwieldy in terms of its scope and length.

Having set aside alternative theoretical frameworks for these reasons, let me note plainly and clearly that there certainly are other theoretical frameworks that analysts can and should bear in mind as they consider the role of economic factors in world politics. Marxism and constructivism are the two candidates that spring most readily to mind.

The beginning of Chapter 8 outlined my assessment that Marxism has significant flaws that impair its usefulness for understanding world politics. However, having shown in this book that liberal political economy has been misunderstood and that it contains a heretofore unrecognized conceptualization, I am open to the idea that Marxist theory may also have more things to say about security affairs than is currently realized. As such, I welcome theoretical efforts to more fully develop or even reformulate what Marxism has to say about the influence of economic factors on world politics. For scholars who are inclined to undertake such a theoretical project, a central question will be whether they would be inclined and able to shift Marxism away from its underlying determinism, a characteristic that to this point has inherently limited its potential usefulness.

At first blush, one might think that constructivism would have little to say about the role of economics in world politics since it focuses on the role of ideas and discounts the significance of material factors.[10] As such, economic factors generally—and certainly the kinds of structural economic factors featured in a Smithian theoretical framework—would seem to fall outside constructivism's purview. After all, the kinds of structural changes in domestic and global production that were highlighted in this book involve shifts in the physical world that we can see: new or modified factories and research and development facilities; new roles for knowledge-based workers that center largely on the development and use of novel technologies; and new forms of production, research, and distribution linkages between global firms, both domestically and internationally. Moreover, all these economic changes result in measurable outputs that we can observe.

However, constructivism stresses that the economic factors we see in the world, including structural ones, ultimately depend on ideas. In this understanding, very little, if anything, is "purely" material: we can always go back—sometimes way back—and find that the origin and/or meaning of almost any material factor or constraint is at least partly dependent upon some idea(s). Along these lines, constructivists would maintain that if decision-makers had not long accorded vital importance to augmenting economic efficiency and technological advancement, then then the kinds of economic factors this book highlighted would not exist in the form they do today or would not create the same kinds of pressures on state behavior. And while one could argue that the great priority placed on the advancement of economic and technological capacity is purely due to evolutionary dynamics, most would readily agree that discursive shifts have been very important in this respect.

Although it has long been commonplace for decision-makers to accord great importance to augmenting economic efficiency and rapid technological advancement, constructivism helpfully reminds us that this could potentially change at some point. Gaining leverage on why, whether, and to what extent such a shift in interests could occur is a crucial task that constructivism highlights which should be carefully explored. Of particular note in this regard is that the world is beset by dramatic environmental challenges that would likely become less acute if decision-makers prioritized economic efficiency and technological progress to a lesser extent by than they do now.

Constructivism also directs us to consider that not all decision-makers may accord the same significance to economic factors. While decision-makers overall have accorded great importance to economic efficiency, there is clearly variation across leaders on this dimension that warrants attention; indeed, sometimes such emphasis varies within an individual leader over time. Key to recognize is that if a given leader downgrades the significance of economic efficiency in order to place a greater emphasis on nonmaterial interests such as status or prestige, then they will be prone to respond to pressures and incentives flowing from economic factors in a different way. Along these lines, a question that future research can and should address is whether the agency of leaders to deemphasize economic efficiency in favor of nonmaterial interests is now generally lower in today's era due to the recent dramatic rise in both technological complexity and competitive pressures in the global economy.

Two Conceptions of Liberal Political Economy

The final point to raise concerns an issue that future research should *not* focus on. In the theoretical half of this book, I stressed that there are three core conceptual questions that analysts need to keep in mind when they undertake future analyses of how economic factors influence security affairs: (a) How do economic goals relate to security goals? (b) What kinds of economic factors are important to study when analyzing world politics? and (c) How and how much do economic actors influence policies regarding international security affairs? I stressed that these conceptual questions do not have set, agreed-upon answers and that analysts are accordingly prone to look for guidance about how to consider them from general theoretical frameworks. I maintained that the two most prominent theoretical frameworks that bear on the role of economics factors in international affairs—liberal political economy and realist/mercantilist political economy—produce very different answers to these conceptual questions and, in turn, that paying attention to these varying responses provides the best means for differentiating these frameworks. From there, I then noted that there is more diversity in liberal political economy than has been understood to this point and that Adam Smith provides the basis for an understanding that stands apart from the conventional one.

Having made the case for two conceptions of liberal political economy that bear on the influence of economic factors on security affairs—conventional liberal political economy and the Smithian alternative—what should be done now? Should they coexist, or should future researchers place them in competition with each other?

Reflecting my learning from Karl Popper and others regarding the great value of theoretical pluralism, I firmly reject the idea these two conceptions of liberal political economy should be in competition—that analysts should seek in future research to figure out which one is "better" and eliminate the "less useful" one. I believe Popper is correct that having more, rather than fewer, theoretical frameworks available as guides for empirical inquiry will prove helpful for scientific progress.[11] In my view, conventional liberal political economy hardly has the "wrong" approach regarding the role of economic factors in world politics: it has one approach, and Smith points to another. The key problem is that while the former has long existed as a prominent guide for analysts, the existence and significance of the latter has lamentably been obscured from view. Smith's unique theoretical insights on the role of economic factors in world politics should not be ignored; he puts forward a theoretical understanding that stands apart from the conventional understanding of liberal political economy that can and should serve as an alternative potential guide for future analysts.

Chapter 1. Introduction

1. Robert Gilpin, *The Political Economy of International Relations* (Princeton: Princeton University Press, 1987), p. 3.

2. Stephen Brooks, *Producing Security: Multinational Corporations, Globalization, and the Changing Calculus of Conflict* (Princeton: Princeton University Press, 2005), p. 1.

3. Montesquieu, *The Spirit of the Laws* (Cambridge: Cambridge University Press, 1989), p. 338.

4. John Stuart Mill, *Principles of Political Economy* (London: Longman, Green and Co, 1920), p. 582.

5. Alexander Hamilton, "The Federalist No. 6," in *The Federalist Papers*, edited by C. Rossiter (New York: Mentor, 1961), pp. 56–57.

6. Friedrich List, *The National System of Political Economy* (Wilmington: Vernon Press, 2013).

7. Vladimir Lenin, *Imperialism: The Highest Stage of Capitalism* (New York: International Publishers, 1917).

8. Most notably, see Erik Gartzke, "The Capitalist Peace," *American Journal of Political Science*, Vol. 41, No. 1 (2007), pp. 166–191.

9. The term *political economy* has multiple meanings. Following Robert Gilpin, my usage of the term *political economy* refers to "the interaction of economics and politics" and not to "the application of economic models to an understanding of political phenomena." See Gilpin, *U.S. Power and the Multinational Corporation: The Political Economy of Foreign Direct Investment* (New York: Basic Books, 1975), p. 263.

10. As Andrew Walter stresses, the "the conventional view is that Smith is firmly within the liberal internationalist tradition in international relations . . . is mistaken and owes more to a tendency to read back nineteenth-century ideas into Smith than to a close analysis of Smith's own works." See Walter, "Adam Smith and the Liberal Tradition in International Relations," *Review of International Studies*, Vol. 22, No. 1 (January 1996), p. 607. In turn, Edwin van de Haar underscores: "there is not much acknowledgment of the fact that Smith held different views on international relations from those of later liberal writers including those who referred to him such as Richard Cobden." See Edwin van de Haar, *Classical Liberalism and International Relations Theory: Hume, Smith, Mises, and Hayek* (New York: Palgrave Macmillan, 2009), p. 2. For a discussion of the overall interpretive problem here—in which a theorist is brought into conformity with a theoretical framework that subsequently emerged, leading to a distortion of the original thinker's views—see Richard Rorty, "The Historiography of Philosophy: Four Genres," *Philosophy in History: Essays on the Historiography of Philosophy*, ed. Richard Rorty, J. B. Schneewind, and Quentin Skinner (Cambridge: Cambridge University Press, 1984), p. 61.

11. As I will discuss in more detail in the concluding chapter, economic factors can also influence security affairs *indirectly* by changing an alternative independent variable that then produces shifts in security dynamics.

12. Although the bulk of Smith's thoughts on world politics are contained in *The Wealth of Nations*, his other works—most notably *The Theory of Moral Sentiments*—also contain a number of important insights on this topic.

13. Pierre Manent, *An Intellectual History of Liberalism* (Princeton: Princeton University Press, 1996), p. xv.

14. For a useful discussion of grand theory, see Kalevi Holsti, "Retreat from Utopia: International Relations Theory, 1945–1970," *Canadian Journal of Political Science*, Vol. 4 (1971), pp. 165–177.

15. Holsti, "Retreat from Utopia," p. 171.

16. In deriving these roles, I rely on the discussion in Robert Merton, *Social Theory and Social Structure* (New York: The Free Press, 1957), esp. pp. 13–15. That it is Merton I draw upon to construct this list of functions that grand theory can play will strike many readers as ironic, since he is regarded as one of the most ardent defenders of middle-range theory in the social sciences (in fact, he coined the term).

17. Merton, *Social Theory and Social Structure*, p. 88.

18. For a more complete discussion of this line of argument, see Stephen Brooks, "Distinguishing a Minimalist Role for Grand Theorizing," *International Relations*, Vol. 31, No. 1 (March 2017), pp. 85–90.

Chapter 2. The Global Economy and War

1. Montesquieu, *The Spirit of the Laws* (Cambridge: Cambridge University Press, 1989), p. 338.

2. Immanuel Kant, *Perpetual Peace*, translated by Lewis White Beck (1795; repr. New York: Bobbs-Merrill, 1957), p. 32.

3. The particular quote from Smith is as follows: "commerce and manufactures gradually introduced order and good government, and with them, the liberty and security of individuals, among the inhabitants of the country, who had before lived almost in a continual state of war with their neighbours, and of servile dependency upon their superiors. This, though it has been the least observed, is by far the most important of all their effects." WN,III.iv.4, p. 412. Some analysts have highlighted this quote as a basis for concluding that Smith saw commerce as having a pacifying effect on world politics. However, this quote is drawn from a section of the book titled "How the Commerce of the Towns Contributed to the Improvement of the Country" where Smith discussed how commerce improved the prospects for security and order within states. In this section, Smith emphasizes that internal security and stability was lacking during the period in which feudalism flourished. But after feudalism ended (which Smith argues was due in significant part to the introduction of commerce), then internal stability and security greatly improved. In short, this quote does not actually concern *interstate* security relations but instead pertains to the effects of commerce on the prospects for security and order *within* states.

4. Edwin van de Haar, *Classical Liberalism and International Relations Theory: Hume, Smith, Mises, and Hayek* (New York: Palgrave Macmillan, 2009), p. 145.

5. Dale Copeland, "Economic Interdependence and War: A Theory of Trade Expectations," *International Security*, Vol. 20, No. 4 (Spring 1996), pp. 10–11.

6. The most notable treatment is Erik Gartzke, "The Capitalist Peace," *American Journal of Political Science*, Vol. 51, No. 1 (2007), pp. 166–191.

7. In one article, Gartzke maintains that "Smith argued that market interests abominate war." Gartzke, "Capitalist Peace," p. 170. In another article, Gartzke asserts that "Smith anticipated that markets that span borders would have pacific effects." Erik Gartzke and Quan Li, "War, Peace, and the Invisible Hand: Positive Political Externalities of Economic Globalization," *International Studies Quarterly*, Vol. 47, No. 4 (December 2003), p. 562.

8. For this assessment, see Edward Mansfield and Brian Pollins, "The Study of Interdependence and Conflict: Recent Advances, Open Questions, and Directions for Future Research," *Journal of Conflict Resolution*, Vol. 45, No. 6 (December 2001), pp. 834–859.

9. See, for example, Bruce Russett and John Oneal, "The Classical Liberals Were Right: Democracy, Independence and Conflict, 1950–1985," *International Studies Quarterly*, Vol. 41, No. 2 (June 1997), pp. 267–293.

10. See Nathaniel Beck, Jonathan Katz, and Richard Tucker, "Taking Time Seriously: Time-Series-Cross Section Analysis with a Binary Dependent Variable," American Journal of Political Science, Vol. 42, No. 4 (October 1998), pp. 1260–1288; Donald Green, Soo Yeon Kim, and David Yoon, "Dirty Pool," *International Organization*, Vol. 55, No. 2 (Spring 2001), pp. 441–468; and D. Scott Bennett and Allan Stam, *The Behavioral Origins of War* (Ann Arbor: University of Michigan Press, 2003), esp. pp. 95–98.

11. Most notably, see Dale Copeland, *Economic Interdependence and War* (Princeton: Princeton University Press, 2014). Copeland argues that trade enhances the prospects for peace when leaders have positive expectations of the future trade environment, but that the incentive to initiate crises are enhanced when trade expectations become negative.

12. Two pioneering analyses of this kind were Gartzke, Li, and Boehmer, "Investing in the Peace"; and Richard Rosecrance and Peter Thompson, "Trade, Foreign Investment, and Security," *Annual Review of Political Science*, Vol. 6 (2003), pp. 377–398. The Gartzke, Li, and Boehmer study sought as part of their analysis to broaden the notion of interdependence beyond an exclusive focus on trade flows between countries to also include foreign direct investment linkages. However, their study used the total amount of inward and outward FDI as a proportion of a country's GDP, which is of no help in determining the extent of FDI linkage between each pair of states (that is, the level of FDI from country A in country B and vice versa). In the end, therefore, the dyadic test this study uses can tell us little about the actual effect of FDI linkages on conflict. The analysis by Rosecrance and Thompson did contain a measure of FDI interdependence. As they note, however, the scope of their analysis of FDI interdependence was greatly circumscribed by data limitations: "Unfortunately, few nations except the United States collect data on FDI flows with particular countries. Thus . . . we had to limit ourselves to looking at data on U.S. FDI and conflict with other countries over the period 1950–1992" (p. 389). A notable recent study with better, albeit far from systematic, data coverage is Hoon Lee and Sara McLaughlin

Mitchell, "Foreign Direct Investment and Territorial Disputes," *Journal of Conflict Resolution*, Vol. 56 No. 4 (August 2012), pp. 675–703. A principal limitation with their analysis is that although dyadic FDI data exists for OECD countries, this is not the case for non-OECD countries.

13. Brooks, *Producing Security*.

14. Brooks, *Producing Security*, pp. 12–13.

15. The exact boundaries of this region are not clear cut. For the purpose of this discussion, I consider the developing world to include all countries outside of North America, Western Europe, and Eastern Europe with the exception of Japan, Singapore, South Korea, Taiwan, Australia, New Zealand, and Israel.

16. See Brooks, *Producing Security*, pp. 220–231. As I discuss, the reasons why the globalization of production promotes stability among the great powers do not apply to developing countries since they have been exposed to this global production shift to a far lesser extent.

17. For a complete discussion of the reasons why it will be structurally harder for a great power to "run the tables" when they cannot effectively go it alone in defense production and the economic benefits of conquest are low, see Brooks, *Producing Security*, pp. 207–217.

18. See the discussion in Stephen Brooks and William Wohlforth, "The Myth of Multipolarity: American Power's Staying Power," *Foreign Affairs*, Vol. 102, No. 3 (May/June 2023), pp. 87–89; and Ben Vagle and Stephen Brooks, *Command of Commerce: America's Enduring Economic Power Advantage over China* (New York: Oxford University Press, 2025), esp. pp. 203–204.

19. See Gartzke, Li, and Boehmer, "Investing in the Peace," pp. 391–438; and Gartzke and Li, "War, Peace, and the Invisible Hand," pp. 561–586. Gartzke and Zhang succinctly summarize this theoretical line of argument as follows: "[A]s the degree of interdependence increases, the costs involved in threatening war rise as well (as investors abandon markets when and where war becomes more likely), ensuring that leaders more credibly communicate resolve. Economies that are well integrated into the global markets face the risk of capital flight when conflict is on the horizon. Markets are thus a credible mechanism for revealing information, because they offer leaders a way to signal resolve that is costly but also short of military violence." Erik Gartzke and Jiakun Jack Zhang, "Trade and War," in *Handbook of the Politics of International Trade,* ed. Lisa Martin (Oxford: Oxford University Press, 2015), p. 431.

20. Thomas Friedman, *The Lexus and the Olive Tree* (New York: Farrar, Straus, and Giroux, 1999), p. 257. See also Jonathan Kirshner's analysis which argues that bankers and other financial actors favor cautious foreign policies and have a marked aversion to war; Jonathan Kirshner, *Appeasing Bankers: Financial Caution on the Road to War* (Princeton, Princeton University Press, 2008).

21. Gartzke and Zhang, "Trade and War," p. 431.

22. See, for example, Amelie Brune, Thorsten Hens, Marc Oliver Rieger, and Mei Wang, "The War Puzzle: Contradictory Effects of International Conflicts on Stock Markets," *International Review of Economics*, Vol. 62, Issue 1 (2015), pp. 1–21; and Christo Kollias, Stephanos Papadamou, and Apostolos Stagiannis, "Armed Conflicts and Capital Markets: The Case of the Israeli Military Offensive in the Gaza Strip," *Defence and Peace Economics*, Vol. 21, No. 4 (August 2010), pp. 357–365.

23. See, for example, Scott Helfstein, "Liabilities of Globalization: Sovereign Debt, International Investors and Interstate Conflict with Other People's Money," *International Finance*, Vol. 15, Issue 3 (Winter 2012), pp. 277–288; and Matthew DiGiuseppe, "The Fiscal Autonomy of Deciders: Creditworthiness and Conflict Initiation," *Foreign Policy Analysis*, Vol. 11, Issue 3 (July 2015), pp. 317–338.

24. The Gartzke and Li 2003 article shows up twice in this table since it examines two different kinds of financial independent variables.

25. Thomas Chadefaux, "Market anticipation of conflict onsets," *Journal of Peace Research*, Vol. 54, No. 2 (2017), p. 322.

26. In Huh and Ju Hyun Pyun, "Does Nuclear Uncertainty Threaten Financial Markets? The Attention Paid to North Korean Nuclear Threats and Its Impact on South Korea's Financial Markets," *Asian Economic Journal*, Vol. 32, No. 1 (2018), pp. 55–82.

27. Kollias, Papadamou, and Stagiannis, "Armed Conflicts and Capital Markets."

28. Not discussed here are studies that ask related, but different questions, such as how stock returns are influenced by international crises.

29. On this point, see especially Guidolin and La Ferrara, "The Economic Effects of Violent Conflict," who conclude (p. 682) that "while the reactions of other national indices are typically mixed, the US market tends to systematically react positively to the onset of conflicts rather than negatively."

30. Guidolin and La Ferrara, "The Economic Effects of Violent Conflict," p. 679.

31. Jeffrey Gerlach and Youngsuk Yook, "Political Conflict and Foreign Portfolio Investment," *Federal Reserve Board Finance and Economics Discussion Series*, April 2016, p. 178. Available at: https://www.federalreserve.gov/econres/feds/political -conflict-and-foreign-portfolio-investment-evidence-from-north-korean-attacks .htm.

32. Gerlach and Yook, "Political Conflict and Foreign Portfolio Investment," p. 185.

33. Smith, WN,IV.vii.c.80, p. 626.

34. Edward Mead Earle, "Adam Smith, Alexander Hamilton, and Friedrich List: The Economic Foundations of Military Power," in *Makers of Modern Strategy from Machiavelli to the Nuclear Age*, ed. Peter Paret (Princeton: Princeton University Press, 1986). p. 229.

35. See, for example, Richard Rosecrance, *The Rise of the Trading State* (New York: Basic Books, 1987).

36. Much of the material in the remainder of this section is drawn from Stephen Brooks, "Economic Actors' Lobbying Influence on the Prospects for War and Peace," *International Organization*, Vol. 67, Issue 4 (2013), pp. 863–888.

37. See the discussion in Brooks, *Producing Security*, pp. 38–40.

38. Brooks, *Producing Security*, p. 42.

39. Brooks, *Producing Security*, pp. 40–42, 248.

40. Brooks, *Producing Security.*, pp. 251–252.

41. Geoffrey Jones, *The Evolution of International Business* (London: Routledge, 1996), pp. 32, 55.

42. See Jeffry Frieden, "International Investment and Colonial Control: A New Interpretation," *International Organization*, Vol. 48, No. 4 (1994), pp. 559–593; and Miles Kahler, "Political Regime and Economic Actors: The Response of Firms to the End of Colonial Rule," *World Politics*, Vol. 33, No. 3 (1991), pp. 390–401.

43. Frieden, "International Investment," pp. 567–568.

44. Christopher Thorne, *The Limits of Foreign Policy: The West, the League, and the Far Eastern Crisis of 1931–1933* (New York: Putnam, 1973), p. 32.

45. Michael Brecher and Jonathan Wilkenfeld, *A Study of Crisis (Book and CD-ROM edition)* (Ann Arbor: University of Michigan Press, 2000).

46. Hoon Lee and Sara McLaughlin Mitchell, "Foreign Direct Investment and Territorial Disputes," *Journal of Conflict Resolution,* Vol. 56 No. 4 (August 2012), p. 3.

47. Lee and Mitchell, "Foreign Direct Investment and Territorial Disputes," pp. 6, 9.

48. Lee and Mitchell, "Foreign Direct Investment and Territorial Disputes," p. 29.

49. Smith, WN,IV.ii.23, p. 463

50. Smith, WN,IV.ii.24, p. 463.

51. Brooks, *Producing Security*, Chapter 4.

52. Brooks, *Producing Security*, p. 78. I have added here the word "consistently" to the phrasing of this hypothesis to clearly reflect that what is of interest is a state's general ability to remain competitive, not the ability to remain competitive in particular systems.

53. The degree of complexity of weapons production by the end of the 20th century is best revealed by a landmark 1992 Commerce Department study, which undertook an exhaustive examination of the supply chain for three weapons systems—the HARM missile, the Mark-48 ADCAP torpedo, and the Verdin communication system—that were chosen as "representative" weapons used by the US Navy. A stunning finding emerged: for just these three weapon systems, a total of "15,000 companies were identified at the subcontractor level, with 11,638 companies still serving as active suppliers to the prime contractors for the three weapons systems" (6,818 for the HARM missile, 1,483 for the Verdin, and 3,336 for the Mark-48 torpedo); U.S. Department of Commerce, *National Security Assessment of the Domestic and Foreign Subcontractor Base: A Study of Three U.S. Navy Weapons Systems* (Washington: U.S. Department of Commerce, 1992), pp. 6, 10, 14, 16.

54. Brooks, *Producing Security*, pp. 29, 34.

55. Brooks, *Producing Security*, p. 126.

56. Brooks, *Producing Security*, p. 13.

57. Brooks, *Producing Security*, pp. 13, 125–126.

58. Brooks, *Producing Security*, p. 126.

59. Mark Devore, "Arms Production in the Global Village: Options for Adapting to Defense-Industrial Globalization," *Security Studies,* Vol. 22, No. 3 (2013), pp. 569–570, 572.

Chapter 3. Societal Actors, Economics, and War

1. For a useful overview of this literature, see Jack Levy and William Thompson, *Causes of War* (New York: Wiley-Blackwell, 2010), pp. 99–104.

2. See John Mueller, *War, Presidents, and Public Opinion* (New York: John Wiley, 1973).

3. John O'Neal and Jaroslav Tir, "Does the Diversionary Use of Force Threaten the Democratic Peace? Assessing the Effect of Economic Growth on Interstate Conflict, 1921–2001," *International Studies Quarterly,* Vol. 50, No. 4 (2006), p. 756.

4. Charles Ostrom and Brian Job, "The President and the Political Use of Force," *American Political Science Review* Vol. 80, No. 2 (June 1986), pp. 541–566.

5. Smith, WN,V.iii.37,50, pp. 919, 925–926.

6. Gustavo Flores-Macias and Sarah Kreps, "Borrowing Support for War: The Effect of War Finance on Public Attitudes toward Conflict," *Journal of Conflict Resolution*, Vol. 61, No. 5 (2017), pp. 997–1020.

7. Rosella Cappella Zielinski, *How States Pay for Wars* (Ithaca: Cornell University Press, 2016), p. 3.

8. Cappella Zielinski, *How States Pay for Wars*, p. 17.

9. Douglas Kriner, Breanna Lechase, and Rosella Cappella Zielinski, "Self-interest, Partisanship, and the Conditional Influence of Taxation on Support for War in the USA," *Conflict Management and Peace Science*, Vol. 35, No. 1 (2018), pp. 1–22. As they note, "From observational data alone, it is all but impossible to isolate the causal impact of war taxation policies from potential confounders," p. 6.

10. Kriner, Lechase, and Cappella Zielinski, "Self-interest, Partisanship, and the Conditional Influence of Taxation on Support for War in the USA," p. 2.

11. Kriner, Lechase, and Cappella Zielinski, "Self-interest, Partisanship, and the Conditional Influence of Taxation on Support for War in the USA," p. 4.

12. Benjamin Page, "Democratic Responsiveness?" *PS: Political Science and Politics*, Vol. 27, No. 1 (1994), p. 26.

13. Michael Tomz, Jessica Weeks, and Keren Yarhi-Milo, "Public Opinion and Decisions about Military Force in Democracies," *International Organization*, Vol. 74, No. 1 (2020): 119–143.

14. For a useful discussion of this point, see Benny Geys, "Wars, Presidents, and Popularity: The Political Cost(s) of War Re-Examined," *Public Opinion Quarterly*, Vol. 74, No. 2 (Summer, 2010), pp. 357–374.

15. Neta Crawford, "United States Budgetary Costs and Obligations of Post-9/11 Wars Through FY2020: $6.4 Trillion," Brown University working paper, November 13, 2019. Available at: https://watson.brown.edu/costsofwar/files/cow/imce/papers/2019 /US%20Budgetary%20Costs%20of%20Wars%20November%202019.pdf

16. Geys, "Wars, Presidents, and Popularity," p. 3.

17. Geys, "Wars, Presidents, and Popularity," p. 6.

18. Geys, "Wars, Presidents, and Popularity," p. 7.

19. Most notably, on September 2, 1987, Trump paid $95,000 to take out a full-page ad in the *New York Times* to explain why "America should stop paying to defend countries that can afford to defend themselves." *The New York Times*, September 2, 1987, p. A28.

20. An additional reason for the neglect of burden sharing is that public opinion scholars within IR—and indeed within political science generally—have a very one-dimensional view of fairness. Public opinion scholars are prone to conceptualize fairness in terms of equality (equality focuses only on outcomes, where something is fair if everyone receives the same payoff or distribution) while ignoring fairness conceptualized in terms of equity (equity factors in effort, with something being seen as fair if outputs are proportional to inputs). For a discussion of the neglect of fairness as equity and an attempt to rectify this oversight by taking seriously a multidimensional concept of fairness, see Kathleen Powers, Joshua Kertzer, Deborah Brooks,

and Stephen Brooks, "What's Fair in International Politics? Equity, Equality, and Foreign Policy Attitudes," *Journal of Conflict Resolution*, Vol. 66, No. 2 (February/ March 2022), pp. 217–245.

21. A prominent example is Richard Eichenberg's important analysis of all public opinion polls on the use of military force between 1981 and 2005. See Richard Eichenberg, "Victory Has Many Friends: U.S. Public Opinion and the Use of Military Force, 1981–2005," *International Security*, Vol. 30, No. 1 (Summer 2005), pp. 140–177. In his analysis, Eichenberg separates out the results for survey questions that examine "multilateral participation." Overall, he finds that mention of multilateral participation in a question increases U.S. public support for the use of force by approximately 5 percentage points. Yet these results do not distinguish between a preference on the part of the public for institutional support versus a preference for burden sharing.

22. Numerous studies have addressed the question of when and why burden sharing occurs. See, for example, Keith Hartley and Todd Sandler, "NATO Burden-Sharing: Past and Future," *Journal of Peace Research*, Vol. 36, No. 6 (November 1999), pp. 665–680; Andrew Bennet, Joseph Lepgold, and Danny Unger, "Burden-sharing in the Persian Gulf War," *International Organization*, Vol. 48, No. 1 (Winter 1994), pp. 39–75. However, I am aware of no published analysis that specifically focuses on the influence of burden sharing on public opinion and has a direct empirical analysis of its effects. An article by Reiter and Chapman does examine burden sharing as part of their analysis, but they measure it in a very problematic way: they use a count of the number of countries participating in a war alongside the United States but do not have any gauge of the level of money or troops that are actually provided by foreign governments; see Terrence Chapman and Dan Reiter, "The United Nations Security Council and the Rally 'Round the Flag Effect," *Journal of Conflict Resolution*, Vol. 48, No. 6 (2004), p. 887.

23. Adam Berinsky, *In Time of War: Understanding Public Opinion, from World War II to Iraq* (Chicago: University of Chicago Press, 2009).

24. Polls are effective at measuring attitudes about specific policies, but they perform far less well in analyzing situations that differ from the current state of affairs. Americans' support for U.S. military actions in Afghanistan, for example, was shaped by a combination of assessments of various factors, including their assessment of the goals of the war, the stakes involved (that is, what would happen if the United States lost the war), and the ability to afford the war financially. Thus, it is impossible to infer from survey data collected on the Afghanistan conflict what level of support U.S. public would give in a future war that differed in terms of the goals, stakes, or cost. One seeming solution to this problem would be to simply ask people directly about the underlying reasons for their views on the use of force in a series of different situations. Yet asking people to choose from a range of options regarding a given military action—for example, between the provision of substantial troops and money for the action by other states or the absence of any such assistance from other countries—has no equivalent in real life; if given such an abstract choice, people, not surprisingly, will tend to state a strong preference for the "best" available option.

25. The next four paragraphs and the tables below are drawn from Deborah Brooks and Stephen Brooks, "Burden Sharing, Institutions, and Public Opinion," Dartmouth College typescript.

26. The experiment consists of seven, not eight, conditions, since it is impossible for burden sharing to exist if no other countries support the mission.

27. Smith, WN,IV.iii.c.8, p. 493.

28. Smith, WN,IV.iii.c.9, p. 493.

29. Much of the material in the remainder of this section is drawn from Stephen Brooks, "Economic Actors' Lobbying Influence on the Prospects for War and Peace," *International Organization*, Vol. 67, No. 4 (Fall 2013), pp. 863–888.

30. Patrick McDonald, *The Invisible Hand of Peace: Capitalism, the War Machine, and International Relations Theory* (New York: Cambridge University Press, 2009); and Kevin Narizny, *The Political Economy of Grand Strategy* (Ithaca: Cornell University Press, 2007). Although the particulars of their arguments differ, both scholars have the same overall conceptual argument regarding the influence of economic actors on the prospects for war and peace: whether these actors enhance or decrease the likelihood of conflict ultimately depends on the balance of political power between those groups that are hostile toward war versus those that are favorable toward war because it will advance their interests.

31. See, for example, McDonald, *Invisible Hand of Peace*, pp. 4, 38, 70, 166–168; Narizny, *Political Economy of Grand Strategy*, pp. 43–44, 86–88.

32. See, for example, McDonald, *Invisible Hand of Peace*, p. 166; Narizny, *Political Economy of Grand Strategy*, p. 52.

33. See, for example, McDonald, *Invisible Hand of Peace*, pp. 4, 38, 113, 295–296; Narizny, *Political Economy of Grand Strategy*, p. 92.

34. See, for example, Narizny, *Political Economy of Grand Strategy*, pp. 16–18, 20.

35. As McDonald notes, "By slowing imports, military conflict raises the domestic price of traded goods and enables import-competing firms to expand their domestic market share." McDonald, *Invisible Hand of Peace*, p. 64; also, for example, p. 69.

36. John Hobson, *Imperialism: A Study* (Ann Arbor: University of Michigan Press, 1902); Eugene Staley, *War and the Private Investor: A Study in the Relations of International Politics and International Private Investment* (Garden City: Doubleday, 1935).

37. For example, in one case that McDonald reports from the end of the nineteenth century, he notes that western farming economic interests saw war with Britain as valuable since it might drive the United States off the gold standard; see McDonald, *Invisible Hand of Peace*, esp. pp. 174–175. For other examples, see pp. 132, 144, 147, 148, 155, 156, 157, 161, 165, 166–168, 170–171, 172, 174–175, 180, 192.

38. McDonald, *Invisible Hand of Peace*, pp. 248, 250.

39. McDonald, *Invisible Hand of Peace*, pp. 253, 257.

40. The one recent empirical analysis I am aware of that sheds light on this issue, an examination of how domestic politics influences foreign policy in the United States, is consistent with this overall assessment. See Helen Milner and Dustin Tingley, *Sailing the Water's Edge: The Domestic Politics of American Foreign Policy* (Princeton: Princeton University Press, 2016). As one part of their analysis, Milner and Tingley gathered data on who testified before Congress regarding U.S. military deployments from the past few decades. Their examination of this congressional testimony found that "economic interest groups accounted for only 3.3%, showing the low rate of interest group engagement with this policy instrument" (p. 102). In a second analysis,

Milner and Tingley undertook a systematic examination of recent lobbying reports by economic interest groups to see if they contained any mention of Syria, Iraq, Iran, Afghanistan, or Libya since they were "all countries that had some degree of military contestation or involvement by the United States during the time span of our lobbying data." Overall, they found that these five countries "were mentioned in only 0.38% of the total lobbying reports" (p. 102).

41. That being said, even if economic actors do not directly engage in security lobbying in advanced states, they may nevertheless subvert or enhance peace through their actions, perhaps unwittingly, by helping to set in motion processes that ultimately alter the likelihood of conflict. For one thing, they may alter security affairs unintentionally through their economic behavior rather than intentionally through their political actions. Their political actions regarding non-security matters can also matter. That is, even if economic actors do not directly lobby for war or for peace, it is possible that they may create pressure for other kinds of policies or actions that lead to conditions that make war more or less likely.

Chapter 4. Domestic Economic Structure and War

1. Donald Winch, *Adam Smith's Politics: An Essay in Historiographic Revision* (Cambridge: Cambridge University Press, 1978), p. 112.

2. Andrew Coe and Jonathan Markowitz, "Crude Calculations: Productivity and the Profitability of Conquest," *International Organization*, Vol. 75 (Fall 2021), p. 1064.

3. Andrew Francis, "The Human Capital Peace: Development and International Conflict," *Defense and Peace Economics*, Vol. 20, No. 5 (2009), pp. 395–411.

4. Winch, *Adam Smith's Politics*, p. 112.

5. See Smith, LJ (A), i.64–66, pp. 28–29.

6. In previous work, I outlined a series of theoretical arguments for why these two structural economic shifts alter the benefits of conquest; I posited that a conqueror, even a ruthless one, would be unable to effectively extract economic gains from the occupation of a vanquished country with a globalized economy and a knowledge-based workforce. The discussion in the next several paragraphs is largely drawn from this previous work. See Stephen Brooks, "The Globalization of Production and the Changing Benefits of Conquest," *Journal of Conflict*, Vol. 43, No. 5 (October 1999), pp. 646–670; Stephen Brooks, *Producing Security: Multinational Corporations, Globalization, and the Changing Calculus of Conflict* (Princeton: Princeton University Press, 2005), pp. 57–71, 161–206.

7. Richard Rosecrance, *The Rise of the Trading State: Commerce and Conquest in the Modern World* (New York: Basic Books, 1986), pp. 48, 58; Richard Rosecrance, *The Rise of the Virtual State: Wealth and Power in the Coming Century* (New York: Basic Books, 1999), esp. pp. 30–31.

8. Stephen Van Evera, "Primed for Peace: Europe After the Cold War," *International Security*, Vol. 15, No. 3 (Winter 1990–91), pp. 14–15.

9. See Brooks, *Producing Security*, pp. 66–69; Brooks, "Globalization of Production and the Changing Benefits of Conquest," pp. 658–659.

10. See Brooks, "Globalization of Production and the Changing Benefits of Conquest," pp. 657–658; Brooks, *Producing Security*, p. 65.

11. See Brooks, *Producing Security*, pp. 60–64; Brooks, "Globalization of Production and the Changing Benefits of Conquest," pp. 660–663. Significantly, to take control of the car's entire value-added chain would require conquering many countries, which would become extremely expensive and difficult very quickly, thereby reducing the overall benefits of conquest. Moreover, the geographic dispersion of production means that a conqueror would not be in a position to simply shift a significant portion of the vanquished country's industrial capacity back to their homeland.

12. Key here is that the level of investment within an economy is strongly influenced by the credibility of commitment of the governing authority not to confiscate a society's wealth or extract excessive rents. Mancur Olson compellingly argues that the form of government with the lowest credibility of commitment regarding wealth confiscation is an external invader that engages in economic extraction, which he aptly terms a "roving bandit." Olson notes that even if an invader only wishes to extract a very minimal level of economic wealth from the vanquished country, they cannot credibly commit to refrain from pursuing a more comprehensive means of wealth extraction since they have no institutional or electoral constraints on their power within the vanquished country. See Mancur Olson, "Dictatorship, Democracy, and Development," *American Political Science Review*, Vol. 87 (1993), p. 568.

13. Charles Boehmer and David Sobek, "Violent Adolescence: State Development and the Propensity for Militarized Interstate Conflict," *Journal of Peace Research*, Vol. 42, No. 1 (2005), pp. 5–26. Boehmer and Sobek use a "monadic" approach rather than a "directed dyadic" approach.

14. GDP per capita is the standard measure of development that is used in the fields of political science and economics, as well as by international organizations, as a means of classifying countries. Using energy consumption per capita as a measure of development is especially problematic in the contemporary period, given that many advanced countries in recent decades have been striving to reduce the intensity of their energy consumption.

15. The material in the next three paragraphs along with the figure below is drawn from Stephen Brooks and Brian Greenhill, "Wealth and War," Dartmouth College typescript.

16. The control variables are joint democracy, contiguity, distance, alliance, bilateral trade, and power. For the full details regarding the statistical model, see Brooks and Greenhill, "Wealth and War."

17. See Andrew Gelman, "Graphs Showing Regression Uncertainty: The Code!" Department of Statistics, Columbia University, August 26, 2012, http://andrewgelman.com/2012/08/26/graphs-showing-regression-uncertainty-the-code/. Taking this approach has the advantage of making it possible to visualize a complex nonlinear relationship and its associated uncertainty without being forced to focus on arbitrary significance thresholds. The figure here does this by presenting the results of a simulation exercise in which 1,000 independent estimates of the model coefficients were taken from the multivariate normal distribution described by the coefficients and variance-covariance matrix estimated from the model. Each set of parameter estimates was then used to plot a line showing the relationship between GDP per capita and the probability of conflict onset, while the values of all other covariates were held constant at their median levels. The graph therefore consists of 1,000 very thin black lines.

18. As one would expect, the degree of uncertainty around the estimated probabilities of conflict is much higher toward these extreme ends of the GDP per capita scale given the current dearth of these kinds of states (see the histogram at the bottom of the figure).

19. Note that because a logarithmic transformation of GDP per capita in the models was used, the GDP per capita scale on the x-axis is nonlinear.

20. See the discussion in Brooks, *Producing Security*, pp. 208–210.

21. Coe and Markowitz, "Crude Calculations," p. 1060.

22. Coe and Markowitz, "Crude Calculations," p. 1068.

23. Coe and Markowitz, "Crude Calculations," pp. 1061, 1079.

24. Coe and Markowitz, "Crude Calculations," p. 1060.

25. The best overall discussion of this dynamic is Coe and Markowitz, "Crude Calculations."

26. Winch, *Adam Smith's Politics*, p. 112.

27. Smith, WN,V.i.f.59, p. 787.

28. Smith, LJ (B), 331, p. 540.

29. John Mueller, *Retreat from Doomsday: The Obsolescence of Major War* (Rochester: University of Rochester Press, 1989); see also James Lee Ray, "The Abolition of Slavery and the End of International War," *International Organization*, Vol. 43, No. 3 (Summer 1989), pp. 405–439.

30. Ronald F. Inglehart, "Changing Values among Western Publics From 1970 to 2006," *West European Politics*, Vol. 31, No. 1–2 (2008), pp. 130–146.

31. Smith, WN,V.i.a.44, pp. 707–708.

32. Erik Gartzke, "The Capitalist Peace," *American Journal of Political Science*, Vol. 41, No. 1 (2007), p. 172. See also Erik Gartzke and Dominic Rohner, "The Political Economy of Imperialism and Development," *British Journal of Political Science*, Vol. 41, No. 3 (2011), pp. 525–556.

33. For notable treatments that recognize the significance of competing dynamics but do not systematically theorize about their interaction, see Boehmer and Sobek, "Violent Adolescence"; Gartzke, "The Capitalist Peace." Coe and Markowitz present the most theoretically sophisticated examination of the interaction of competing dynamics, but they apply this analysis only to the specific issue of measuring the gains of conquest; Coe and Markowitz "Crude Calculations."

34. Existing studies of how development influences conflict have not sufficiently explored this theoretically. Boehmer and Sobek do undertake a nonlinear analysis and they also do recognize that development has both an inhibitory effect and facilitating effect on conflict; see Boehmer and Sobek, "Violent Adolescence." However, their theoretical analysis models each of these effects in linear terms. What is not clear from their analysis, then, is how the interaction of two linear effects could produce the inverse U-shaped relationship they highlight.

35. The material in the next three paragraphs along with the figure below is drawn from Brooks and Greenhill, "Wealth and War."

36. Gartzke, "The Capitalist Peace," p. 172; and Gartzke and Rohner, "The Political Economy of Imperialism and Development."

37. Full details regarding the statistical model are delineated in Brooks and Greenhill, "Wealth and War."

38. Boehmer and Sobek, "Violent Adolescence," pp. 14–15.

39. Boehmer and Sobek, "Violent Adolescence," pp. 5, 22.

40. See, for example, Thomas Homer-Dixon, "Environmental Scarcities and Violent Conflict: Evidence from Cases," *International Security*, Vol. 19, No. 1 (Summer, 1994), pp. 5–40; and Michael Klare, *Rising Powers, Shrinking Planet: The New Geopolitics of Energy* (New York: Metropolitan Books, 2008).

41. Coe and Markowitz, "Crude Calculations," p. 1059.

42. Francesco Caselli, Massimo Morelli, and Dominic Rohner, "The Geography of Interstate Resource Wars," *The Quarterly Journal of Economics*, Vol. 130, No. 1 (2015), pp. 267–315.

43. Emily Meierding, "Dismantling the Oil Wars Myth," *Security Studies*, Vol. 25 (2016), p. 258. See also Emily Meierding, *The Oil Wars Myth: Petroleum and the Causes of International Conflict* (Ithaca: Cornell University Press, 2020); Emma Ashford, *Oil, The State, and War: The Foreign Policy of Petro States* (Georgetown University Press, 2022); and Kenneth Schultz, "Mapping Interstate Territorial Conflict: A New Data Set and Applications," *Journal of Conflict Resolution*, Vol. 61, No. 7 (2017), p. 1581.

44. Schultz, "Mapping Interstate Territorial Conflict," p. 1582.

45. Georg Struver and Tim Wegengast, "The Hard Power of Natural Resources: Oil and the Outbreak of Militarized Interstate Disputes," *Foreign Policy Analysis*, Vol. 14, Issue 1 (Jan. 2018), pp. 86–106.

46. Cullen Hendrix, "Oil Prices and Interstate Conflict Behavior," *Conflict Management and Peace Science*, Vol. 34, Issue 6 (2017), pp. 575–596.

47. Jeff Colgan, "Oil, Domestic Politics, and International Conflict," *Energy Research and Social Science*, Vol. 1 (March 2014), pp. 198–205; and Jeff Colgan, "Oil and Revolutionary Governments: Fuel for International Conflict," *International Organization*, Vol. 64, Issue 4 (2010), pp. 661–694.

48. Jonathan Markowitz, *Perils of Plenty: Arctic Resource Competition and the Return of the Great Game* (New York: Oxford University Press, 2020); Jonathan Markowitz, Benjamin Graham, Suzie Caldwell, and Christopher Fariss, "Productive Pacifists: The Rise of Production-Oriented States and the Decline of Profit-Motivated Conquest," *International Studies Quarterly*, Vol. 64, Issue 3 (September 2020), pp. 558–572; Jonathan Markowitz, Christopher Fariss, and R. Blake McMahon, "Producing Goods and Projecting Power: How What You Make Influences What You Take," *Journal of Conflict Resolution*, Vol. 63, No. 6 (2019), pp. 1368–1402.

49. Markowitz, *Perils of Plenty*, p. 2, emphasis in original.

50. Markowitz, *Perils of Plenty*, p. 3.

51. Markowitz et al., "Productive Pacifists," pp. 35–36.

Chapter 5. How Do Economic Factors Influence Terrorism and Civil Conflict?

1. To be clear on terminology, domestic terrorism is "a single-country affair where the victims and perpetrators hail from the venue country, where the attack occurs." In contrast, "if the nationalities of the victims or the perpetrators involve more than one country, or if the venue country differs from that of the victims or perpetrators, then

the terrorist attack is a transnational incident." See Walter Enders, Gary Hoover, and Todd Sandler, "The Changing Nonlinear Relationship between Income and Terrorism," *Journal of Conflict Resolution*, Vol. 60, No. 2 (2016), p. 199.

2. The most prominent analysis is Alan Krueger and Jitka Malečková, "Education, Poverty and Terrorism: Is There a Causal Connection," *Journal of Economic Literature*, Vol. 17, No. 4 (Fall 2003), pp. 119–144.

3. Michael Wolfowicz, Yael Litmanovitz, David Weisburd, and Badi Hasisi, "What Is the State of the Quantitative Literature on Risk Factors for Radicalization and Recruitment to Terrorism?," in Weisburd D., Savona E., Hasisi B., Calderoni F. (eds) *Understanding Recruitment to Organized Crime and Terrorism* (New York: Springer, 2020).

4. David Weisburd, Ernesto Savona, Badi Hasisi, and Francesco Calderoni, "Introduction," in Weisburd D., Savona E., Hasisi B., Calderoni F. (eds) *Understanding Recruitment to Organized Crime and Terrorism* (New York: Springer, 2020), p. 5.

5. Wolfowicz et al., "What Is the State of the Quantitative Literature on Risk Factors for Radicalization and Recruitment to Terrorism?" p. 48.

6. See Khusrav Gaibulloev and Todd Sandler, "What We Have Learned about Terrorism since 9/11," *Journal of Economic Literature*, Vol. 57, No. 2 (2019), p. 313; and Jonathan Kenyon, Christopher Baker-Beall, Jens Binder, "Lone-Actor Terrorism—A Systematic Review," *Studies in Conflict and Terrorism* (2021), p. 7, who underscore that there is a "general consensus regarding the lack of a single comprehensive socio-demographic profile for lone-actor terrorists. Lone actors have been found to come from a variety of educational, socioeconomic, ethnic and family backgrounds, with differences in education levels, operational ability, training and access to financing."

7. On this point, see Enders, Hoover, and Sandler, "Changing Nonlinear Relationship between Income and Terrorism," p. 199.

8. Dongfang Hou, "The Formation of Terrorist Groups: An Empirical Analysis," *Defence and Peace Economics*, Vol. 32, Issue 6 (2021), pp. 698–707.

9. Luis de la Calle and Ignacio Sánchez-Cuenca, "Rebels without a Territory: An Analysis of Nonterritorial Conflicts in the World, 1970–1997," *The Journal of Conflict Resolution*, Vol. 56, No. 4 (2012), pp. 580–603.

10. See, for example, Lai, "'Draining the Swamp.'"

11. As Ghatak and Gold put it, "The destitute want material benefits like food and shelter, not policy changes." See Sambuddha Ghatak and Aaron Gold, "Development, Discrimination, and Domestic Terrorism: Looking Beyond a Linear Relationship," *Conflict Management and Peace Science*, Vol. 34, No. 6 (2017), pp. 620–621.

12. Gaibulloev, Khursav, and Todd Sandler, "What Have We Learned about Terrorism Since 9/11," *Journal of Economic Literature*, Vol. 57, No. 2 (2019), p. 314. See also Ghatak and Gold, "Development, Discrimination, and Domestic Terrorism," p. 621.

13. Enders, Hoover, and Sandler, "Changing Nonlinear Relationship between Income and Terrorism," p. 201.

14. Ghatak and Gold, "Development, Discrimination, and Domestic Terrorism," p. 621.

15. Audrey Kurth Cronin, "Behind the Curve: Globalization and International Terrorism," *International Security*, Vol. 27, No. 3 (Winter, 2002–2003), p. 30.

16. Stanley Hoffman, "The Clash of Globalizations," *Foreign Affairs*, Vol. 81, No. 4 (July/August 2002), p. 112.

17. Inmee Baek and Maxim Bouzinov, "Does Democratic Progress Deter Terrorist Incidents?" *European Journal of Political Economy*, Vol. 66 (2021), p. 2.

18. S. Brock Blomberg and Gregory Hess, "The Lexus and the Olive Branch: Globalization, Democratization, and Terrorism," in *Terrorism, Economic Development, and Political Openness*, ed. P. Keefer and N. Loayza (Cambridge: Cambridge University Press, 2008), p. 134.

19. Hess and Blomberg, "Lexus and the Olive Branch," pp. 122, 134.

20. Joseph Stiglitz and Leif Pagrotsky, "Blocking the Terrorists' Funds: The Global Financial System Provides Hiding Places for Dirty Money. It Must Be Reformed," *Financial Times*, December 7, 2001, p. 23.

21. Khusrav Gaibulloev and Todd Sandler, "What We Have Learned about Terrorism since 9/11," *Journal of Economic Literature*, Vol. 57, No. 2 (2019), p. 313.

22. Drakos and Gofas, "In Search of the Average Transnational Terrorist Venue," p. 91.

23. Blomberg and Hess, "Lexus and the Olive Branch," p. 134.

24. Martin Gassebner and Simon Luechinger, "Lock, Stock, and Barrel: A Comprehensive Assessment of the Determinants of Terror," *Public Choice*, Vol. 149 (2011), pp. 235–361.

25. Gassebner and Luechinger, "Lock, Stock, and Barrel"; Li and Schaub, "Economic Globalization and Transnational Terrorism."

26. Gries and Meirrieks examine the influence of banking crises on domestic terrorism; they conclude that banking crises lead to a subsequent increase in domestic terrorism, but only in less developed countries; see Thomas Gries and Daniel Meirrieks, "Do Banking Crises Cause Terrorism?" *Economic Letters*, Vol. 119 (2013), pp. 321–324.

27. Mascarenhas and Sandler, "Remittances and Terrorism."

28. A study examining how FDI influences domestic terrorism finds that FDI has a non-linear effect on the likelihood of terrorism: FDI enhances domestic terrorism for low-income countries, whereas FDI decreases terrorism for high-income countries; see Glen Biglaiser, Lance Hunter, and Ronald McGauvran, "The Double-Edge Sword of Foreign Direct Investment on Domestic Terrorism," *Journal of Conflict Resolution* (2023).

29. Respectively, Sanso-Navarro and Vera-Cabello, "The Socioeconomic Determinants of Terrorism"; Robinson, Crenshaw, and Jenkins, "Ideologies of Violence."

30. The first group is Li and Schaub, "Economic Globalization and Transnational Terrorism"; and Sanghamitra Bandyopadhyay and Abdullah Ijaz, "Is There a Relationship Between Inequality and Terrorism? Evidence from a Semi-Parametric Approach," *Applied Economics Letters*, Vol. 29, No. 9 (2022), pp. 855–860. The second group is Sanso-Navarro and Vera-Cabello, "The Socioeconomic Determinants of Terrorism"; and Mascarenhas and Sandler, "Remittances and Terrorism."

31. Kendall Hoyt and Stephen Brooks, "A Double Edged-Sword: Globalization and Biosecurity," *International Security*, Vol. 28, No. 3 (Winter 2003/04), pp. 123–124.

32. See, for example, Ethan Bueno de Mesquita, "The Quality of Terror," *American Journal of Political Science*, Vol. 49, No. 3, pp. 515–530.

33. Charles Boehmer and Mark Daube, "The Curvilinear Effects of Economic Development on Terrorism," *Peace Economics, Peace Science and Public Policy*, Vol. 19 (No. 3), pp. 359–368. See also, for example, Robinson, Crenshaw, and Jenkins, "Ideologies of Violence," pp. 2009–2026.

34. Orlandrew E. Danzell, Yao-Yuan Yeh, and Melia Pfannenstiel, "Determinants of Domestic Terrorism: An Examination of Ethnic Polarization and Economic Development," *Terrorism and Political Violence*, Vol. 31, No. 3 (2019), p. 539.

35. Atin Basuchoudhary and William Shughart, "On Ethnic Conflict and the Origins of Transnational Terrorism," *Defence and Peace Economics*, Vol. 21, No. 1 (2010), pp. 65–87; Krisztina Kis-Katos, Hedge Liebert, and Günther G. Schulze, "On the Heterogeneity of Terror," *European Economic Review*, Vol. 68, (May 2014), pp. 116–136; Alan Krueger and David Laitin, "Kto Kogo? A Cross-Country Study of the Origins and Targets of Terrorism," in *Terrorism, Economic Development, and Political Openness*, ed. P. Keefer and N. Loayza (Cambridge: Cambridge University Press, 2008), pp. 148–173; Peter Kurrild-Klitgaard, Mogens K. Justesen, and Robert Klemmensen, "The Political Economy of Freedom, Democracy and Transnational Terrorism," *Public Choice*, Vol. 128, No. 1/2 (Jul. 2006).

36. Kis-Katos, Liebert, and Schulze, "On the Heterogeneity of Terror," p. 121.

37. Kis-Katos, Liebert, and Schulze, "On the Heterogeneity of Terror," pp. 118–119.

38. Kis-Katos, Liebert, and Schulze, "On the Heterogeneity of Terror," p. 122.

39. See, for example, Muhammad Shahbaz, Muhammad Shahbaz Shabbir, Muhammad Nasir Malik, and Mark Edward Wolters, "An Analysis of a Causal Relationship between Economic Growth and Terrorism in Pakistan," *Economic Modelling*, Vol. 35 (September 2013), p. 26.

40. Seung-Whan Choi, "Economic Growth and Terrorism: Domestic, International, and Suicide," *Oxford Economic Papers*, Vol. 67, Issue 1 (January 2015), p. 162.

41. Henrik Urdal, "A Clash of Generations? Youth Bulges and Political Violence," *International Studies Quarterly*, Vol. 50, No. 3 (September 2006), p. 612.

42. Krueger and Laitin, "Kto kogo? A Cross-Country Study," p. 148.

43. Smith, WN.III.iv.9, p. 418.

44. Smith, WN.III.iv.15, p. 421.

45. Smith, WN.III.iv.17, p. 422.

46. Tor Georg Jakobsen, Indra De Soysa, and Jo Jakobsen, "Why Do Poor Countries Suffer Costly Conflict? Unpacking Per Capita Oncome and the Onset of Civil War," *Conflict Management and Peace Science*, Vol. 30, No. 2 (2013), p. 140.

47. Michael Ward, Brian Greenhill, and Kristin Bakke, "The Perils of Policy by P-value: Predicting Civil Conflicts," *Journal of Peace Research*, Vol. 47, No. 4 (2010), pp. 363–375. Hegre, Allansson, and Vestby note that the Ward, Greenhill, and Bakke article marked an important "turning point" in the literature. See Håvard Hegre, Marie Allansson, and Jonas Vestby, "VIEWS: A Political Violence Early-Warning System," *Journal of Peace Research*, Vol. 56, No. 2 (March 2019), p. 156.

48. Ward, Greenhill, and Bakke, "Perils of Policy by P-value," p. 363.

49. GDP per capita of course is not the only way of measuring economic development. The composition of the economy also matters, and many studies in the civil war literature have taken this approach. For a useful review of the literature on how natural resources influence civil war, see Michael Ross, "What Do We Know About

Natural Resources and Civil War?" *Journal of Peace Research*, Vol. 41, No. 3 (2004), pp. 337–356.

50. A May 5, 2021, search on Google Scholar revealed 476 citations to the Ward, Greenhill, and Bakke article that were systematically reviewed.

51. David Muchlinski, David Siroky, Jingrui He, and Matthew Adam Kocher, "Comparing Random Forest with Logistic Regression for Predicting Class-Imbalanced Civil War Onset Data," *Political Analysis*, Vol. 24 (2016), pp. 87–103.

52. Jakobsen, De Soysa, and Jakobsen, "Why Do Poor Countries Suffer Costly Conflict?" p. 140.

53. See the discussion in Christopher Magee and Tansa George Massoud, "Openness and Internal Conflict," *Journal of Peace Research*, Vol. 48, No. 1 (2011), pp. 59–61; Katherine Barbieri and Rafael Reuveny, "Economic Globalization and Civil War," *Journal of Politics*, Vol. 67, No. 4 (2005), pp. 1229–1234.

54. United Nations Conference on Trade and Development (UNCTAD), "More Than 100 Countries Depend on Commodity Exports," September 8, 2021, available at https://unctad.org/news/more-100-countries-depend-commodity-exports.

55. Katherine Barbieri and Rafael Reuveny, "Economic Globalization and Civil War," *Journal of Politics*, Vol. 67, No. 4 (2005), pp. 1229–1247.

56. Bussmann, Schneider, and Wiesehomeier, "Foreign Economic Liberalization and Peace."

57. Blanton and Apodaca, "Economic Globalization and Violent Civil Conflict."

58. Sorens and Ruger, "Globalisation and Intrastate Conflict."

59. Andreea S. Mihalache-O'Keef, "Whose Greed, Whose Grievance, and Whose Opportunity? Effects of Foreign Direct Investments (FDI) on Internal Conflict," *World Development* Vol. 106 (June 2018), pp. 187–206.

60. Ashan Kibria, Oldi Reza, and Akhundjanov B. Sherzod, "Foreign Direct Investment and Civil Violence in Sub-Saharan Africa," *The World Economy*, Vol. 43, No. 4 (2020), pp. 948–981.

61. Sorens and Ruger, "Globalisation and Intrastate Conflict"; Blanton and Apodaca, "Economic Globalization and Violent Civil Conflict."

62. Barbieri and Reuveny, "Economic Globalization and Civil War."

Chapter 6. Comparing Liberal Political Economy and Mercantilist/Realist Political Economy

1. Benjamin Cohen, *International Political Economy: An Intellectual History* (Princeton: Princeton University Press, 2008), pp. 34–35.

2. In his 1975 book, Gilpin defined mercantilism in a very generic sense and noted it was synonymous with the economic nationalist perspective; Robert Gilpin, *U.S. Power and the Multinational Corporation: The Political Economy of Foreign Direct Investment* (New York: Basic Books, 1975), p. 25. In his 1987 book, Gilpin then switched away from using the term *mercantilism* to employ the term *economic nationalism,* which he posits is synonymous with the realist perspective. Gilpin underscores that his theoretical position had been realist in the 1970s but was not something he had acknowledged then: "Although I did not fully appreciate it at the time, I had returned to a realist conception of the relationship between economics

and politics that had disappeared from postwar American writings." See Gilpin, *The Political Economy of International Relations* (Princeton: Princeton University Press, 1987), pp. xii, xiii. In 2001, Gilpin then clarified his theoretical position further, arguing that realism and economic nationalism have the same underlying theoretical core but do not necessarily overlap in terms of their normative policy prescriptions. As Gilpin notes, "while all nationalists are realists in their emphasis on the crucial role of the state, security interests, and power in international affairs, not all realists are nationalists in their normative views regarding international affairs. Therefore, in this book I employ the broader term 'realism' or, more specifically, 'state-centric realism' to characterize my approach." Gilpin, *Global Political Economy: Understanding the International Economic Order* (Princeton: Princeton University Press, 2001), p. 14.

3. Gilpin, *U.S. Power and the Multinational Corporation*, p. 29.

4. Gilpin, *U.S. Power and the Multinational Corporation*, pp. 27–28, emphasis in original.

5. To his credit, in his later work Gilpin admits that he did not properly distinguish the analytic and normative elements of the theories he was comparing. See Gilpin, *Global Political Economy*, p. 14.

6. Gilpin, *War and Change in World Politics*, p. 129.

7. Smith, WN,IV.ii.30, pp. 464–465.

8. Gilpin, *U.S. Power and the Multinational Corporation*, pp. 26–27.

9. Gilpin himself acknowledges this in a later essay. See Robert Gilpin, "No One Loves a Political Realist," *Security Studies*, Vol. 5, No. 3 (1996), p. 4.

10. As Harlen notes, "Despite their reputations as staunch advocates of laissez-faire policies, the early Liberals, especially Smith, recognized the need to make exceptions to free trade. Similarly, Hamilton and List recognized the need to place restrictions on protectionism." See Christine Margerum Harlen, "A Reappraisal of Classical Economic Nationalism and Economic Liberalism," *International Studies Quarterly*, Vol. 43, No. 4 (December 1999), p. 742.

11. Particularly helpful on this point is István Hont, *Jealousy of Trade: International Competition and the Nation-State in Historical Perspective* (Cambridge: Harvard University Press, 2005).

12. As Gilpin notes, "The problem with the liberal theory of free trade and the principle of comparative advantage is that these ideas neglect the economic costs of free trade and are based on a liberal image of society, that is, a society composed of individuals. In the real world of states and conflict groups, free trade has other effects that frequently override its universal benefits." See Gilpin, "No One Loves a Political Realist," p. 10.

13. Andrew Walter, "Adam Smith and the Liberal Tradition in International Relations," *Review of International Studies*, Vol. 22, No. 1 (January 1996), p. 14; see also Eric Helleiner, "Economic Nationalism as a Challenge to Economic Liberalism? Lessons from the Nineteenth Century," Trent International Political Economy Center (TIPEC) Working Paper No. 02-3, TIPEC, Peterborough, Ontario, 2002, p. 312.

14. Gilpin, *U.S. Power and the Multinational Corporation*, p. 27.

15. David A. Baldwin, *Economic Statecraft* (Princeton: Princeton University Press, 1985), pp. 83–84; Jonathan Kirshner, "The Political Economy of Realism," in

Unipolar Politics: Realism and State Strategies After the Cold War, ed. Ethan Kapstein and Michael Mastanduno (New York: Columbia University Press, 1999).

16. Gilpin, *U.S. Power and the Multinational Corporation,* p. 28.

17. On this point, see, for example, Andrew S. Skinner, *Adam Smith and the Role of the State* (Glasgow: Glasgow University Press, 1974), p. 22.

18. On this point, see, for example, Baldwin, *Economic Statecraft;* Walter, "Adam Smith and the Liberal Tradition in International Relations."

19. Gilpin, *U.S. Power and the Multinational Corporation,* p. 32.

20. This is actually inconsistent with Gilpin's earlier statement that liberalism sees economic changes as leading to shifts in security affairs: "For liberals the long-term trend is toward world integration. . . . The logic of economic and technological development, it is argued, has set mankind on an inexorable path toward global political unification and world peace." Gilpin, *U.S. Power and the Multinational Corporation,* p. 29. Although Gilpin is correct that liberalism sees economic shifts as having the potential to alter security affairs, he is wrong in positing that all liberals see the direction of change as always positive.

21. Gilpin's framework is more helpful for clarifying *his* own underlying theoretical conception. Yet even for this self-referential purpose, his conceptualization suffers because it is underspecified in a number of important ways.

22. Walter, "Adam Smith and the Liberal Tradition in International Relations," p. 6.

23. Walter, "Adam Smith and the Liberal Tradition in International Relations," p. 76.

24. See Baldwin, *Economic Statecraft,* p. 81.

25. Kirshner, "Political Economy of Realism," p. 74.

26. Kirshner, "Political Economy of Realism," p. 76.

27. In Kirshner's analysis, the root of this underlying distinction seems to be different views about the extent to which fear of conflict shapes state behavior—see the discussion of this issue below.

28. Smith, WN,IV.ii.30, pp. 464–465.

29. Kirshner, "Political Economy of Realism," p. 72.

30. Kirshner, "Political Economy of Realism."

31. Kirshner, "Political Economy of Realism," p. 72, quoting Friedrich List, *The National System of Political Economy* (Wilmington: Vernon Press, 2013), p. 347.

32. Kirshner, "Political Economy of Realism," p. 91, footnote 17, quoting List, *National System,* p. 120.

33. Edward Mead Earle, "Adam Smith, Alexander Hamilton, Friedrich List: The Economic Foundations of Military Power," in *Makers of Modern Strategy: From Machiavelli to the Nuclear Age,* ed. Peter Paret (Princeton: Princeton University Press, 1986), pp. 222–223; see also Edwin van de Haar, *Classical Liberalism and International Relations Theory: Hume, Smith, Mises, and Hayek* (New York: Palgrave Macmillan, 2009); Helleiner, "Economic Nationalism as a Challenge to Economic Liberalism?"

34. On this point, see, for example, van de Haar, *Classical Liberalism and International Relations Theory;* Hont, *Jealousy of Trade;* Harlen, "Reappraisal of Classical Economic Nationalism and Economic Liberalism"; Walter, "Adam Smith and the Liberal Tradition in International Relations."

35. Kirshner, "Political Economy of Realism," pp. 72–73.

36. Kirshner, "Political Economy of Realism," pp. 73–74.

37. Kirshner, "Political Economy of Realism," p. 77.

38. Kirshner, "Political Economy of Realism," p. 78.

39. Kirshner, "Political Economy of Realism," pp. 75–76.

40. Kirshner, "Political Economy of Realism," p. 75.

41. Based on his categorization scheme and how he codes realism, Kirshner also implicitly suggests that liberalism regards states as not being very concerned about being dependent on others for defense capabilities.

42. A useful discussion of this point is Earle, "Adam Smith, Alexander Hamilton, and Friedrich List." Among realists, Kenneth Waltz is the notable exception in recognizing that Smith differs from standard liberal views. Waltz notes that Smith's thoughts "on international relations are uniformly more perspicacious than those of most liberals of the period," but he does not explore the point any further. See Waltz, *Man, the State, and War: A Theoretical Analysis* (New York: Columbia University Press, 2001), p. 96, footnote 33.

Chapter 7. How Do Economic Goals Relate to Security Goals?

1. For a useful discussion that helpfully emphasizes this point, see James Fearon, "Two States, Two Types, Two Actions," *Security Studies*, Vol. 20, No. 3 (2011), pp. 436–438.

2. Stephen Brooks, "Dueling Realisms," *International Organization*, Vol. 51, No. 3 (Summer 1997), esp. pp. 463–467. See also James Fearon, "Cooperation, Conflict, and the Costs of Anarchy," *International Organization*, Vol. 72 (Summer 2018), pp. 523–559; Robert Powell, "Guns, Butter, and Anarchy," *American Political Science Review*, Vol. 87, No. 1 (1993), pp. 115–132.

3. Jonathan Kirshner, "The Political Economy of Realism," in *Unipolar Politics: Realism and State Strategies after the Cold War*, ed. Ethan B. Kapstein and Michael Mastanduno (New York: Columbia University Press, 1999).

4. Kirshner, "Political Economy of Realism," p. 76.

5. Kirshner, "Political Economy of Realism," p. 76.

6. Mark Zacher and Richard Matthew, "Liberal International Relations Theory: Common Threads, Divergent Strands," in *Controversies in International Relations Theory*, ed. Charles Kegley (New York: St. Martin's Press, 1995), p. 119.

7. Andrew Moravcsik, "Taking Preferences Seriously: A Liberal Theory of International Politics," *International Organization*, Vol. 51, No. 4 (Autumn 1997), p. 539.

8. Smith, WN,II.v.31, p. 372.

9. István Hont, *Jealousy of Trade: International Competition and the Nation-State in Historical Perspective* (Cambridge: Harvard University Press, 2005), p. 78.

10. Hont, *Jealousy of Trade*, pp. 75–76. In light of his views regarding the intensity of international economic competition, it is perhaps not surprising that Smith "approved of retaliatory tariffs as a means of forcing another country to open up its trade." Perhaps more surprising is that Smith was willing "to approve even of measures to promote certain types of business activity. . . . Smith sanctioned the

government's granting of temporary monopolies in cases where merchants might not otherwise be willing to take the great risks necessary to establish a branch of trade" See Christine Margerum Harlen, "A Reappraisal of Classical Economic Nationalism and Economic Liberalism," *International Studies Quarterly*, Vol. 43, No. 4 (December 1999), pp. 737, 738.

11. Robert Prasch, "The Ethics of Growth in Adam Smith's Wealth of Nations," *History of Political Economy*, Vol. 23, No. 2 (1991), p. 346. See also the discussion in David A. Baldwin, *Economic Statecraft* (Princeton: Princeton University Press, 1985), p. 85.

12. For an overview, see Donald Winch, *Adam Smith's Politics: An Essay in Historiographic Revision* (Cambridge: Cambridge University Press, 1978), pp. 103–120.

13. Harlen, "Reappraisal of Classical Economic Nationalism and Economic," p. 737.

14. Winch, *Adam Smith's Politics*, p. 104.

15. Smith, WN,V.i.a,13–14, pp. 696–697.

16. Smith, WN,IV.ii.24,30, pp. 463–465.

17. Kirshner, "Political Economy of Realism," pp. 75–76.

18. Smith, WN,IV.ii.23–24, p. 463.

19. Harlen, "Reappraisal of Classical Economic Nationalism and Economic," p. 740.

20. As O'Neill notes, "almost all the applications of risk aversion and risk acceptance have a problem. When we label someone as risk-averse we are comparing the person to a standard of risk neutrality. However, international applications do not usually specify a standard, or they cite the economics definition, which can be applied only when the goal of the decision involves money or some other measurable commodity. The economics definition states that a risk-neutral person is indifferent between playing a gamble and receiving the gamble's average face value for sure, but international goals almost never allow a reasonable way to calculate 'average face value.' They involve an element that is not measurable as a quantity or they include multiple scales. In this case risk neutrality, acceptance, and aversion are undefined." See Barry O'Neill, "Risk Aversion in International Relations Theory," *International Studies Quarterly*, Vol. 45, No. 4 (December 2001), p. 618.

21. O'Neill, "Risk Aversion in International Relations Theory," p. 618.

22. O'Neill, "Risk Aversion in International Relations Theory," pp. 627, 625, emphasis in original. O'Neill underscores that "IR analyses have tended to treat risk attitude as a character trait, determined by the decision-maker's personality rather than the particular decision being faced. By the economics definition, however, the party's risk attitude can change depending on arbitrary aspects of how the given decision is stated, so its notion of risk attitude is not determined by personality. The comparative definition given here allows risk to be seen as a personality characteristic" (p. 618).

23. O'Neill, "Risk Aversion in International Relations Theory," p. 627.

24. O'Neill, "Risk Aversion in International Relations Theory," pp. 618–621.

25. On this point, see the discussion of the literature in Andrew Walter, "Adam Smith and the Liberal Tradition in International Relations," *Review of International Studies*, Vol. 22, No. 1 (January 1996), p. 14; Eric Helleiner, "Economic Nationalism

as a Challenge to Economic Liberalism? Lessons from the Nineteenth Century," Trent International Political Economy Center (TIPEC) Working Paper No. 02–3, TIPEC, Peterborough, Ontario, 2002, p. 312.

26. Martin Wight, *International Theory: The Three Traditions*, ed. Gabriele Wight and Brian Porter (New York: Holmes and Meier, 1992), pp. 114–115, 263.

27. Richard Rosecrance, "The Political Socialization of Nations," *International Studies Quarterly*, Vol. 20, No. 3 (September 1976), p. 441.

28. Walter, "Adam Smith and the Liberal Tradition in International Relations," p. 6. On this point, see also Edwin van de Haar, *Classical Liberalism and International Relations Theory: Hume, Smith, Mises, and Hayek* (New York: Palgrave Macmillan, 2009), p. 145.

29. Helleiner, "Economic Nationalism as a Challenge to Economic Liberalism?" p. 312.

30. Helleiner, "Economic Nationalism as a Challenge to Economic Liberalism?" p. 21. Similarly, van de Haar notes that, in Smith's view, "[i]nsufficient defense was a danger to the stability of the state, which in its turn would lead to a loss of national wealth." See van de Haar, *Classical Liberalism*, p. 142.

31. Hont, *Jealousy of Trade*, p. 52.

32. Smith, TMS,VI.ii.2.4,7,11, pp. 229–231.

33. Smith, TMS,VI.ii.2.3, p. 228.

34. Walter, "Adam Smith and the Liberal Tradition in International Relations," p. 18. As Harlen similarly notes, "For Smith, nationalistic antagonisms were powerful enough to overcome economic interests." See Harlen, "Reappraisal of Classical Economic Nationalism and Economic," p. 736. See also Robert Manzer, "The Promise of Peace? Hume and Smith on the Effects of Commerce on War and Peace," *Hume Studies*, Vol. 22, No. 2 (1996), p. 377.

35. Van de Haar, *Classical Liberalism*, pp. 60–61.

36. Walter, "Adam Smith and the Liberal Tradition in International Relations," p. 22. Similarly, van de Haar concludes that "Smith was pessimistic about the actual binding force of international law." See van de Haar, *Classical Liberalism*, p. 61.

37. Smith, LJ (B),339, p. 545.

38. Smith, TMS,VI.ii.2.3, p. 228.

39. Smith, WN,V.i.a.1, p. 689. To emphasize the point, a few pages later Smith again notes that "the first duty of the sovereign" is "that of defending the society from . . . violence and injustice." See Smith, WN,V.i.a.42, p. 707.

40. Walter, "Adam Smith and the Liberal Tradition in International Relations," p. 22.

41. Smith, TMS,VI.ii.2.6, p. 230.

42. Baldwin, *Economic Statecraft*, p. 80.

43. Walter, "Adam Smith and the Liberal Tradition in International Relations," p. 14.

44. Smith, WN,IV.iii.c.11,13, pp. 494, 496.

45. Smith does outline some statements that would *seem* to provide a succinct encapsulation of his understanding of the economics-security trade-off. The problem is that these statements do not properly capture the subtleties of his overall perspective. Most notably, Smith's famous phrase that "defence . . . is of much more importance than opulence" can make it seem like his conception of the economics-security

trade-off coincides with that of realist political economy. But as we see in this chapter, Smith's conception of this trade-off only partially overlaps with that of realist political economy.

Chapter 8. The Role of Economic Factors in World Politics

1. For a useful overview and assessment of Marxist empirical propositions concerning security affairs, see Jack Levy and William Thompson, *Causes of War* (New York, Wiley-Blackwell: 2010), pp. 85–91.

2. Robert Gilpin, *The Political Economy of International Relations* (Princeton: Princeton University Press, 1987), p. 58; Kenneth Waltz, "Globalization and American Power," *National Interest*, Vol. 59 (Spring 2000), p. 52.

3. John Stuart Mill, *Principles of Political Economy* (1920; repr. London: Longman, Green and Co, 1848), p. 582.

4. See, for example, John R. Oneal and Bruce M. Russet, "The Classical Liberals Were Right: Democracy, Interdependence, and Conflict, 1950–1985," *International Studies Quarterly*, Vol. 41, No. 2 (June 1997), pp. 267–294.

5. Smith, LJ (A), i.27, p. 14.

6. Smith, LJ (A), i.28, p. 14.

7. Smith, LJ (A), i.28, pp. 14–15.

8. Smith, LJ (A), i.31, p. 15.

9. Smith, LJ (A), i.31, pp. 15–16.

10. John Dunning, "Regions, Globalization, and the Knowledge Economy: The Issues Stated," in *Regions, Globalization, and the Knowledge Economy*, ed. John Dunning (Oxford: Oxford University Press, 2000), p. 8.

11. See, for example, Stephen Brooks, *Producing Security: Multinational Corporations, Globalization, and the Changing Calculus of Conflict* (Princeton, Princeton University Press: 2005), p. 208.

12. Jonathan Markowitz, *Perils of Plenty: Arctic Resource Competition and the Return of the Great Game* (New York: Oxford University Press, 2020); Jonathan Markowitz, Benjamin Graham, Suzie Caldwell, and Christopher Fariss, "Productive Pacifists: The Rise of Production-Oriented States and the Decline of Profit-Motivated Conquest," *International Studies Quarterly*, forthcoming; Jonathan Markowitz, Christopher Fariss, and R. Blake McMahon, "Producing Goods and Projecting Power: How What You Make Influences What You Take," *Journal of Conflict Resolution*, Vol. 63, No. 6 (2019), pp. 1368–1402.

13. Markowitz et al., "Productive Pacifists."

14. Markowitz et al., "Productive Pacifists," pp. 24–25.

15. Smith, WN,IV.i.31, pp. 446–447.

16. Smith, WN,IV.ix.41, pp. 680–681.

17. István Hont, *Jealousy of Trade: International Competition and the Nation-State in Historical Perspective* (Cambridge: Harvard University Press, 2005), p. 304.

18. Hont, *Jealousy of Trade*, p. 79.

19. I fully delineate the globalization of production in a previous book. See Brooks, *Producing Security*, ch. 2.

20. Gordon Hanson, Raymond Mataloni, and Mathew Slaughter, "Expansion Strategies of U.S. Multinational Firms," *NBER Working Paper #8433* (2001), p. 20.

21. United Nations Conference on Trade and Development (UNCTAD), *Key Trends in International Merchandise Trade* (Geneva: United Nations, 2014), p. 9.

22. United Nations Conference on Trade and Development (UNCTAD), *World Investment Report, 1995: Transnational Corporations and Integrated International Production* (Geneva: United Nations, 1995), p. 39.

23. For a more complete discussion, see Brooks, *Producing Security*, pp. 38–44.

24. Quddus Snyder, "Integrating Rising Powers: Liberal Systemic Theory and the Mechanism of Competition," *Review of International Studies*, Vol. 39 (2013), pp. 220–221.

25. For example, my 2005 book does recognize that the globalization of production can influence security behavior by altering the nature of dyadic linkages between states, and I do formulate one proposition along these lines. See Brooks, *Producing Security*, pp. 257–261. However, this dyadic proposition is not a central focus of my analysis (I devote just a few pages to it and concentrate instead on a series of structural theories), and I do not evaluate it empirically. Conversely, in *The Invisible Hand of Peace* Patrick McDonald does recognize that the qualitative nature of economic globalization has shifted in recent decades and that this new global economic structure has the potential to alter how economic factors influence the likelihood of conflict. However, he devotes just a few pages to this issue and does not examine it empirically, focusing instead on a series of dyadic theories. See McDonald, *The Invisible Hand of Peace: Capitalism, the War Machine, and International Relations Theory* (New York: Cambridge University Press, 2009), pp. 293–295.

26. Andrew Walter, "Adam Smith and the Liberal Tradition in International Relations," *Review of International Studies*, Vol. 22, No. 1 (January 1996), pp. 23, 28.

Chapter 9. How Do Economic Actors Affect Security Policy?

1. Jonathan Kirshner, "The Political Economy of Realism," in *Unipolar Politics: Realism and State Strategies After the Cold War*, ed. Ethan Kapstein and Michael Mastanduno (New York: Columbia University Press, 1999).

2. Andrew Moravcsik, "The New Liberalism," in *The Oxford Handbook of Political Science*, ed. Robert Goodin (New York: Oxford University Press), p. 711.

3. Mark Zacher and Richard Matthew, "Liberal International Relations Theory: Common Threads, Divergent Strands," in *Controversies in International Relations Theory*, ed. Charles Kegley (New York: St. Martin's Press, 1995), p. 118.

4. Moravcsik, "New Liberalism," p. 712.

5. Zacher and Matthew, "Liberal International Relations Theory," p. 119.

6. See the discussion in Stephen Brooks, "Economic Actors' Lobbying Influence on the Prospects for War and Peace," *International Organization*, Vol. 67, No. 4 (Fall 2013), pp. 863–888.

7. See, for example, Adam Berinsky, *In Time of War: Understanding American Public Opinion from World War II to Iraq* (Chicago: University of Chicago Press, 2009).

8. David Baldwin, *Economic Statecraft* (Princeton: Princeton University Press, 1985), pp. 83–84.

9. Andrew Skinner, *Adam Smith and the Role of the State* (Glasgow: Glasgow University Press, 1974), p. 17.

10. Skinner, *Adam Smith and the Role of the State*, pp. 18–19, 22, emphasis in original.

11. Andrew Walter, "Adam Smith and the Liberal Tradition in International Relations," *Review of International Studies*, Vol. 22, No. 1 (January 1996), p. 12.

12. Smith, WN,I.xi.p.10, p. 266.

13. Smith, WN,IV.iii.c.10, p. 494.

14. Smith, WN,I.xi.p.10, p. 267.

15. Smith, WN,IV.iii.c.10, p. 494.

16. Smith, WN,I.xi.p.10, p. 267.

17. As Walter notes, "in *The Wealth of Nations*, he [Smith] was above all preaching to British legislators to reform their practices and institutions." See Walter, "Adam Smith and the Liberal Tradition in International Relations," p. 26.

18. David McNally, *Political Economy and the Rise of Capitalism: A Reinterpretation* (Berkeley: University of California Press, 1988), pp. 208–209.

19. Smith, WN,IV.ii.45, p. 472.

20. Smith, WN,IV.iii.c.9, p. 493.

21. Skinner, *Adam Smith and the Role of the State*, p. 23.

22. Smith, WN,III.ii.4, p. 383.

23. Skinner, *Adam Smith and the Role of the State*, pp. 12, 14.

24. István Hont, *Jealousy of Trade: International Competition and the Nation-State in Historical Perspective* (Cambridge: Harvard University Press, 2005), p. 304.

25. Smith, WN,II.iii.36, p. 346, WN,II.iii.31, p. 343.

26. Smith, WN,IV.ii.43, p. 471.

27. Smith, WN,IV.iii.c.9, p. 493.

28. For useful discussions of political entrepreneurship, see Douglass North, *Institutions, Institutional Change, and Economic Performance* (New York: Cambridge University Press, 1990); Douglass North, "Institutional Change: A Framework for Analysis," in *Institutional Change: Theory and Empirical Findings*, ed. Sven-Erik Sjostrand (New York: Routledge, 1993); Paul Joskow and Roger Noll, "Economic Regulation," in *American Economic Policy in the 1980s*, ed. Martin Feldstein (Chicago: University of Chicago Press, 1994); Adam Sheingate, "Political Entrepreneurship, Institutional Change, and American Political Development," *Studies in American Political Development*, Vol. 17, No. 2 (October 2003).

29. Sheingate, "Political Entrepreneurship, Institutional Change, and American Political Development," p. 188.

30. Joskow and Noll, "Economic Regulation," 376–377.

31. William Riker, *The Art of Political Manipulation* (New Haven: Yale University Press, 1986), p. 64.

32. Robert Dahl, *Who Governs? Democracy and Power in an American City* (New Haven: Yale University Press, 1963), p. 6.

33. Smith, TMS,VI.ii.2.11,14, pp. 231–232.

34. Smith, WN.IV.vii.c.44, p. 606.

35. Hont, *Jealousy of Trade*, pp. 56, 62.

36. For a particularly incisive discussion of this point, see Hont, *Jealousy of Trade*, ch. 5.

37. Smith, TMS.VI.ii.2.16–17, pp. 233–234.

38. Smith, TMS,VI.ii.2.16, p. 233.

39. Smith, WN,IV.ii.43–44, p. 471.

40. Douglass North, "Institutions, Transaction Costs, and Productivity in the Long Run," p. 2, available at https://econwpa.ub.uni-muenchen.de/econ-wp/eh/papers/9309/9309004.pdf.

41. North, "Institutional Change," p. 38.

42. Hont, *Jealousy of Trade*, p. 7.

43. Smith, WN.IV.iii.c.9, p. 493.

44. Smith, WN.IV.iii.c.9, p. 493.

45. Hont, *Jealousy of Trade*, pp. 115–116, 117, 119. Hont explains further that "by contrasting national emulation to national animosity, Smith demonstrated that commercial reciprocity and intense competition were compatible" (p. 120).

46. Douglass North, "Constraints on Institutional Innovation: Transaction Costs, Incentive Compatibility, and Historical Considerations," in *Agriculture, Environment, and Health: Sustainable Development in the 21st Century*, ed. Vernon Ruttan (Minneapolis: University of Minnesota Press, 1994), p. 65.

47. See David Kang, "South Korean and Taiwanese Development and the New Institutional Economics," *International Organization*, Vol. 49, No. 3 (Summer 1995), pp. 555–587; David Kang, *Crony Capitalism: Corruption and Development in South Korea and the Philippines* (New York: Cambridge University Press, 2002).

48. North, "Institutional Change," p. 38.

49. For a useful analysis that makes this point, see Quddus Snyder, "Integrating Rising Power: Liberal Systemic Theory and the Mechanism of Competition," *Review of International Studies*, Vol. 39 (2013), pp. 209–231.

Chapter 10. The Significance of the Theoretical Analysis

1. Alexander Wendt, *Social Theory of International Politics* (Cambridge: Cambridge University Press, 1999), p. 4.

2. Based on a search in Google Scholar performed on October 30, 2024.

3. Stephen Brooks and William Wohlforth, "Power, Globalization, and the End of the Cold War: Reevaluating a Landmark Case for Ideas," *International Security*, Vol. 25, No. 3 (Winter, 2000/01), pp. 5–53. The literature on this case through 2000, and a discussion of economic factors within it, is thoroughly delineated therein.

4. Although the theoretical framework outlined here is not one I have previously outlined explicitly, it is the one that has always guided my empirical analyses. Chapter 3 of my dissertation is an early, preliminary attempt to delineate its core features. See Stephen G. Brooks, "The Globalization of Production and International Security," PhD dissertation, Yale University, 2001. It was only many years after writing my dissertation—after I had read *The Wealth of Nations* for the second time—that I belatedly came to realize the significant correspondence between the analysis in Chapter 3 of my dissertation and Smith's underlying theoretical framework.

5. The discussion in this chapter that follows is largely drawn from Brooks and Wohlforth, "Power, Globalization, and the End of the Cold War"; Stephen Brooks, *Producing Security: Globalization, Multinational Corporations, and the Changing Calculus of Conflict* (Princeton: Princeton University Press, 2005), ch. 4. See those publications for a more complete discussion of the lines of evidence discussed below as well as all relevant citations (in the analysis here, citations are only provided for direct quotes).

6. Interview with Valery Boldin, February 24, 1999, conducted by Oleg Skvortsov, head of the Cold War Oral History Project at the Institute of General History, Moscow (on file at the Institute of General History and the Mershon Center at Ohio State University).

7. As Rosecrance underscores, the transformation of many of the most advanced states toward knowledge-based economies was greatly facilitated by new geographic dispersion strategies of MNCs. See Richard Rosecrance, "The Rise of the Virtual State," *Foreign Affairs*, Vol. 75, No. 4 (July–August, 1996), pp. 45–61.

8. As cited in Gertrude Schroeder, "The Implementation and Integration of Innovations in Soviet-Type Economies," *Cato Journal*, Vol. 9, No. 1 (1989), p. 47.

9. William Schmickle, "Soviet Foreign Trade Reforms Under Gorbachev," in *The U.S.S.R. and the World Economy: Challenges for the Global Integration of Soviet Markets Under Perestroika*, ed. Deborah Palmieri (Westport: Praeger, 1992), p. 30.

10. William Odom, "The Soviet Military in Transition," *Problems of Communism*, Vol. 39, No. 3 (May 1990), pp. 52–53, 63–64.

11. Gareev as quoted in Sergei Belanovsky, "The Arms Race and the Burden of Military Expenditures," in *The Destruction of the Soviet Economic System: An Insider's Account*, ed. Michael Ellman and Vladimir Kontorovich (Armonk: M.E. Sharpe, 1998), p. 63.

12. Moiseev quoted in Thomas Nichols, *The Sacred Cause: Civil-Military Conflict over Soviet National Security* (Ithaca: Cornell University Press), p. 213.

13. Interview with Valery Boldin, February 24, 1999, conducted by Oleg Skvortsov, head of the Cold War Oral History Project at the Institute of General History, Moscow (on file at the Institute of General History and the Mershon Center at Ohio State University).

14. Politburo session of October 4, 1986, in National Security Archive Briefing Book, *Understanding the End of the Cold War: The Reagan/Gorbachev Years* (Providence: Brown University, 1998), Doc. 32.

15. William Odom, *The Collapse of the Soviet Military* (New Haven: Yale University Press, 1998), p. 115.

16. Mikhail Sergeevich Gorbachev, *Memoirs*, 1st ed. (New York: Doubleday, 1996), p. 564.

17. Odom, *Collapse of the Soviet Military*, p. 225.

18. Interview with Dmitry Yazov, December 16, 1998, conducted by Oleg Skvortsov, head of the Cold War Oral History Project at the Institute of General History, Moscow (on file at the Institute of General History and the Mershon Center at Ohio State University).

19. Sergei Akhromeev and Georgy Kornienko, *Glazami Marshala i Diplomata: Kriticheskii Vzgliad na Vneshniuiu Politiku SSSR do i Posle 1985 Goda* [Through

the Eyes of a Marshal and a Diplomat: A Critical Look at the Foreign Policy of the USSR Before and After 1985] (Moscow: Mezhdunarodnye Otnosheniia, 1992), pp. 314–315.

20. Within the Soviet political system, consumers as well as civilian firms were not positioned to directly lobby the leadership for an improvement in their plight. Yet the conventional liberal understanding is that leaders need not act only in response to direct appeals but can also be motivated by the likely expected response of consumers and firms to policy change.

21. Gorbachev quoted in Jerry Hough, *Russia and the West: Gorbachev and the Politics of Reform* (New York: Simon and Schuster, 1988), p. 11.

22. Zaikov quoted in Anders Aslund, *Gorbachev's Struggle for Economic Reform* (Ithaca: Cornell University Press, 1989), p. 46.

Chapter 11. Looking Forward

1. David Baldwin, *Economic Statecraft* (Princeton: Princeton University Press, 1985).

2. Google Scholar search conducted on August 16, 2022.

3. David Baldwin, "Evaluating Economic Sanctions," *International Security*, Vol. 23, No. 2 (Autumn 1998), p. 193.

4. See German Parliamentary Commissioner for the Armed Forces, *Annual Report of the Parliamentary Commissioner for the Armed Forces*, January 28, 2020, p. 42.

5. Nava Ashraf, Colin Camerer, and George Loewenstein, "Adam Smith, Behavioral Economist," *Journal of Economic Perspective*, Vol. 19, No. 3 (Summer 2005), p. 132.

6. See, for example, Douglass North, "Institutional Change: A Framework for Analysis," in *Institutional Change: Theory and Empirical Findings,* ed. Sven-Erik Sjöstrand (New York: Routledge, 1993).

7. Lake notes that provided we are willing to assume that that governments anticipate the reactions of others and makes choices accordingly, then "decision theoretic results appear to converge on game theoretic equilibria" and that "[t]his is intuitively plausible but lacks, as far as I know, a formal proof. It is unlikely to hold under *all* circumstances." See David Lake, *Entangling Relations: American Foreign Policy in its Century* (Ithaca: Cornell University Press, 1999), p. 44, emphasis in original.

8. See Stephen Brooks and William Wohlforth, *America Abroad: The United States' Global Role in the 21st Century* (New York: Oxford University Press, 2016), chs. 9 and 10.

9. As noted in Chapter 2, Gilpin's prominent categorization scheme did not merely seek to compare and realist and liberal political economy, but also sought to contrast each of them with Marxism. See Robert Gilpin, *U.S. Power and the Multinational Corporation: The Political Economy of Foreign Direct Investment* (New York: Basic Books, 1975), pp. 20–43; Robert Gilpin, *The Political Economy of International Relations* (Princeton: Princeton University Press, 1987), pp. 25–64. Gilpin's decision to develop a tripartite categorization scheme is, in my view, a key reason why the categories he created are ill equipped for properly differentiating realist and liberal political economy.

10. I thank Alex Wendt for numerous helpful conversations regarding the theoretical issues examined in the next three paragraphs. For a useful discussion of the role of ideas and material factors within international relations theory, see Alexander Wendt, *Social Theory of International Politics* (Cambridge: Cambridge University Press, 1999), esp. ch. 3.

11. Popper emphasizes that it would be a grave mistake to have all scientists in a field working within the same theoretical framework in part because this would impair creativity. In his writings, Popper emphasizes the overriding importance of permanent open critical discussion, stressing that a researcher should always seek out discussion with those in disagreement with them and be prepared to change their views following these conversations; in his view, having a range of contrasting general theoretical frameworks both encourages and facilitates such discussions. As Popper maintains: "It is often asserted that discussion is only possible between people who have a common language and accept common basic assumptions. I think this is a mistake. All that is needed is a readiness to learn from one's partner in the discussion, which includes a genuine wish to understand what he intends to say. If this readiness is there, the discussion will be the more fruitful the more the partners' backgrounds differ. Thus the value of a discussion depends largely on the variety of the competing views. Had there been no Tower of Babel, we should invent it." See Karl Popper, *Conjectures and Refutations: The Growth of Scientific Knowledge* (New York: Routledge & Kegan Paul, 1963), p. 352.

A NOTE ON THE TYPE

———◆———

THIS BOOK has been composed in Miller, a Scotch Roman typeface designed by Matthew Carter and first released by Font Bureau in 1997. It resembles Monticello, the typeface developed for The Papers of Thomas Jefferson in the 1940s by C. H. Griffith and P. J. Conkwright and reinterpreted in digital form by Carter in 2003.

Pleasant Jefferson ("P. J.") Conkwright (1905–1986) was Typographer at Princeton University Press from 1939 to 1970. He was an acclaimed book designer and AIGA Medalist.

GPSR Authorized Representative: Easy Access System Europe - Mustamäe tee
50, 10621 Tallinn, Estonia, gpsr.requests@easproject.com